Keeping

the

Circle

Keeping the Circle

American Indian Identity in
Eastern North Carolina, 1885–2004

Christopher Arris Oakley

University of Nebraska Press
Lincoln and London

Library of Congress Cataloging-in-Publication Data
Oakley, Christopher Arris.
Keeping the circle : American Indian identity in eastern North Car-
olina, 1885–2004 / Christopher Arris Oakley.
p. cm.—(Indians of the Southeast)
Includes bibliographical references and index.
ISBN-13: 978-0-8032-3574-8 (cloth : alk. paper)
ISBN-10: 0-8032-3574-7 (cloth : alk. paper)
ISBN-13: 978-0-8032-5069-7 (electronic)
ISBN-10: 0-8032-5069-x (electronic)
ISBN-13: 978-0-8032-2253-3 (paper : alk. paper)
1. Indians of North America—North Carolina—History—20th
century. 2. Indians of North America—North Carolina—Ethnic
identity. 3. Indians of North America—North Carolina—Politics
and government. I. Title. II. Series.
E78.N74035 2005
305.897'0756—dc22
2005008694

Set in Minion by Kim Essman.
Designed by Debra Turner.

To my parents, Alton and Loretta Oakley

Contents

Illustrations

Maps

Photographs

Acknowledgments

This book would not have been possible without the help of numerous friends, colleagues, family members, and total strangers. In particular, John Finger, my adviser and mentor, carefully guided me through my dissertation, which became the first draft of this book. Lorri Glover, Jeff Norrell, and Benita Howell offered important criticism and advice, making the work much better than it was originally. In addition, I would like to thank the following individuals, all of whom contributed in one way or another, often without even knowing it: David La Vere, Linda Oxendine, Malinda Maynor, Karen Blu, W. McKee Evans, Walt Wolfram, Stanley Knick, Bruce Wheeler, Susan Becker, Todd Diacon, Palmira Brummett, Wayne Cutler, Elaine Breslaw, Penny Hamilton, Kim Harrison, Alice Cotton, H. G. Jones, Mary Frances Morrow, and Richard King. Denise Jones of the *Raleigh News and Observer*, Davie Hinshaw of the *Charlotte Observer*, David Weaver of the *Rocky Mount Telegram*, and Steve Massengill of the North Carolina State Archives helped with the location of relevant photographs and illustrations. I would also like to thank the staffs at the following libraries for their courteous and patient assistance: Hodges Library in Knoxville (especially the Inter-Library Loan staff), the Southern Historical Collection in Chapel Hill, the North Carolina Collection in Chapel Hill, the North Carolina State Archives in Raleigh, the North Carolina State Library in Raleigh, the Sampson-Livermore Library in Pembroke, the National Archives and Records Administration in Washington, the Outer Banks History Center in Manteo, the Thomas Hackney Braswell Library in Rocky Mount, and the Perkins Library in Durham.

Several organizations provided funding for research. The American Philosophical Society kindly awarded the project a grant through its Phillips Fund for Native American Research. The North Caroliniana Society provided an Archie

K. Davis grant that financed a research trip to Chapel Hill. The History Department at the University of Tennessee provided aid via the Bernadotte Schmitt Research Fellowship, and the Graduate School at the University of Tennessee funded a year of writing through the Arthur Yates Dissertation Fellowship.

And finally, very special thanks go to my parents, for whom this work is dedicated, and to the numerous North Carolina Indians who graciously opened their doors to a naive but curious graduate student.

Series Editors' Introduction

In *Keeping the Circle: American Indian Identity in Eastern North Carolina, 1885–2004*, Christopher Arris Oakley describes the process by which Indian communities in eastern North Carolina organized themselves into tribes, which became central to their identity as Indians by the end of the twentieth century. Like many Native people in the South, Indians in eastern North Carolina do not have federal recognition, but they do have long histories as Indian people. During the segregation era, they struggled to maintain their ethnic identity, and when Jim Crow ended, they began to express themselves politically and culturally in bold new ways. Oakley demonstrates how, in some respects, the history of eastern North Carolina Indians paralleled that of Native Americans throughout the country, but he also focuses on the ways in which their experiences are unique. The South's obsession with race provides a framework for exploring those differences, but only North Carolina provided for three-way segregation that acknowledged Indian ethnicity. Furthermore, each Native community in North Carolina has a distinct history, and Oakley's narrative does not lose sight of these separate strands that form his narrative. Based on research in North Carolina documents, federal records, newspapers, and oral history collections, this book reveals a little-known history. By contextualizing that history in terms of national policy, culture, and events, Oakley makes a significant contribution to the study of American Indians as a whole.

Theda Perdue
Michael D. Green
University of North Carolina

Introduction
Defining Indian Identity

I wouldn't change for anything in the world. I'd rather be a dead Indian than no Indian at all. – Reuben R. Lewis (Meherrin)

To most Americans, and many historians, Native American history ended in 1890 at Wounded Knee, South Dakota, where federal soldiers shot more than 150 Sioux men, women, and children, a tragic event that symbolically marked the end of the Plains Wars. Consequently, for most of the twentieth century, both scholars and laypersons have traditionally viewed American Indians as relics of the past rather than contemporary survivors. Native American history, of course, did not stop at Wounded Knee. But, in many ways, the popular and scholarly image of Indian culture remains based on late-nineteenth-century stereotypes such as the brave warrior, the stoic chief, and the mystical shaman, epitomized by historical figures like Crazy Horse, Sitting Bull, and Geronimo. As a result, modern Native Americans continue to be overshadowed by their more famous ancestors.

In the latter half of the twentieth century, some scholars attempted to correct this historical oversight by reinserting the original Americans into American history. At first, historians concentrated on federal Indian policy and official efforts to "civilize the savages," a process that demanded both acculturation, the adoption of European culture, and assimilation, the loss of a separate tribal identity. In the late 1900s authors adopting more of a "bottom-up" technique focused on how Native Americans reacted to these civilization campaigns, emphasizing their tenacity and persistence. Most recently, Indian identity has become a popular subtopic within the broader field of Native American studies, with some authors tackling a series of difficult questions regarding Native American identity, such as who is an Indian, and what exactly does that mean. Most everyone agrees that Native Americans are still living in the United States, but just who they are is a very difficult and controversial question made even more complicated by a variety of economic and political factors, such as the recent spread of reservation gambling.

Traditionally, Americans of European descent defined Indians primarily in racial terms. That is, Native Americans were biologically characterized as a subgroup within the human species. This was also true for other minority groups, such as African Americans and Asian Americans. To Indians, this race-based system of social classification often made little sense. Native Americans did not see themselves as part of a single group or people, whether it was defined biologically or not. Prior to contact with Europeans, there was no such thing as an "Indian," but rather hundreds of peoples living in North and South America with a variety of different cultures. Nevertheless, first Europeans and later white Americans categorized Indians as a single racial group.

This racial definition of Indianness reached its peak in the early twentieth century. During the first few decades of the 1900s, Social Darwinism dominated thought in America. In the late 1800s the British philosopher Herbert Spencer applied Charles Darwin's theories on evolution to human societies, arguing that only the fittest of these societies would survive. The American William Graham Sumner imported Spencer's ideas and applied them to laissez-faire capitalism in the United States. According to Sumner, the rich prospered because they were more highly evolved, while the poor suffered because they could not compete. Sumner and others also believed that races could be ranked from highest evolved, Caucasian, to lowest, Negroid; all others, including American Indians, fell somewhere in between. Furthermore, Social Darwinists argued that races carried certain traits in their blood that determined various characteristics, such as intelligence and personality. Sumner's theories flourished in the late nineteenth and early twentieth centuries, a time of rapid industrialization, American imperial expansion, and widespread poverty among the immigrants and lower classes in the exploding cities of the Northeast. At the same time, Social Darwinism also dovetailed nicely with the establishment of Jim Crow segregation in the mostly rural and agrarian South. In fact, Sumner's theories not only justified but also demanded separation of the races.[1]

A few academics dared to criticize these theories of racial essentialism. The anthropologist Franz Boas challenged the philosophy behind Social Darwinism as early as the 1890s. Boas revolutionized the science of anthropology, advocating extensive fieldwork, observation, the study and use of indigenous languages, and the collection of life histories. From 1888 to 1903 Boas coordinated the accumulation of statistical information from more than eighteen thousand Native Americans, a data bank that scholars continue to mine for raw material. Based on his research, Boas argued that biology and culture were different, and that cultures should be analyzed on their own merits, not ranked from most civilized to least. Building on Boas's work, members of the "Chicago School of Sociology," led by Robert E. Park, also questioned Social Darwinism in the 1920s.[2]

Despite these noteworthy challenges, Spencer and Sumner, not Boas and Park, dominated the argument during the first few decades of the twentieth century. The consequences of this debate were not limited to the halls of academia; these theories on race and identity trickled down from the intelligentsia into popular culture and affected the way that groups defined themselves. Therefore, some Native Americans and members of other minority groups also defined their own identity in racial and biological terms. For many Indians, this was new and controversial. In many Indian societies, kinship defined tribal or community identity. Traditionally, kinship was not limited to one's "blood" relatives, but rather was based on a more complex system of social responsibilities and obligations. It also included those who married into the society, as well as others who became members of the community in various ways, such as adoption. Thus, it was quite possible to be fully considered a member of the community or tribe, and therefore an Indian, without being biologically related to others. Moreover, in the late 1800s and early 1900s, the federal government began to require that tribes maintain official rolls in order to determine who was eligible for benefits from previous land treaties. This led to the use of blood quantum, which is a measurement of Native American ancestry expressed as a fraction, to determine Indianness. For example, someone who has one Indian parent and one non-Indian parent would be considered "one-half" Indian.

World War II, however, marked a major turning point in the way that Americans thought about and wrote about racial identity. The defeat of Nazi Germany compelled many Americans to question the racialist assumptions that had dominated mainstream thought since the late 1800s. In the 1940s and 1950s, scholars such as Gunnar Myrdal, Horace Kallen, and Frederik Barth, building on the earlier work of Boas and Park, attacked the last vestiges of Social Darwinism by contending that race was constructed socially rather than biologically. Because of the constant interaction of humans over the previous few centuries, the concept of race was becoming meaningless as an analytical tool for examining group formation and social interaction. Consequently, ethnicity replaced race as the best technique for studying group formation. A racial group was simply a group of people who shared a common biological lineage. An ethnic group, by contrast, was a self-conscious group of people who shared a common identity that was based on, among other factors, history, culture, religion, and language.

In subsequent years scholars began to build on these new ideas. In doing so, they challenged Americans' fundamental assumptions regarding identity. Before World War II America was often described as a "melting pot," wherein separate racial and ethnic groups would eventually assimilate into a homogeneous American society. The millions of immigrants who entered the United States in the late 1800s and early 1900s would eventually blend in with other Americans and lose their cultural or ethnic identity. But in the 1950s and 1960s, authors questioned the accuracy of this metaphor. For example, Horace Kallen, a social psychologist, argued in *Cultural Pluralism and the American Ideal* that ethnicity was a basic feature of self-identity and that distinct ethnic cultures could survive in a liberal democracy. The anthropologist Frederik Barth took Kallen's argument even further. Barth contended that distinct ethnic groups could maintain their separate identities despite frequent interaction with other groups. In fact, interaction actually cultivated and encouraged the preservation of ethnicity. According to Barth, ethnic groups that lived in multicultural states developed markers, or signs of distinctiveness, to separate themselves from others. Barth found that members of ethnic groups regarded some features of their culture as vital to maintaining a separate identity, while they rejected other less meaningful elements. Some groups, for example, might deem religion an important component of their distinctiveness but reject the need or significance of a common language or traditional dress. In other groups, the opposite might be true, with language and dress more culturally significant than religion. Barth labeled these markers "boundaries" and argued that they kept ethnic groups from fully assimilating and losing their identity. Boundaries did not have to be physical or geographical; they could be cultural, material, or even ideological. Therefore, ethnic groups, even if rather small, could maintain their identity in large multiethnic nation-states. In essence, Barth replaced the analogy of the melting pot with the jigsaw puzzle, where boundaries defined the individual pieces that ultimately fit together, creating a unique cultural landscape that more accurately pictured American society.[3]

These new theories influenced all Americans, not just academics. According to the authors Michael Omi and Howard Winant, for the first time in American history, scholars in the postwar years adopted and sustained the notion of racial equality. The new social science filtered down through all levels of society and eventually altered the way that most Americans thought about race and ethnicity. But there was also an interesting side effect. Prior to the war, identity was defined exclusively by biology. After the war, however, Americans began to define identity by ethnicity and culture. Black and Indian, which were previously racial categories, essentially became ethnic categories. But African Americans and Native Americans were as ethnically and culturally diverse as European Americans. There was just as much cultural difference between Cherokees and Navajos, for example, as between Italians and Irish, perhaps even more. Nevertheless, Native American and African American became, in essence, ethnicities, which, according to stereotypes, carried certain common cultural characteristics. All Indians and blacks, therefore, were supposedly members of the same ethnic group and thus shared basic cultural characteristics. There was, of course, no historical basis for this. According to Omi and Winant, "There [was], in fact, a subtly racist element in this substitution—in which whites are seen as variegated in terms for group identities, but blacks [and Indians] 'all look alike.'"[4]

These changes influenced the way that Native Americans maintained and exhibited their unique identity. One consequence was an emerging pan-Indian or supratribal ethnic identity. Previously most Indians defined themselves solely in tribal terms. For example, one was a Cherokee or a Navajo; but few saw themselves as part of a larger ethnic group. In the postwar years, however, this changed as Indians began to form multitribal groups, which led to the development of a broader ethnic consciousness, a move partly designed to increase their political power to effect change within the American democratic system. Most Indians still defined themselves tribally, especially when dealing with other Indians, but they also embraced this broader identity as "Native Americans," particularly when dealing with outsiders.

The emergence of a broader pan-Indian ethnic identity subsequently led to a political renaissance. In the post–World War II era, Native Americans pooled their political and economic capital to agitate for reform. From the fish-ins in the Pacific Northwest to the occupation of the Bureau of Indian Affairs office building in Washington DC, Native American activism spread across the country in the 1960s and 1970s. Almost acting as a political action committee, Indians pressured politicians in local, state, and federal offices to address their needs. In *Return of the Native*, Stephen Cornell analyzed this explosion in Indian political activity. Cornell argued that a variety of factors, including New Deal legislation and the threat of tribal termination in the 1950s, sowed the seeds for the flowering of a broader supratribal Indian identity, which in turn led to the protests and demonstrations of the 1960s and 1970s. This activism continued into the 1990s. Fergus Bordewich noted the changes in his book *Killing the White Man's Indian*. To Bordewich, it became clear that a "revolution was underway in Indian country . . . an upheaval of epic proportions that encompassed almost every aspect of Indian life, from the resuscitation of moribund tribal cultures and the resurgence of traditional religions, to the development of aggressive tribal governments determined to remake the entire relationship between Indians and the United States."[5]

Because of these changes, the definition, or definitions, of Indian identity evolved in the second half of the twentieth century into a complex mishmash of biological and cultural ideas. By the turn of the century, there were numerous definitions of Indianness. For example, according to the U.S. Census, anyone who claimed to be an Indian was an Indian, at least when determining population. But in order to qualify for government programs and benefits, Indians must be enrolled members of federally recognized tribes. Native Americans themselves are also divided regarding definitions of identity. Some define Indianness in cultural terms; others base it on genealogy. Today each tribe sets its own guidelines for defining membership. Some continue to carry biological components, partly basing identity on blood quantum, whereas others rely on behavioral characteristics or kinship when defining Indianness.

With so many different definitions of Indianness, an obvious problem emerges: just who gets to decide who is an Indian, and what criteria do they use? The short answer is everyone and no one. Anyone can claim to be a Native American when the census taker comes to the door. But, in the end, there is no final arbiter of Indian identity. For the government, Native American identity is a legal issue. Federal acknowledgment of an Indian tribe is based on a historical relationship between the tribe and the government. In the eighteenth and nineteenth centuries, many Indian tribes signed treaties with the federal government regarding land ownership. These treaties were based on language in the Constitution that characterized Indians as dependent domestic nations within the United States. Therefore, treaties established a government-to-government relationship between Native American tribes and the federal government. Ostensibly, official federal recognition continued that tradition. The reality, however, became much more complex, especially in the late twentieth century. Today, recognition is partly about cultural pride and political sovereignty, though tribal governments actually have very little real power, but it is also about economic benefits, such as aid for housing and education. To Indian tribes and communities mired in poverty, this money is very attractive. In the late twentieth century, consequently, several Native American communities organized and pursued acknowledgment.

Federal recognition, however, also carries certain negatives that somewhat offset the economic benefits. Tribes seeking acknowledgment have to conform to government definitions of Indianness. In other words, they define themselves according to government-imposed definitions that are often complex and based on outdated stereotypes of Native Americans. Moreover, some critics contend that by participating in certain federal programs, American Indians are becoming just another minority group within American society. Some Indians resist this process by continuing to define their own identity internally while trying to exist outside of the system established by the government, a very difficult proposition given the poor economic situation in many Indian communities.

As Native Americans debated their own conceptions of identity, the new postwar theories on Native American race, ethnicity, and culture generated disagreement and controversy among academics. Some authors criticized scholars and federal policy makers for inventing modern Indians based on cultural fictions. As the federal government passed Indian legislation in the postwar era to redress past grievances, and as the interest in Indian culture increased in the 1960s and 1970s, critics contended that many individuals merely pretended to be American Indians to reap financial benefits or to appear socially fashionable; and even worse, some critics challenged the authenticity of whole tribes.

Cultural pluralists countered these criticisms by arguing that American Indians were the only people required to prove, often with detailed documentation, who they were. The invention of culture and identity, pluralists further contended, was natural and promoted social cohesion by establishing a set of common values. Other groups, not just Native Americans, have historically redefined their identity. Most current ethnicities evolved over centuries, as separate groups often coalesced to form new ethnic groups and nations, and therefore also constituted cultural inventions. Furthermore, they contended that ethnicity, by its very nature, was constantly evolving. In other words, identity was a process, not a constant.

But to many Americans, Indians were not supposed to change or evolve. The sociologist Angela Gonzales argued that in the late twentieth century, Indian identity was still primarily based on a handful of outdated cultural stereotypes. "Real" Indians lived on reservations, were enrolled members of a federally recognized tribe, had long straight black hair and dark eyes, wore leather moccasins and beads, spoke a tribal language, and practiced "traditional" Indian spirituality. To many twentieth-century Americans, nineteenth-century Plains Indian culture, a lifestyle limited to a specific place and time, still defined Native American identity. Furthermore, other groups were allowed to evolve—few whites lived in log cabins, grew their own food, or wore powdered wigs in the 1990s—while Indians were required to stay trapped in time or risk losing their authenticity. According to Fergus Bordewich, "To see change as failure, as some kind of cultural corruption, is to condemn Indians to solitary confinement in a prison of myth that whites invented for them in the first place."[6]

Southeastern Indians

The concept of modern Native American identity becomes even more complex when applied to the American South, a region where three races have intermingled for the past four hundred years. During the seventeenth century European settlers and Indians regularly interacted—sometimes peacefully, sometimes violently—in what would later become "the South." Colonials often traded with Native Americans, exchanging manufactured goods for deerskins, a mutually beneficial practice. Some white traders married Indian women to facilitate their business, thus establishing closer relationships between Indians and Europeans. Unfortunately, the less scrupulous ones also enslaved Native Americans, sending many to the West Indies to work on the sugar plantations; other Indian slaves labored on tobacco plantations in Virginia and the Carolinas. When Native Americans proved to be a poor source of labor—they were highly susceptible to disease and could easily run away and hide—European colonists began importing African slaves, adding a third ingredient to the region's flavorful cultural stew.

After American independence, the new U.S. government tried to deal with "the Indian question." At first federal officials attempted to "civilize" Native Americans by trying to turn them into small independent farmers and landowners. Many southern Native Americans adopted elements of European material culture but, at the same time, chose to maintain their Indianness. For the most part, this "civilization campaign" failed, as Indians continued to live on communal land under tribal governments. With the massive immigration of new European settlers in the early 1800s, the friction between white farmers and Native Americans in the South intensified, especially regarding the ownership of farmlands. Whites argued that Indians underutilized their land, and therefore it should be opened up for settlement. Indians countered that whites illegally poached on land guaranteed them through federal treaties. After Eli Whitney's cotton gin rejuvenated the sagging textile market, white farmers with newfound dreams of getting rich pushed westward looking for fertile soil in order to plant "king cotton." Native Americans resented the arrival of the new farmers, and tension increased and occasionally led to violence.

In the 1830s President Andrew Jackson decided to solve the problem by removing southern Indians to lands in the West where they could reside peacefully until "civilized" enough to assimilate into American culture. What followed was one of the saddest chapters in U.S. history, as the federal army rounded up thousands of Indians and forced them down the Trail of Tears, an appropriately named death march. For some tribes, one-fourth of the population died on the undersupplied and poorly planned journey. In many American history textbooks, Indian history in the southeastern United States ended with the removal of the "Five Civilized Tribes" (Cherokees, Choctaws, Chickasaws, Creeks, and Seminoles) from the South. But not all Indians relocated to the West; some remained, hiding out in the mountains, swamps, and other undesirable areas of the region. These holdouts can be broadly divided into two categories: small "remnant" communities, such as the Eastern Band of Cherokees, who managed to resist removal by hiding in isolated areas; and "unremoved" communities, or the dozens of small Indian settlements that managed to avoid removal altogether, mostly because they lived on remote and infertile land. These Indian communities persevered relatively isolated from their neighbors throughout the rest of the nineteenth century.

In the early twentieth century, southern Native Americans reemerged, once again attracting attention from non-Indians. Railroads, automobiles, paved highways, and telephones decreased the physical and symbolic space between the previously isolated Indian communities and their neighbors. The dramatic post–World War II shift from an agricultural to an industrial economy in the South pushed Native Americans further into mainstream America. According to the anthropologist J. Anthony Paredes, the twentieth-century South became a testing ground for defining contemporary Indianness. After all, many Native Americans in the region lived very much like their non-Indian neighbors. Still, they retained a distinctive racial and social identity. Jim Crow legislation in the 1800s had tried to divide all Southerners into either whites or "coloreds." Because of this biracial social system, many experts predicted that Native Americans in the region would eventually "disappear" by integrating into society either as whites or blacks. In 1945 the scholar Julian H. Steward, echoing the thoughts of many others, argued that "the Indian is virtually extinct in the eastern United States . . . it is solely a question of a few years before the last survivors will disappear without leaving any important cultural or racial mark on the national population."[7]

But Steward, like so many before him, underestimated Native American persistence and resolve. Indians in the southeastern United States, as well as those in the Northeast, refused to disappear. As Walter L. Williams has noted, cultural persistence and survival, rather than assimilation and absorption, better characterized southern Native American history in the twentieth century. Moreover, the American Indian experience constituted a vital component of Southern history and merited more investigation. According to Williams, "The

South, an area of three cultural and racial groups, cannot really be understood without a knowledge of the Indian experience in the region. Southern Indians are not on a 'road to disappearance,' and it is time to ask if they ever were."[8]

In the South, as well as elsewhere, modern Indian identity is based on both environmental and biological factors. Therefore, one's identity is not completely ascribed at birth but is, at least partially, a matter of choice. Yet, at the same time, one's choices are certainly limited by biological factors. American Indian identity is usually transferred from parent or guardian to progeny during early childhood. One is Native American, therefore, because one is raised Native American by a Native American. In a letter to Senator Daniel Inouye of the Select Committee on Indian Affairs, the anthropologist Karen Blu summarized this definition, arguing that "Indian identity . . . is profoundly cultural, a piece of a moral universe for those who hold it. It is not carried on a gene, it is not lost when Indians change their ways of making a living or use a different language. It is a way of seeing, a mode of understanding, a way of being in the world."[9]

The Indians of Eastern North Carolina

At more than one hundred thousand, North Carolina has the largest Native American population of any state in the South, and one of the largest in the country. Although Indians live throughout the state, their population is concentrated in three regions: a federal reservation in the western mountains, a cluster of several counties in the southeastern coastal plain, and a smaller area in the northeastern and central portion of the state along the Virginia border. About ten thousand of the thirteen thousand members of the Eastern Band of Cherokees reside in the Great Smoky Mountains on the fifty-six-thousand-acre Qualla reservation. The other ninety thousand North Carolina Indians, the focus of this book, live mostly in small rural communities that dot the Piedmont and coastal regions of the state, though a growing number reside in urban areas, such as Raleigh, Greensboro, Fayetteville, and Charlotte.

Surprisingly, North Carolina Indians have seldom attracted scholarly attention, especially when compared to tribes in the West. Those who have written about them have usually concentrated on the colonial era, when Native Americans and Europeans clashed over land and the deerskin trade. Authors examining more recent history have often focused on the Eastern Band of Cherokees, the most well known group in the state. Today, however, the Cherokees account for only about 13 percent of the state's Indian population. Moreover, because the Cherokees are federally recognized, their story is somewhat different.

By comparison, the other North Carolina Indians, who reside mostly in the

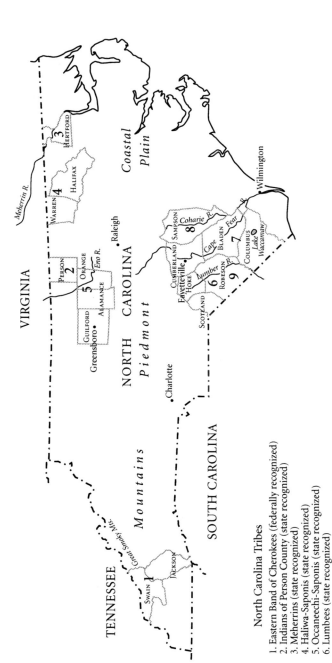

North Carolina Tribes

1. Eastern Band of Cherokees (federally recognized)
2. Indians of Person County (state recognized)
3. Meherrins (state recognized)
4. Haliwa-Saponis (state recognized)
5. Occaneechi-Saponis (state recognized)
6. Lumbees (state recognized)
7. Waccamaw-Siouans (state recognized)
8. Coharies (state recognized)
9. Tuscaroras (unrecognized)

Indians currently living in North Carolina. The map shows the location of Indian tribes currently residing in North Carolina, counties with significant Indian populations, and notable geographic features of the state. Urban Indian organizations are found in Charlotte, Greensboro, Fayetteville, and Raleigh.

eastern half of the state, remain relatively unexplored. Despite their relative obscurity, all of these communities have maintained a strong Indian identity. At the core of that identity is the belief that they are the descendants of the original inhabitants of what is today eastern North Carolina. Just exactly who is and who is not an actual descendant of the indigenous peoples of the region remains a controversial question. But to Indians in the eastern part of the state, this connection is very important. Most Native Americans, including those in North Carolina, place tremendous importance on a sense of place—they came from here, whereas everyone else came from somewhere else. Therefore, their identity is intertwined with the local geography. In Frederik Barth's terms, this belief is the primary boundary that separates Indians from others in North Carolina. Moreover, this conviction of common origin unites Indians in the state.

At the same time, this unity regarding their common origin masks a constant tension both within and between these communities over the specific components of Indian identity. Belief in common origins may create a bond, but North Carolina Native Americans have continuously debated what specific characteristics define them as Indians. Other than a common ancestry, just exactly what constitutes Indianness? Is it biological or is it cultural? All ethnic groups, not just Indians, define themselves by employing boundaries, whether real or symbolic, that distinguish them from others. And those boundaries can change over time, as they did in eastern North Carolina from the late 1800s to the present. Moreover, the evolution of group identity is not simply an insular process—it does not occur in a vacuum. Consequently, the formation of Indian identity is also a dialectical process, a combination of internal assertions of identity (who Indians think they are) with external expectations of identity (who others think they are). Therefore, conceptions of identity are also partially affected by broader trends in society, even for Native Americans living in rural North Carolina in the late 1800s. This, of course, is not unique to Native Americans but applies to all groups. In short, defining identity is a continual process, and Indians in eastern North Carolina have continuously reshaped and redefined their identity in the twentieth century in response to changes around them. Ultimately, this process would lead to the formation—or perhaps more accurately reformation—of eight Native American tribes: the Coharies, the Haliwa-Saponis, the Lumbees, the Meherrins, the Occaneechi-Saponis, the Person County Indians, the Tuscaroras, and the Waccamaw-Siouans. With the exception of the Tuscaroras, who are related to the Lumbees but claim a separate identity, all of these tribes are recognized by the North Carolina state government. This book is partly the story of the formation of these tribes. But, I hope, it is also something more. For the past 120 years, Native Americans in eastern North Carolina have struggled to survive as a separate people. Despite pressure to give up this fight and assimilate, they have thus far succeeded in maintaining their identity as the descendants of North Carolina's indigenous population. This is a truly remarkable achievement. How they accomplished such a feat is the real focus of this book.

The use of several terms in this work may offend some readers. Throughout the text, I have tried to be as specific as possible when using names—it is always preferable to refer to someone as a Coharie or a Haliwa rather than simply an Indian. In a work such as this, however, general statements are necessary. The terms Native American, American Indian, and Indian are used interchangeably, mostly to avoid repetition. American Indian is probably the best choice of the three, and the one that most Indians currently prefer, at least in North Carolina. Native American can be confusing, as it also defines anyone born in the United States, and Indian alone can also be misleading, referring to citizens of the Asian country. Of course, prior to Columbus's geographical blunder, there was no such thing as an Indian; and prior to the twentieth century, most Native Americans referred to themselves as Cherokees, Cheyennes, or Tuscaroras, rather than as Indians. But in the last few decades, many have openly adopted a more general pantribal identity, proudly calling themselves Indians or Native Americans. In fact, they have used it to their advantage, as have other minority groups. Readers will also find troublesome terms such as "mixed-blood" and "blood quantum." I use them hesitantly, understanding the problems associated with such loaded and culturally biased jargon. I also refer to the organized Native American groups in North Carolina as tribes. Recently scholars have argued that the concept of "tribe" is mostly a product of the postcontact period and actually the creation of Europeans. Of course, for that matter, so were "blood quantum" and "Indian." But Native Americans have taken these European terms and concepts and tried to use them to their advantage. Hence my decision to use them, as do many North Carolina Indians.

CHAPTER ONE

Acculturated but Not Assimilated

Appearance doesn't have anything to do with it. No anthropologist can tell us what is an Indian. It's how you feel about it. . . . An Indian is always an Indian. – Lew Barton (Lumbee)

In 1888 fifty-four Croatan Indians from eastern North Carolina petitioned the federal government for monetary aid to help educate their children. Prior to this request, representatives of the Commission of Indian Affairs in Washington were unaware of any Indian tribe in eastern North Carolina. The Cherokees, of course, lived in the western mountains of the state, but who were these Croatans? According to the federal census, there were only about six thousand Indians in all of North Carolina, and that number included several thousand Cherokees. The Croatans, however, claimed that more than one thousand Indian children lived in Robeson County alone. If the Croatans were indeed Indians, then the federal census had grossly undercounted them. The commissioner of Indian Affairs T. J. Morgan ultimately rejected their request, claiming a lack of funds, though he did not question their Indianness. "The Government is responsible for the education of something like 36,000 Indian children and has provisions for less than half this number," Morgan wrote to W. L. Moore, one of the Croatan petitioners, in August 1890. "So long as the immediate wards of the Government are insufficiently provided for, I do not see how I can consistently render any assistance to the Croatans or any other civilized tribe."[1]

Federal officials should not have been surprised to learn that there was still a significant number of Native Americans living in eastern North Carolina in the late nineteenth century. Despite three hundred years of contact with European colonists, African slaves, and, after independence, Americans, thousands of Indians still lived in the South, including North Carolina. In general, they resided in small, isolated settlements in sparsely populated areas, eking out a living on family farms. Although their daily existence was similar to poor whites in the region, they still considered themselves Indians. They were, in short, "acculturated but not assimilated."

Origins

In the sixteenth century, just before contact with Europeans, about fifty thousand Native Americans lived in present-day North Carolina. These original inhabitants could be broadly divided into three language groups. The Algonkian-speaking tribes, such as the Hatteras, Pamlicos, and Weapemeocs, resided near the coast in numerous small villages. The Iroquoian speakers consisted mostly of the Tuscaroras and the Cherokees, though there were also several others, such as the Meherrins and the Corees. The third group, the Siouans, lived in the Piedmont region, just above the fall lines of the state's rivers, and in the extreme southeastern portion of the state, near present-day Wilmington. The Siouans included the Waccamaws, Saponis, Occaneechis, and Enos, among others. In general, all three groups inhabited small, politically autonomous villages and towns. They lived in thatched huts and log homes (not tepees) and hunted, fished, and grew crops, primarily corn, beans, and squash. The numerous villages created an extensive trading network that reached from the coast all the way to the mountains. Most precontact Indians who lived in the present-day southern United States traced their ancestry through their mother's side of the family. In this matrilineal kinship system, the mother's relatives, especially her oldest brother, were the most important members of a child's family. Kinship was extremely important in most communities, determining relationships, obligations, rivalries, and even marriage partners.[2]

English settlers first tried to colonize North America in the 1580s. A small group of settlers, backed by Sir Walter Raleigh, established a colony on the Outer Banks of present-day North Carolina near the town of Manteo. Running low on supplies, they sent one of their leaders, John White, back to England. When White returned, he found the word "croatan," supposedly a reference to a nearby Indian village, carved on a tree, but the settlers were gone. They were never found. What happened to the Roanoke colonists remains one of America's great historical mysteries, and authors continue to speculate about their fate. In a book-length study, David Beers Quinn concluded that the settlers moved northward to the Chesapeake Bay area, where they were eventually killed by the Powhatan Confederacy sometime in the early 1600s. In a recent article, the

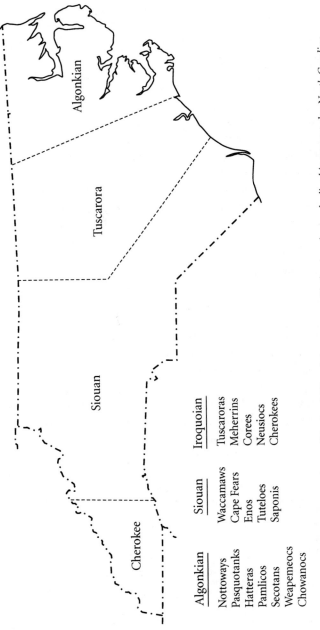

Algonkian

Tuscarora

Siouan

Cherokee

Algonkian

Nottoways
Pasquotanks
Hatteras
Pamlicos
Secotans
Weapemeocs
Chowanocs

Siouan

Waccamaws
Cape Fears
Enos
Tuteloes
Saponis

Iroquoian

Tuscaroras
Meherrins
Corees
Neusiocs
Cherokees

Historical Indians of North Carolina. Partial list of the precontact Native Americans who lived in present-day North Carolina. Historians and archaeologists believe other tribes also existed but were wiped out by European diseases before being documented.

North Carolina historian Thomas Parramore argued that the settlers migrated westward, got entangled in an internal Weapemeoc political struggle, and were killed. Without further archaeological evidence, the mystery most likely will remain unsolved, and scholars will continue to debate the issue based on the scant documentary evidence.[3]

In 1607 the English established another settlement in the Chesapeake Bay area of Virginia. Although this colony ultimately succeeded, it took another sixty years before the English populated in significant numbers what would become North Carolina. When they did arrive, settlers initially established peaceful relations with the local Indians, a strategic move considering that they were heavily outnumbered. White merchants inserted themselves into the indigenous trade network, working their way through the Carolina forests exchanging manufactured goods for deerskins. As the number of colonists increased, the relationship with the local Indians often deteriorated, as both groups competed for land and other resources in the region. The relationship worsened when traders began enslaving Native Americans and sending them to the sugar plantations in the West Indies. In 1711 a contingent of Tuscaroras, angry about the slave trade and the encroachment of settlers, attacked a group of white colonists, killing many, including women and children, and igniting a war. The North Carolina colonists, with the help of both whites and Indians from South Carolina, struck back and defeated the "rebellious" Tuscarora contingent, forcing most to move northward to live with their brethren, where they eventually became part of the Iroquois Confederacy. North Carolina officials used the Tuscarora War as justification to strengthen their control over local Indians, even punishing those who had fought with the colonists.[4]

Following the Tuscarora War, most of the Indians who remained in eastern North Carolina coalesced into new multitribal communities and settled on land that European settlers did not want, such as the swamps of the coastal region. Their numbers, however, had been thinned by warfare, the slave trade, and, most severely, disease. American Indians lacked immunity to European diseases and suffered periodic pandemics, especially from smallpox. The English and other Europeans certainly carried a military technological superiority with them to the "New World," but their most powerful weapon was probably a sneeze or a cough. Neither Native Americans nor Europeans understood germ theory at that time, a problem that placed extra stress on Indian societies. Some Native Americans interpreted the pandemics as curses, wondering what they had done to deserve this horrible malady. Conversely, Europeans saw Indians' susceptibility as a sign of physical and moral inferiority, concluding that God was punishing the heathens while at the same time opening up the "New World" for conquest and colonization.[5]

For the rest of the 1700s and into the 1800s, Native Americans in eastern North Carolina continued to live in isolation in small farming communities. During the early 1800s North Carolina Indians enjoyed many of the same rights as poor whites—they could own guns, testify in court, and even vote, if they owned property. They even managed to avoid forced removal in the 1820s and 1830s because they lived on land that no one wanted. In 1831, however, Nat Turner led a slave rebellion in Virginia that killed more than fifty whites, including women and children. Turner's rebellion sent shock waves throughout the South, scaring whites who feared the potential of a mass slave revolt. As a result of these fears, the North Carolina General Assembly rewrote the state constitution in 1835 and divided all North Carolinians into whites, slaves, and free persons of color, placing Native Americans into the last category and taking away many of their rights, including suffrage. This new arrangement angered Indians, who subsequently retreated further into isolation, choosing to withdraw from society and focus on their own internal needs. In an effort to protect their separateness, Indian communities discouraged interracial relationships, especially with blacks, and ostracized those who married outside of the community. Ironically, the new constitution may have actually preserved and strengthened Indian identity in North Carolina, as Native Americans ardently resisted being classified as "free persons of color" along with African Americans. This trend would repeat itself in the future—the more white Americans tried to assimilate Indians, the harder they fought to maintain their identity.[6]

Henry Berry Lowry

When the first shots of the Civil War were fired in South Carolina in April 1861, most North Carolina Indians initially supported the Confederacy. In fact, many wanted to join the fight. But according to state law, those who could not legally own firearms, including all "free persons of color," could not be issued weapons. Therefore, Native Americans were relegated to manual labor. Since plantation owners were reluctant to give up their slaves, state officials conscripted Native Americans to use as labor. Although willing to fight for the South, Indians in eastern North Carolina were sent to Wilmington to help build Fort Fisher, a large earthen fort designed to protect the mouth of the Cape Fear River. Undersupplied and overworked, many Native Americans fled the work camps and hid in the nearby swamps, where they formed refugee communities with runaway slaves and escaped Union soldiers from the prisoner-of-war camps in South Carolina.[7]

During the war one of these fugitive groups began raiding prominent local planters for provisions. A flamboyant young teenager named Henry Berry Lowry led the group, which included several of his relatives and at least two former slaves. Members of the "Lowry Gang" allegedly killed James Brantley Harris, a prominent white man, in retaliation for the murder of three of Lowry's relatives. The Confederate Home Guard, a local militia charged with keeping the peace during the war, combed the swamps looking for Lowry and his men. Guard members actually captured Lowry several times, but he always managed to escape, sometimes in dramatic fashion. On one occasion white officials imprisoned the outlaw in a high-security "jail within a jail" in Wilmington. One morning the guards found the cell empty, though it was still locked from the outside with no visible signs of escape. In another episode, a group of militia members stumbled upon Lowry alone in a canoe rounding a bend in a river. The pursuers, supposedly safe on land, hid behind some nearby trees and opened fire on the heavily outnumbered Lowry. In a flash, Lowry grabbed his rifle, jumped into the river, and, using his canoe as a shield, actually advanced on his pursuers and wounded two of the men. The bandit's marksmanship so awed his pursuers that they fled into the surrounding forest. Lowry once again escaped.[8]

Wealthy white planters in the Robeson County area, where most of the raids occurred, feared the wrath of the Lowry Gang, but local Indians adored the outlaws. According to legend, Lowry and his followers raided only those who could afford it, treated victims with respect, and shared the spoils with the needy. During one raid, the Lowry Gang interrupted a prominent white family having dinner. Rather than disrupt the meal, they sat down and ate a leisurely dinner with their victims before loading stolen supplies on a wagon led by a mule. Later, Lowry returned the mule and wagon. During another robbery, the gang learned that its victim, who they thought was very rich, was actually quite poor. Rather then deprive the man, the bandits returned what they had taken and disappeared into the swamps empty handed. But the Lowry Gang could also be violent, especially toward those who had mistreated local Indians. On one occasion a raid turned destructive and bloody when the gang consumed too much of the victim's alcohol and resorted to violence, unnecessarily injuring two men.[9]

Even after the end of the Civil War in 1865, local authorities offered enormous bounties for each of the members. By the early 1870s there was a twelve-thousand-dollar reward for the capture, dead or alive, of Henry Berry Lowry. Yet, despite the rewards, Lowry and his men continued to evade authorities and

Henry Berry Lowry, the "Indian Robin Hood" and the
"greatest hero a people ever had." After the deaths of his brother
and father, Henry Berry Lowry and his band wreaked havoc in
southeastern North Carolina until he disappeared in 1872. Courtesy of the
North Carolina Office of Archives and History, Raleigh NC, N.93.11.1.

embarrass local officials. In July 1871 the sheriff ordered deputies to arrest the wives of the bandits and hold them until they surrendered. Upon learning this, Lowry led a raid on a local plantation and told the owner to "go to Lumberton and tell the Sheriff and County Commissioners that if they don't let my wife out of that jail I'll retaliate on the white women of Burnt Swamp Township." Lowry then dictated a note to deliver to the sheriff, demanding that their "wives who were arrested a few days ago, and placed in jail, be released to come home to their families by Monday Morning, and if not, the Bloodiest times will be here that ever was before—the life of every man will be in Jeopardy." The sheriff released the women four days later.[10]

In 1872 Lowry and his men hit the bandit's jackpot. The gang stole a horse and wagon, raided the store of two wealthy merchants, and escaped with more than one thousand dollars' worth of merchandise and twenty-two thousand dollars in cash. Shortly after this job, Lowry disappeared into the Carolina mist, never to be seen again. Some believed that he died from a gunshot wound, while others claimed that he escaped and lived a long life. According to one story, Lowry boarded a train dressed as a federal soldier, rode out of the state, and served four years in the U.S. Army. Whatever his fate, Henry Berry Lowry became a folk hero, the great "Indian Robin Hood" of North Carolina, who sparked fear in wealthy white landowners and made the local authorities appear foolish.[11]

Jim Croatan

In the immediate postwar years, the reconstruction government of North Carolina restored some legal rights to American Indians, allowing them to vote and own arms. But these reforms were short lived. Much to the consternation of Indians in the state, Republicans appeared to be just as disinterested in Indian affairs in the 1870s as white Democrats were before the war, despite the fact that Indians had harbored runaway slaves and Union soldiers. Republicans were too worried about consolidating their political power in North Carolina to advocate radical reforms that might anger white voters. In 1877 the Republican Party abandoned Reconstruction in the South in order to secure the election of Rutherford B. Hayes as president. The end of Reconstruction signaled a return to the past for nonwhite Tar Heels as Democrats "redeemed" their state and reasserted their political and economic authority. In the 1880s and 1890s, conservative legislators passed new laws that protected the property rights of wealthy landowners, politically disempowered "coloreds," and assured white dominance. The general assembly, for example, disfranchised all nonwhites. The Fifteenth Amendment, passed in the wake of the Civil War, supposedly gave all male citizens the right to vote. But conservative whites in North Carolina, as well as other southern states, used a variety of methods to circumvent the amendment. In 1902 the North Carolina legislature passed a law that required all potential voters to pass a literacy test. Specifically, they had to read, write, and interpret a portion of the U.S. Constitution to the satisfaction of the local registrar. To ensure that illiterate whites could still vote, the act included a "grandfather clause" stating that those eligible to vote before 1866, along with all of their descendants, were excluded from the test. Of course, some African Americans and Native Americans could read and write very well. Nevertheless, white registrars, who solely determined whether someone passed, usually failed nonwhites. Across the South, other state legislators passed similar rules, collectively known as Jim Crow laws, designed to create two Souths, one for whites and one for "coloreds."[12]

North Carolina Indians, however, refused to be labeled "coloreds" and chose instead to forge a third racial category in this biracial system. The new state constitution, passed during Congressional Reconstruction, required schooling for children of all races. In the postwar years, a public education movement swept the country as reformers argued that a modern industrialized democracy required a literate and educated citizenry. Public schools also provided a venue for teaching "American" values to the increasing number of immigrants, especially in the Northeast. In the South, these values included racial separation. By the 1880s county governments in North Carolina had established segregated school systems for whites and "coloreds" in the state. Reluctant to enroll their children in colored schools for fear of losing their separate identity, Native American parents in Robeson County convinced the local state representative Hamilton McMillan to introduce legislation in the North Carolina General Assembly to create separate schools for Indians. According to the bill, the Robeson Indians "shall have separate schools for their children, school committees of their own race and color, and shall be allowed to select teachers of their own race."[13] In the legislation, McMillan called the Robeson Indians "Croatans" based on his belief that they were the descendants of Sir Walter Raleigh's "Lost Colony." According to McMillan, before White returned from England, the colonists had migrated westward and settled among the local Algonkian-speaking Indians who resided in the coastal part of North Carolina. There the colonists became mixed with the indigenous peoples of the state. Their descendants, he believed, were currently living in Robeson County.[14]

In 1885 the North Carolina General Assembly passed the Croatan bill and created a third school system in Robeson County. The bill also officially designated the Indians "Croatans." McMillan, an amateur historian, was obviously influenced by the belief that he had solved the mystery of the Lost Colony, but why would other North Carolina legislators support the law? Ironically, the bandit Henry Berry Lowry partially explained the vote. The Lowry War, only a decade in the past, was still fresh in the minds of many whites. Uncomfortable with the idea of a possible Indian-black alliance, state officials chose to characterize the Lowry uprising as an "Indian war." Mary Norment, a contemporary white woman who wrote a history of the events, called the Lowry Gang "modern Robeson county Apaches" and "North Carolina Modocs."[15] In a letter to a federal officer investigating the raids, two white ministers argued that the Lowrys were "free from all taint of Negro blood . . . [and] have always claimed to be Indian & disdained the idea that they are in any way connected with the

African race."[16] Moreover, the federal government was also waging a series of military campaigns in the 1870s and 1880s against Native Americans in the West in order to open the region for expansion. The Plains Wars garnered a lot of attention in the East, as writers romantically documented the heroics of white soldiers against the "savage" Indians. As Norment's reference to the Apaches indicates, some North Carolinians may have been influenced by these events. If the Lowry Gang was indeed comprised of Indians, then, logically, others living in the area must also be Indians. In 1887 the General Assembly passed another law outlawing "all marriages between a [Robeson] Indian and a negro or between an Indian and a person of negro descent to the third generation."[17] In the early 1900s state officials would also establish separate hospitals and jails for Indians in parts of eastern North Carolina, particularly in Robeson County. These acts partly offset the biracial social system that Jim Crow legislation tried to enforce. At the time, these acts probably seemed like a minor concession to the Indians in southeastern North Carolina, but, in future years, they would have significant consequences.[18]

Native American Schools

In the late 1880s and 1890s, the Croatans in and around Robeson County built several small schools. Although they received a modest appropriation from the state, Native Americans supplied all of the labor and paid for a significant portion of the construction costs. To help staff the schools, the General Assembly provided one thousand dollars for the construction of a teacher-training school. The assembly also named W. L. Moore, James Oxendine, James Dial, and Preston Locklear, all Indian men, trustees of the normal school. In the fall of 1887, fifteen students paid four dollars to enroll in the new Croatan Normal School.[19]

Influenced by the Croatans of Robeson County, Native Americans in other counties in eastern North Carolina opened their own schools in the early 1900s. Native Americans in Sampson County petitioned the state government for an Indian-only school. Since Sampson had a much smaller population of Indians than Robeson, state officials initially ignored the request. Unwilling to continue to send their children to "colored" schools, Indian parents in Sampson established New Bethel, a private one-room school that served children in grades one through six. A community farm, where children worked in the afternoons and on weekends, partially financed the school. Both the Sampson County Board of Education and the North Carolina General Assembly eventually capitulated to the demands of the local Indians and incorporated New Bethel into the public school system in 1911. But the state and county offered only minimal monetary aid, forcing the Sampson Native Americans to finance the majority of the budget out of their own pockets, even though some owned property in the county and paid the same property taxes as whites.[20]

Native Americans living in Bladen and Columbus counties attempted to open their own school in the 1890s. Several interrelated Indian communities straddled the border that separated these two counties in southeastern North Carolina. Working together, parents established an Indian-only school using enrollment fees to pay teachers. Not enough parents could afford the fees, however, and the school closed within a few years. In the early 1900s the Bladen and Columbus Indians tried again. A group formed the Council of Wide Awake Indians and petitioned the county governments for educational aid. Influenced by their neighbors in Robeson, the Indians in Bladen and Columbus also claimed to be Croatans. Their request, however, was rejected. According to the anthropologist Patricia Lerch, the establishment of the Wide Awake council was an important step for Native Americans in the area. First, the council helped to unite the communities socially. Second, Wide Awake served as an unofficial governing body for the local Native Americans, a forerunner of what would later become an official tribal government. And finally, through the council, Indian leaders learned how to work with white politicians and government structures, lessons that would serve them well in later years.[21]

During the first decades of the twentieth century, Native Americans living in eastern North Carolina continued to build and maintain their own schools. By 1914 there were twenty-seven Indian-only schools, thirty-six teachers, and eighteen hundred students in Robeson County alone. Gradually, the state government incorporated these schools into the public educational system. Despite this consolidation, most Indian schools received very little financial aid from the state and relied heavily on parents of the students for the necessary resources. People donated time, money, labor, and materials to help construct, staff, and fund the local schools. Yet, despite these efforts, schools constantly suffered from inadequate funding. Lacking paper, students wrote on small chalk slates. Teachers, who instructed children of all ages and academic levels, struggled to find books and other materials, and schools frequently shut down because of the inability to meet payrolls. Nevertheless, some important future leaders received their first formal education in these Indian-only schools.[22]

In 1909 the Croatan Normal School moved to the town of Pembroke. Although the school was part of the North Carolina system, the General Assembly gave Native Americans almost complete control. The all-Indian board of trustees had the power "to employ and discharge teachers, to prevent negroes from attending said school, and to exercise the usual functions of control and management of said school, their action being subject to the approval of the State board of education."[23] The school also enacted a strict moral code, especially for women, and students could be expelled for inappropriate or immoral behavior. In 1921 the state partially financed the construction of a new administrative building, eventually named Old Main, that became the symbolic center of campus. Created to train teachers, the Croatan Normal School primarily acted as a high school until the 1920s. Its graduates, however, taught in Indian elementary schools across the state. The school finally graduated its first class of "normal" teachers in 1928.[24]

Native Americans in eastern North Carolina insisted on keeping their schools Indian-only. In most communities, parents and school administrators, with the support of the state and county governments, formed "blood committees" to prohibit non-Indians, particularly African Americans, from enrolling. Parents who wanted to send their children to Indian schools had to apply to the committees who subsequently ruled on the Indianness of each applicant. The racial standards were strict—most school committees traced the ancestry of applicants back four generations, and only a trace of "African" blood could disqualify a child. Prominent local citizens, often landowners, comprised the school committees and controlled admissions, curriculum, and hiring practices. If a committee member resigned, the remaining members appointed a new representative. Since school positions were among the few white-collar opportunities available for Indians, these committees assumed a great deal of power and prestige in the community.[25]

Implementing strict racial standards for school enrollment proved problematic. In fact, the process of defining Indianness created controversy and occasionally divided communities. In 1913 the Sampson County blood committee rejected a student because he did not meet its requirements. After the parents complained, state officials threatened to cut the school's meager public funding. The committee refused to give in, however, and the General Assembly temporarily suspended aid. In Robeson County, families occasionally filed lawsuits when their children were denied admission to Indian schools. In these cases, local judges made the final decision, legally determining Indian status. Either way, the process ensured that non-Indians would not be allowed to enroll in these schools. Any student attending an Indian school had to prove his or her Indianness to either a committee or a judge. This was obviously an attempt to remove any doubt that these schools were truly Indian-only. The Native American perspective was clear: to enroll even one student who was not undoubtedly of Indian heritage threatened the racial identity of the entire group.[26]

Along with providing education to children, schools also played important

Croatan Indian Normal School and students, 1916. Photo courtesy of the North Carolina Office of Archives and History, Raleigh NC.

social roles in Native American communities. Teachers, who held prestigious if not financially lucrative positions, often became community leaders. They served as unofficial lawyers, giving out advice on a variety of subjects, and helped other Indians with various tasks such as filling out government and legal forms and reading and responding to their mail. Most Indian children attended the same schools with the same students year after year, therefore strengthening community unity. Schools also served as gathering places and hosted a variety of social events, such as holiday celebrations and the annual "school-breaking," a large all-day party commemorating the end of the academic year and the start of summer. About a week before the end of classes, students, parents, and other members of the community would gather for the celebration, which included food, dancing, and games.[27]

Native American Churches

Along with schools, North Carolina Native Americans established their own churches in the late nineteenth and early twentieth centuries. Churches, like schools, socially separated Indians from both whites and blacks in the state. Before the Civil War, many Native Americans, as well as some African Americans, attended church with whites. But when Jim Crow seized control of the South in the late 1800s, most white churches banned all "coloreds." Consequently, many Native American communities financed and built their own churches. In Robeson County, Native Americans founded several churches in the late nineteenth century, such as Union Chapel, Thessalonica, and Saddletree. In nearby Sampson County, Indians established two churches, New Bethel Baptist and Beaver Dam, near the turn of the century. In Alamance County, Native Americans also built two new churches, Martin's Chapel Baptist and Jeffries Cross, in the early 1900s. The practice quickly spread, as other Indian communities in the state also built places of worship.[28]

The process of organizing a local church was similar in most Native American communities. Neighborhoods held local fund-raisers in order to buy the necessary supplies. Occasionally, wealthier Indian individuals donated land or money for the cause, an altruistic act that also enhanced their status in the community. The men supplied the labor, working in the evenings and on weekends, while the women cooked for the workers and performed other tasks. The routine resembled a traditional barn raising, with local Indians overseeing every step of the process, from planning to the grand opening. Most churches were very simple one-room frame structures. Because they required a lot of teamwork and effort, churches helped solidify local Indian unity, bringing communities closer together.[29]

The establishment of Prospect Church and Sandy Plains Church, both Methodist churches in Robeson County, illustrated the trend. In the 1870s Indians living in the Prospect community did not have their own place of worship. They pooled their resources and built a one-room log structure to act as both a church and a school. Prospect quickly grew in the twentieth century and became one of the largest Native American churches in the country. Likewise, Indians living in the Sandy Plains community also lacked a church. Although most of the residents were sharecroppers, a few owned their own farms. In 1906 two prominent farmers donated a tract of land to build a church. With donated lumber, the local Indians founded Sandy Plains Methodist Church and named William Luther Moore the first minister.[30]

Ideologically, Indian churches in North Carolina mirrored other southern Protestant churches. In the early nineteenth century, Evangelical Protestantism swept across much of the South as fiery itinerant preachers converted millions of southerners, including thousands of African Americans and Native Americans. By the late 1800s the majority of North Carolina Indians were Evangelical Christians, mostly Baptists and Methodists. Like other southern Protestants, Native Americans believed in a literal interpretation of the bible. Ministers preached strict piety and the need to develop and nurture a personal relationship with God, while warning parishioners about the evils of a treacherous and active devil. When internal disputes over doctrinal issues arose, factions would sometimes break away from the congregation and form their own church, a practice common throughout the South.[31]

In Native American communities, the Sabbath was strictly a day of worship. On Sunday mornings Indian families would go to their local church for Sunday School, which was followed by the morning service. After the sermon, families would eat lunch and visit with one another for a while, swapping stories and discussing local matters. In the late afternoon the preacher would give another sermon, and the families would go home to rest and prepare for the coming week. In the summers, usually July or August, churches held revivals, which usually lasted about a week, to reenergize the congregation and attract new members.[32]

As the number of Indian churches in eastern North Carolina increased, denominations established religious conferences and associations. Several churches formed the Burnt Swamp Baptist Association in the 1870s, the first documented Native American religious organization in North Carolina. The Burnt Swamp Constitution, passed in 1910, required that member churches establish racial guidelines, stating that "this association shall be comprised of the members chosen by the different churches in our union, who shall be known, designated and styled as Indians or lineal descendants of Indians."[33] Also in the late nineteenth century, several Methodist ministers organized their own conference, which subsequently divided over an internal dispute and split into two separate groups, the North Carolina Conference of the Methodist Church and the Holiness Methodist Conference. Despite the occasional squabbling, churches and conferences served mostly to unite, not divide, Native Americans. They also allowed Indians from different communities to get together, fostering a broader "pan-Indian" identity in the state.[34]

North Carolina Indians tried to keep their churches, like their schools, Indian-only. Church committees voted on whether to allow certain families to join their congregation, and once again the key issue was racial identity. The decisions of the committees occasionally divided communities, as Native Americans debated the definition of Indianness. In the early 1900s, for example, members of the Beaver Dam church in Sampson County became involved in an intense internal fight over the racial identity of several members of their congregation. As tempers increased, a suspicious fire destroyed the church. Some cried foul, arguing that disgruntled parishioners, angry about the admittance of non-Indians, deliberately burned the church in protest. The mystery was never solved and remained a contentious issue in the county.[35]

Like schools, churches performed important social roles in Native American communities. In fact, the same buildings frequently functioned as both schools and churches. Churches hosted secular activities, such as homecomings and picnics, as well as the more traditional choir practices, Bible studies, and youth meetings. Since Native Americans encouraged marriage within the community, church events served as meeting grounds for finding prospective marriage partners. The church also acted as an economic safety net. Congregations raised funds to help fellow parishioners in times of trouble, such as when a crop failed. Ministers, who like teachers held socially prestigious positions, functioned as the moral center of many communities, defining accepted codes of conduct. They frowned on drinking, smoking, and premarital sex, among other vices, and violators faced stiff penalties. In Sampson County, for example, church officials "ex-communicated" congregational members who strayed from the path of the righteous, a harsh punishment for violators, as the church served so many vital community functions. In many ways churches mirrored the traditional precontact Native American kinship system. An Indian without a church in North Carolina in the early twentieth century was very much like one without kin prior to contact with Europeans, lacking identity and a sense of belonging.

Those ostracized for misconduct could eventually return to the church, but only if they convinced officials of their repentance.[36]

One difference was notable between the precontact kinship system and the social structure of the schools and churches in the 1900s: Indian communities had become patrilineal and patriarchal. By the twentieth century North Carolina Indians traced their lineage through their fathers, rather than through their mothers. Moreover, gender roles had changed. Men now tended the fields and occupied most of the official positions of power within the community, serving, for example, on school committees. They still hunted, though this became more of a recreational activity. Boys worked in the fields but also collected firewood and fed stock animals, along with other tasks. Women were limited to their "feminine sphere," cooking, cleaning, and raising children. Girls helped their mothers and aunts and also looked after younger siblings. There was a connection between Protestantism and this "cult of domesticity" that dated back to the second Great Awakening earlier in the 1800s. The shift of gender roles was especially noticeable in Native American churches, where tradition forbade women from holding any official position of power, though many acted with influence behind the scenes.[37]

Both Indian-only schools and churches increased the interaction between various Native American communities in eastern North Carolina and planted the seeds for the growth of a pan-Indian identity in the state. Most of the graduates of the normal school were from Robeson, but there were more teachers than positions in that county. Consequently, some moved to other counties, such as Sampson and Halifax, where they found jobs in other Indian schools. Several married and settled in their new homes, establishing ties between the communities. Indian churches and conferences also led to increased interaction between various Native American communities in eastern North Carolina. Pastors rarely held full-time positions and traveled by foot or mule from one Indian community to the next giving sermons on Sundays, frequently staying as guests in the homes of local families. Gospel-singing groups also visited other counties and congregations to participate in Sunday services and religious gatherings. Because of their relatively large population, the Indians living in Robeson County became the trendsetters and leaders, forging the path for other North Carolina Native Americans.[38]

Sharecropping

While much of the Northeast was industrializing in the late nineteenth and early twentieth centuries, rural agrarianism still characterized the economy of the South. In North Carolina most Native Americans worked as tenant farmers and sharecroppers, growing cash crops, primarily cotton and tobacco, as well as staples for personal use, such as corn and wheat. The end of the Civil War had not destroyed the cotton industry in the state. In fact, king cotton still reigned in the "New South" of the early twentieth century. In 1860, just before the start of the war, North Carolina farmers harvested 145,000 bales of cotton. In 1890 the number was 390,000, an increase of 167 percent in three decades. By 1910 Tar Heel farmers were harvesting more than 665,000 bales per year.[39]

Native Americans participated in this agrarian economy, but primarily as farm workers, not farm owners. In the late 1800s Native Americans in southeastern North Carolina lost much of their land. For most of the nineteenth century, Indians in the state had lived on unwanted lands in isolated communities, eking out a meager existence on small family farms. By the late 1800s, however, population growth and the need for more farmland reduced the physical and social space between Indians and others in the state. At the turn of the twentieth century, the North Carolina General Assembly financed the drainage of swamplands in the eastern part of the state, increasing the value of previously unproductive land. Furthermore, logging companies began buying land in North Carolina from the state government. In 1890 a South Carolina lumber company purchased thousands of acres in southeastern North Carolina, especially in Bladen, Columbus, and Robeson counties, where thousands of Native Americans lived. A Maryland lumber company established a regional office in Brunswick County and also bought large tracts of land from the state. After it was cleared, the companies sold the land to corporate farms and wealthy white landowners. Although their ancestors had occupied the area for decades, if not centuries, most local Indians did not have deeds or other official documents and therefore were unable to establish legal ownership. Consequently, many were dispossessed of their land, perhaps without even knowing it until after the fact.[40]

North Carolina Indians also lost land because of chronic indebtedness. Lacking paper currency, Native Americans had to purchase seeds, fertilizers, housewares, and other farm equipment from area merchants on credit using their potential crop as collateral. In some communities, landowners ran general stores and allowed Indians to buy supplies on credit against future crop yields. The credit price was substantially more than the cash price, and interest rates climbed as high as 10 percent. Since most Indians were illiterate, this process was also open to potential fraud. If at the end of the year the farmer could not pay his bill, he would sink further into debt. When the debts reached a certain level, merchants and bankers would foreclose on the loan and confiscate the land.

Foreclosure, combined with inability to prove ownership, caused Indians to lose land they had farmed on for decades. By the early twentieth century, fewer than 20 percent of Indians in eastern North Carolina owned land. Most worked on farms owned by whites—who may or may not have lived nearby—often on land that was "owned" by their ancestors.[41]

Pushed off of their land, Native Americans became dependent on others for their economic existence. Some became day laborers earning a flat rate for a day's work. Others became tenant farmers, renting land from large farm owners in order to grow cash crops. Native Americans, as well as poor whites and African Americans, preferred tenancy because they controlled their working conditions, giving them some degree of economic freedom. Tenant farmers worked unsupervised, received better returns, enjoyed a higher social status, and owned their crops until they were sold at market. Most Indians in eastern North Carolina, however, became sharecroppers. In sharecropping, landowners provided the basic necessities, including food, shelter, supplies, and land, usually fifteen to twenty acres. But they also took a percentage of the crop, usually between one-third and one-half, depending on the contract, which was renegotiated annually. Landowners and area merchants would also sell sharecroppers goods on credit, usually at a high interest rate. Frequently, the annual provisions cost more than the returns, so the sharecropper actually owed landowners or merchants money at the end of the year. Since few sharecroppers had hard currency, the liability rolled over to the next year, earned interest, and led to a cycle of debt and poverty. Once a sharecropper became indebted to a landowner, he or she might be tied to that farm for years. By nature, the system prevented Indians, as well as blacks and poor whites, from bettering themselves economically. The harder they worked, the more the landowner made. "They own the land and you work the land," explained William Sampson, a Robeson County Indian who grew up on a farm sharecropping. "They furnished the house you stayed in . . . we furnished the labor. At the end of the year, sometimes we could get half the crop, sometimes we would get one third the crop. This means every three dollars we made, we got one, the landowner got two."[42]

As sharecroppers, most North Carolina Indians lived in shabbily constructed houses on land owned by others. These homes were very small, usually only two or three rooms, and lacked plumbing and electricity. A single fireplace provided the only heat, while the windows were usually uncovered, allowing cold air and rain into the house. Since they did not own their homes, Indians rarely renovated or improved the structures, especially since they could be out of a job at the end of the year. Likewise, landowners, who were interested only in profits, rarely improved the buildings, making only the most necessary repairs.[43]

While large landowners profited from the sharecropping system, most Native Americans in eastern North Carolina barely managed to get by. In 1913 a federal agent collected economic data on more than one thousand Indians living in Robeson, Scotland, and Hoke counties. He estimated that less than 25 percent of Indian farmers owned their own land. The rest worked for others and were impoverished. Yet Indians were apparently very good farmers. In 1910 the National Bank in Lumberton established an annual contest for the best corn grown in the area. The first year, most Indians were unaware of the event and only a few entered. Nevertheless, one Native American man placed second. The next year, Indian farmers swept all three prizes. The bank promptly canceled the competition.[44]

A "Convenient" Label

In the early 1900s experts at the Smithsonian Institute deemed the Croatans of North Carolina worthy of an encyclopedic entry in their *Handbook of American Indians North of Mexico*. In the volume, the noted anthropologist James Mooney wrote the entry for the Indians of Robeson County. Disregarding the Lost Colony theory as "baseless," Mooney argued that the five thousand or so Native Americans in southeastern North Carolina were most likely the descendants of colonial-era tribes who had intermixed with Europeans and Africans. Mooney concluded that the name Croatan, although historically inaccurate, served "as a convenient label for a people who combine in themselves the blood of the wasted native tribes, the early colonists or forest rovers, the runaway slaves or other negroes, and probably also of stray seamen of the Latin races from coasting vessels in the West Indian or Brazilian trade."[45]

Despite Mooney's approval of the name, by 1910 North Carolina whites had turned Croatan into a derogatory racial epithet. Questioning their identity, skeptics called Indians in the eastern part of the state "Cros," a nickname that carried a double meaning. Along with being a shortened version of Croatan, "Cro" was also a reference to Jim Crow segregation, not so subtly insinuating that they were really African Americans trying to hide their ancestry. Moreover, the name Croatan was actually a reference to a historical place, not to a people. Some Native Americans expressed their unhappiness with the name to local and state officials. Consequently, the state government passed legislation in 1911 that officially changed their designation from the Croatans to the Indians of Robeson County.[46]

The new name, which lacked a specific historical reference, failed to please most Native Americans in the Robeson County area. As a result, some tried to connect themselves historically with the Eastern Band of Cherokees. In 1913 Angus W. McLean, a white state representative from Robeson County, pushed through a new bill in the North Carolina legislature that changed the designation of the local Indians to the Cherokees of Robeson County. McLean honestly believed that the Native Americans in and around Robeson County were related to both the Eastern Band of Cherokees in North Carolina and the Cherokee Nation of Oklahoma. Despite McLean's conviction, very little evidence supported his claim. Nevertheless, the "Indians of Robeson County" became the "Cherokee Indians of Robeson County," at least according to state law.[47]

After his success at the state level, McLean tried to convince the federal government of the Robeson Indians' Cherokee roots. In a statement given to the House Committee on Indian Affairs, McLean testified that the Robeson Indians were "originally part of the great Cherokee tribe of Indians, which inhabited the western and central portion of Carolina before the advance of the white man."[48] Some Indians in eastern North Carolina supported McLean's efforts, but others, who believed that they were the descendants of the coastal Siouan tribes who had lived in the region, opposed his legislation. Congressional leaders subsequently asked the Department of the Interior to look into the matter. In 1914 the Indian commissioner sent special agent O. M. McPherson to Robeson County to investigate the historical origins of the community and to determine if they were entitled to any special privileges or treaty rights. After completing his research, McPherson contended that the local Indians were in fact the descendants of the Lost Colony and the Hatteras Indians, an Algonkian-speaking tribe that had lived along the coast prior to contact with Europeans. "I have no hesitancy in expressing the belief that the Indians originally settled in Robeson and adjoining counties in North Carolina were an amalgamation of the Hatteras Indians with Governor White's lost colony," McPherson wrote in his report. "The present Indians are the descendants with a further amalgamation continuing down to the present time, together with a small degree of amalgamation with other races."[49] He also concluded that the Robeson Indians did not have any official historical relationship with the federal government, and therefore did not have any special claims or treaty rights.

While all of this was going on, some Indians in eastern North Carolina were also trying to earn federal recognition. If they achieved this, they would receive federal money for their schools. This issue divided communities. Some wanted acknowledgment. In fact, part of the reason that some claimed a connection to the Cherokees was that they were already recognized by the federal government. But others feared that they would lose control of their schools if they earned acknowledgment. Federal money also meant federal mandates and the loss of community oversight. On the Cherokee reservation in western North Carolina, the federal government paid for Indian schools, but it also controlled them, determining who worked there as well as the curriculum. Between 1912 and 1916 congressional representatives from eastern North Carolina introduced at least three bills that would have federally acknowledged the Robeson Indians under a variety of terms. But because of McPherson's report, all of the acknowledgment bills subsequently failed.[50]

Drawing Boundaries

On the eve of the Great Depression, most Native Americans in eastern North Carolina probably appeared, at least to outsiders, completely acculturated. Their daily lives resembled those of poor whites and blacks across the South. Nevertheless, they maintained a separate identity. The cornerstone of that identity was a belief that they were the descendants of North Carolina's original inhabitants. This oral tradition was what made them Native Carolinians, and therefore Native Americans. But other than this belief, what exactly separated these people and communities from others in the state? How did they maintain that identity? In the post–Civil War era, Native Americans in eastern North Carolina established boundaries that marked their distinctiveness. From the 1880s to the 1920s, three characteristics marked the boundaries that separated Indians from others in the region. First, Native Americans maintained a strong attachment to their community and their land—land that in many cases they no longer legally owned. Second, within these communities, an extended network of interrelated families determined Native American identity. And finally, the establishment of Indian-only schools and churches allowed social separation from others and outwardly marked their distinctiveness. Although these factors are interrelated and chronologically overlap, it is easier, and more illustrative, to examine them one by one.

Although the exact tribal origins were somewhat of a mystery, all Native Americans in eastern North Carolina believed, even in the early 1900s, that they were connected to the region's indigenous peoples. That belief was based on oral history. Prior to the arrival of Europeans in the late 1500s, southern Indians, like other nonliterate societies, relied on oral history to chronicle the past. Most Indians in the South remained illiterate well into the twentieth century, forcing communities to rely on oral traditions to pass down their history. These stories, often a mixture of fact and fancy, evoked themes of pride and strength in the face of oppression. Some connected Indian communities to prominent individuals or tribes of the past. Indians living in Sampson County, for example, traced their history back to certain Indians who fought for the colonies during the American Revolution, such as the Tuscarora James Cohary. Other stories involved "trickster" tales, where Indians outsmarted foolish white authorities, a theme also prevalent in African American slave oral tradition. Most important, though, oral history provided a connection with precontact Indian peoples. Native Americans in Bladen and Columbus counties passed down two legends related to their origins. According to the first, many years ago, two lovers got into an argument. The woman prayed for help to Great Eagle, who responded by creating Lake Waccamaw to protect her. According to the second one, a meteor struck the ground in southeastern North Carolina, creating a huge crater. The waters of the surrounding swamps and rivers quickly filled the hole and created a lake. In either case, Lake Waccamaw became the culture hearth and namesake of both the colonial-era tribe and the modern Indian community.[51]

The most common oral tradition among the various Indians in the eastern part of North Carolina involves the "Lost Colony" of the 1580s. As noted above, the mystery of the colony remains unsolved. But some North Carolina Native Americans contend that they know the truth. Every Indian community in the state has, at one time or another, claimed a relationship to the ill-fated settlement. The most popular version is that, facing starvation, the colony left Roanoke and settled among the nearby Algonkian tribes, thus explaining the European features of some modern Indians in the eastern part of the state. Indeed, many of the surnames of the colonists appeared in Indian communities, including Lowry, Cole, Locklear, Moore, and Dare, the latter the last name of the first English child born in America, Virginia Dare. Despite a lack of hard evidence, many Indians became convinced of their connection to the colony. According to one Coharie man, "We have always been told by our fathers and others that we are mixed with the lost colony of Roanoke. We, therefore, are a mixture of Governor White's colony and the original Indians."[52] In the 1980s Adolph Dial, a Lumbee and a professor at the University of North Carolina at Pembroke, pointed to the fact that about one-half of the English surnames of the Lost Colony were still present in Robeson County. "I firmly believe that part of the Lost Colony's blood is here in Robeson County among the Lumbee people," Dial told a reporter.[53] Others disagreed. "It [Dial's claim] doesn't have any basis in fact," William Powell, a historian at the University of North Carolina, Chapel Hill, told the same reporter. "The only evidence he presents is purely traditional . . . and dates from 1880. If he has any documented evidence I'd sure like to see it."[54]

More than any other oral tradition, however, the legend of Henry Berry

Lowry united Native Americans in southeastern North Carolina, especially those in Robeson County. During the twentieth century the tale of the Lowry Gang continued to grow. In addition to those mentioned earlier in this chapter, there are numerous tales in the local history of Lowry and his men. Oral tradition described Lowry as an imaginative and creative escape artist who often avoided capture by making his pursuers look like buffoons. According to one story, Lowry, wearing a disguise, offered to help the homeguard hunt himself and spent several days leading the posse on a wild chase before once again vanishing into the Carolina swamps. In another chapter, a posse surrounded and apparently trapped Lowry in his cabin. A fierce shoot-out followed. After a while Lowry's pursuers noticed that the return fire had stopped. At some point during the standoff, Lowry, his wife, a wounded man, and several other members of his gang escaped through a secret door and fled to the nearby swamps, once again artfully evading capture.[55]

Community membership also helped Native Americans define their boundaries. During the late nineteenth and early twentieth centuries, Indians in eastern North Carolina lived in distinct and separate communities in several different counties. In Sampson County, for example, Indians resided in the small municipalities of Herrings and Dismal. In Bladen, Columbus, Harnett, Hoke, Person, and Scotland counties, they lived, respectively, in the townships of Carvers Creek, Bolton, Averesboro, Antioch, Holloway, and Stewertsville. In Robeson County, Native Americans occupied several small settlements, such as Fairgrove, Magnolia, and Prospect. In Alamance County, Indians lived near Pleasant Grove Township in a community known locally as "Little Texas," while in Halifax County, Indians inhabited "The Meadows" near Hollister. Most of these communities were quite small, ranging from a few dozen families to perhaps several hundred residents. Families and individuals who lived in the places were considered Indians because they lived there. Residence in one of these numerous small settlements, therefore, was a component in defining identity.[56]

Native Americans in eastern North Carolina developed a strong attachment to these communities. The most obvious example of this was Robeson County. To local Indians, Robeson represented a culture hearth, and they considered the county, particularly the Lumber River, the geographical center of their identity. Even when they moved to other communities and states, local Indians referred to Robeson as home and spoke of it reverentially as "God's country." Indians in Sampson, Bladen, Person, and Halifax counties nurtured similar attachments to their communities. In general, Native Americans grew up, married, had children, and died on the same farms in the same communities. Few migrated out of their communities, and fewer still moved into them. Only a handful of poorly maintained dirt roads led into most of these settlements, where ten miles was still considered a great distance to travel. Too poor to buy automobiles, most Indians walked wherever they needed to go, limiting interaction with outsiders.[57]

Within these communities, an extended network of interrelated families also helped define Indian identity. Native Americans often worked and lived on neighboring farms, creating a tightly knit group of related kin. The small number of surnames within an Indian community illustrated the interconnectedness and insularity. In Halifax County, for example, a large number of Indians carried the last names of Richardson and Mills. In southeastern North Carolina, Indians living in Robeson and Sampson counties shared common family names, such as Chavis, Locklear, Lowry, Maynor, Oxendine, and Brewington. In Columbus and Bladen counties, a large number of Indians had the surnames Freeman, Moore, and Jacobs. In Orange and Alamance counties, Jeffries, Enoch, and Watkins were common Indian family names, and in Person County, six family surnames encompassed the entire Indian community.[58]

Although lacking official government structures, Native American communities were nevertheless politically organized. In most communities, school and church committees served as powerful political structures. In addition, the elder men of prominent families frequently emerged as leaders, even if they held no official position of power. Other community members would go to these men for guidance and assistance. Occasionally, leaders formed social groups that also carried informal political power, such as the aforementioned Council of Wide Awake Indians in Bladen and Columbus counties. In the late 1800s Indians in Robeson County founded the Order of the Red Man Lodge, which lasted into the 1930s, when several members organized a new group, the Siouan Tribal Council. Sixteen communities in Robeson elected men to represent them at the general council, which in turn elected officers to run the organization. Similar groups would be created in other communities in future years.[59]

An attachment to place and extended kinship helped North Carolina Native Americans preserve and define their identity, but segregated schools and churches allowed them to separate themselves from others in the state. In schools and churches, Indians used race to protect their identity, and they took their racial standards very seriously, as noted by white outsiders. In 1932 the former governor Angus W. McLean, who was from Robeson County, wrote in a letter to the North Carolina senator Josiah Bailey, "The overwhelming majority of the Indian race has . . . been very jealous in their efforts to keep their blood pure. When special schools were established for the Indians about 1885, they insisted upon excluding from these schools, as the law requires, persons of the negro blood, however remote the strain."[60] In a 1936 memo, the Indian scholar

D'Arcy McNickle, after visiting southeastern North Carolina, noted that "the visitor among these Indians will find them desperately anxious to maintain their racial identity. They resent the fact that Negroes, in one matter or another, have become intermixed with them."[61]

The interesting case of the "Smilings" further illustrated the connection, and the tension, between race and Indian identity in eastern North Carolina. In the early 1900s a group of families claiming Native American heritage moved from Sumter County, South Carolina, into Robeson County. Many of the new arrivals shared the surname of Smiling. Robeson Native Americans doubted their claim of Indian ancestry, however, and barred them from both their schools and churches. The Smilings, who refused to worship with blacks, established their own congregation, and the local school board, unsure what to do with them, built them a separate school. Consequently, for a while, four distinct school systems operated in the county—one for blacks, whites, Indians, and Smilings.[62]

That North Carolina Indians relied on racial arguments to define their identity should not be surprising given the context of the times. As noted above, Social Darwinism reigned in the United States in the late 1800s and early 1900s. Consequently, identity was primarily defined by biology. In the South, Americans were divided along racial lines. While white southerners created Jim Crow biracial segregation, North Carolina Indians actively responded by asserting and protecting their own racial identity. They were not "coloreds," but rather Indians, and demanded recognition as such.[63]

Just as significant as what did define Native American identity in eastern North Carolina during the early twentieth century was what did not. Although most likely the descendants of Tuscaroras, Hatteras, and other colonial-era tribes, Indians no longer referred to themselves by these names. Moreover, they were not federally recognized, they did not live on reservations, they did not wear feathers or warbonnets, and they did not dress or talk "like Indians." In general, they did not fit the typical stereotype of what a Native American should look or act like. And yet, they were still Indians.

Conclusion

When Reconstruction ended in the late 1870s, white southerners began the process of "redeeming" their state governments. With the Republican Party only a minor presence, conservative Democrats regained control of local, county, and state governments across the South, including North Carolina. Although slavery had been abolished, redeemers looked for other ways to control the African American population in the South. They used literacy tests and poll taxes to disfranchise nonwhites, while the system of sharecropping, which still exploited black labor, replaced slavery as the dominant characteristic of the southern agricultural economy.

To separate socially whites and blacks, state governments passed a series of segregation laws that, in effect, created two Souths. In the 1880s the vast majority of North Carolinians could easily be divided into white and black. Though, of course, there was the awkward problem—at least from the perspective of many whites, especially former plantation owners—of what to do with individuals who had both European and African "blood." In most cases, southerners adopted a "one drop rule," defining those with any known African ancestry as "colored." Under the lurking shadow of Social Darwinism, biology defined one's place in southern society.

Not everyone fit neatly into these categories, however. North Carolina and other southern states also contained a small but significant population of American Indians. The Cherokees, a well-known tribe, resided in the Great Smoky Mountains of western North Carolina, while several thousand Native Americans lived in the eastern part of the state. In general, these Indians worked as farmers in small communities of interrelated families. Some owned their own farms, but many others had lost, and were losing, their land to outsiders. Consequently, sharecropping became common in these Indian communities, as it was across the South. To outsiders, their daily life resembled that of other poor North Carolinians, both black and white. But, at the same time, they maintained their identity as Native Americans.

At first the North Carolina government tried to label the Indians living in eastern North Carolina "coloreds." They refused the label, however, and challenged the biracial system of social classification by adamantly refusing to give up their status as the descendants of North Carolina's original inhabitants. The key to their Indian identity, therefore, was this connection to the indigenous peoples of the region. But this connection only internally defined these communities. With the external pressure to assimilate by accepting a legal status as "coloreds," Indians living in these communities needed to find a way to separate themselves physically from others. Consequently, they built their own churches and demanded their own public schools. Ironically, the external threat of legal and political forced assimilation—that is, being labeled simply "colored"—led to new efforts to exhibit publicly their Indian identity. Biracial segregation became, at least in part of eastern North Carolina, triracial. A social system based on biology and race had to acknowledge the fact that there were three racial groups in the state. Jim Crow had adopted a Native American brother: Jim Croatan.

CHAPTER TWO

From Pitchforks to Time Cards

Well, I couldn't see myself being a second-class citizen. I had tasted . . .
what it was like to be a first-class citizen. I was with whites and I had
heard them talk about their opportunities, opportunities that I didn't
have. – James Locklear (Lumbee)

On Black Thursday in October 1929, brokers, financiers, and businessmen in New York City watched helplessly as the stock market spiraled downward. Five days later, on October 29, the market completely collapsed. Billions of dollars' worth of stock became virtually worthless in a matter of hours. Crowds gathered outside on Wall Street to watch the carnage, while traders started fistfights on the floor of the exchange. Although the stock market crash did not cause the subsequent economic crisis, it came to symbolize the beginning of the Great Depression, a decade-long period of poverty and suffering that challenged the limits of democracy and capitalism in the United States.

Eastern North Carolina was several hundred miles and a world away from Wall Street. To Indians living in the Tar Heel state, Manhattan would have looked like an alien world with its motor cars, skyscrapers, electric lights, and teeming masses of immigrants. Nevertheless, North Carolina Indians were part of the national economy, whether they knew it or not, and the subsequent depression affected them as much as it did any group of Americans. The year 1929 marked the beginning of a transitional period for Native Americans in eastern North Carolina, as it did for many other Americans. During the next two decades, the economic, political, and social world of North Carolina Indians would change, and they would have to change with it.

The Great Depression

The Great Depression devastated the agrarian economy in North Carolina. During the 1930s crop prices plummeted and surpluses increased, leaving many farmers with thousands of pounds of nearly worthless harvests. In the 1920s the two main cash crops in North Carolina were still tobacco and cotton. In 1920 tobacco averaged 20 cents and cotton averaged 22.5 cents per pound in the state. At the peak of the Depression, in the mid-1930s, those prices had plummeted to, respectively, 8.6 cents and 6 cents per pound. Facing accumulating debts and unable to sell their crops, thousands of farmers lost their homes and their lands to creditors and bankers. Consequently, sharecroppers and tenant farmers, who relied on landowners for work, found themselves unemployed, and in some cases homeless.[1]

The Great Depression was color-blind and affected all North Carolinians, including Native Americans. In fact, because most were poor farmers, Indians were especially hard hit. Those who did own land often had to sell it because of the inability to pay their mortgages; banks and creditors foreclosed on others. Sharecroppers and tenant farmers lost their jobs and their homes when landowners became unwilling or unable to pay them. Those who were fortunate enough to keep employment usually earned less as crop prices continued to fall. Of course, while their income dropped, their debts continued to mount. Times were hard, and Indians eked out an existence as best they could. "People didn't have but a few clothes and what they raised was the only food they had," one North Carolina Indian man later recalled. "There was no money [and] many of our people didn't have farms and gardens where they could grow food."[2]

Because the census at that time did not keep detailed records for non–federally recognized Native Americans, the exact statistics for Indians in eastern North Carolina are difficult to determine. But an examination of Robeson County, which at that time was about one-fourth Indian, illustrates the effects of the Depression on Native American farmers during the early 1930s. According to the U.S. Department of Commerce, the number of farm owners in Robeson decreased from 1925 to 1935 by 3.4 percent, while the number of sharecroppers went up more than 36 percent. From 1930 to 1935 the average value of a farm decreased 21 percent, and the total acreage harvested went down 3.2 percent. Moreover, there was a significant change in what was being grown. In 1929 farmers in the county allocated 64,000 acres to corn, 97,800 acres to cotton, and 24,300 acres to tobacco. In 1934 those numbers were 87,000, 60,000, and 19,600, respectively. The reliance on the cash crops of cotton and tobacco decreased significantly in relation to corn, an important food crop.[3]

For several reasons, the competition for sharecropping and tenant jobs in eastern North Carolina increased dramatically in the 1930s, especially for Native Americans. First, as farm owners lost their land, they were forced to become workers. Second, the birth rate for Indians had gone up dramatically in the 1920s, causing the ratio of people to land also to increase. The total Robeson population grew from 54,674 in 1920 to 66,512 in 1930, an increase of almost 22 percent in ten years. Consequently, while there were 52.5 inhabitants per square mile in Robeson in 1920, there were 65 per square mile in 1930. And finally, large white landowners actively recruited white farm families from other counties in the state to compete for jobs. The Robeson County farm owner Paul McNeill, for example, brought in eight white families from a Piedmont county in 1934 to work on his land. McNeill and others did this for two reasons. First, during the Depression, they preferred to give jobs to needy white families rather than to needy Indian families; and second, the recruitment increased job competition, allowing them to negotiate better yearly contracts. By the mid-1930s Indian farmers, many of whom had been working the same land for years, were rapidly losing their jobs to outsiders. Some estimated that as many as 30 percent of Native American sharecroppers were unable to renew their contracts in 1936. According to one white overseer, as many as thirty Indians would apply for each job opening on his farm.[4]

By the middle of the 1930s, Native Americans in eastern North Carolina were in a desperate situation. John Pearmain, an assistant specialist representing the Indian Rehabilitation Division of the Resettlement Administration, noted the problem when he visited Robeson and surrounding counties in November 1935. Pearmain conducted more than fifty interviews with local farmers, mostly Native Americans. According to his report, Indians scratched out a living on annual contracts that paid them little and left them in debt to either the owner or a local merchant. Wash Bell was typical. A sharecropper, Bell borrowed two hundred dollars during World War I to purchase supplies; but at 10 percent interest, he still owed two hundred in 1935, despite nearly two decades of hard work and attempts to pay down his debt. Nathaniel Dial's case was more extreme. In 1926 he had borrowed five hundred dollars to buy needed provisions; nine years later, he owed more than two thousand. Because of this debt, Dial subsequently lost his farm. Dial contended that some local white creditors lent Indians money then intentionally prevented them from repaying the loan in order to foreclose on their land. Others echoed his complaint. In his report, Pearmain concluded that outsiders, corporate farmers, and white businessmen were foreclosing on debts in order to purchase large tracts of land in Robeson County. By the late 1930s Butters Lumber Company, Pates Supply Company, and the Beaufort County Lumber Company all owned land in Robeson, as did a few wealthy families who did not live in the county. The president of Pates Supply, for example, owned more than 430 acres in Robeson. According to one Indian man, "Anyone who gets in debt to them is fairly sure to lose his place."[5]

Pearmain's report also noted the terrible living conditions among Native Americans in eastern North Carolina. Many owned very few clothes, usually just the rags on their backs, and children often went shoeless. He also examined twenty-nine Indian houses, classifying ten as good, seven fair, and twelve poor. Moreover, Pearmain's standards for rating the houses were pretty low— none of them, even the ones he rated good, had either indoor plumbing or electricity. On average, there were 3.29 rooms and 7.15 persons per dwelling, and extended families often shared the same residence. Sixteen people lived in Sheldon Bullard's five-room house, while Lindsey Revels shared his three-room home with ten family members. Pearmain described Henry Locklear's home as "mighty sorry; leaky; no chimney [hence no heat]; the wind goes through it." When evicted from their homes, some Indians stayed in tobacco barns. During the winters, pneumonia ravaged the homeless and the poor, while during the summers, malaria plagued all.[6]

Even the whites Pearmain interviewed noticed the exceptional misery among Native Americans. J. T. Moore and his wife moved to Robeson County in the 1920s when he took a job as the overseer on the eleven-hundred-acre Fletcher Plantation. At any given time, about eighteen Indian families worked on the plantation's land as either tenant farmers or sharecroppers. Moore told Pearmain in 1935 that destitute Native Americans asked him daily for jobs. Moore admitted that white landowners were recruiting white farmers from other counties and that large corporate farms were buying up land through foreclosures. His wife, who was a relief worker for the North Carolina Emergency Administration, also described the poverty among Indian people in Robeson County. Both Moores blamed the problems on the inequities of sharecropping, arguing that the system was "ruining this country." Many poor Indians, blacks, and whites probably agreed.[7]

An Indian New Deal

Shortly after taking office in 1933, President Franklin D. Roosevelt declared the South the nation's number one economic problem. Through his New Deal, FDR implemented policies to reduce both crop production and the total amount of acreage farmed, which would bolster prices while dealing with the problem of overproduction. New legislation, such as the Agricultural Adjustment Act (AAA), encouraged the growth of large-scale mechanized farming, igniting a

Indian family at home in Robeson County, ca. 1930. Photo courtesy of the National Archives and Records Administration, Washington DC.

southern agricultural revolution. These programs benefited large landowners at the expense of many smaller farmers and sharecroppers, though that was not the intention of the optimistic New Dealers. With access to low-interest loans, wealthy farmers shifted from labor-intensive to capital-intensive farming by investing in heavy equipment, specializing in one crop, and adopting new scientific techniques. Unburdened of their previous labor needs, large planters promptly fired tenant farmers and eventually drove many smaller family farms out of the market. The New Deal ultimately contributed to the development of agribusiness while destroying the traditional family farm, a cultural institution and a way of life in the rural South. Ironically, the New Deal, in some ways, actually accelerated what the Great Depression had started.[8]

Aware of the economic problems plaguing reservations, Roosevelt sought to include Native Americans in his New Deal coalition. In April 1933, FDR boldly appointed John Collier commissioner of Indian Affairs. Unlike most of his predecessors, Collier was actually familiar with, and respected, Native American history and culture. Born in Georgia in 1884, Collier devoted much

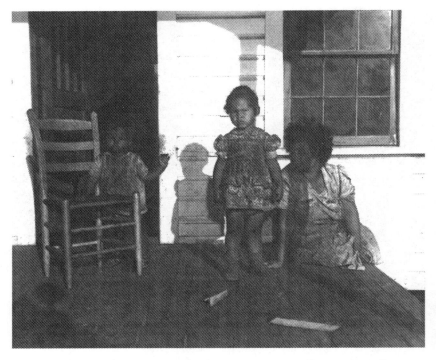

*Indian family at home in Columbus County, ca. 1940. Photo courtesy of
the North Carolina Office of Archives and History, Raleigh NC.93.11.1.*

of his life to studying and helping American Indians. In the 1920s he cofounded
the American Indian Defense Association (AIDA), a group of white scholars,
writers, and reformers dedicated to assisting Native Americans. AIDA criticized
the current federal Indian policy of allotment, which, since the 1880s, had been
designed to break up reservations, dissolve tribal governments, and turn Indians
into small economically self-sufficient farmers. At the same time, the federal
government was confiscating millions of acres of Indian land, selling or giving it
away to white individuals and corporations. Allotment was a disaster for Native
Americans. In the late 1800s and early 1900s, the federal government seized more
than ninety million acres, or approximately two-thirds of all land held by Native
American tribes. In the 1920s AIDA and other groups financed and authored
several reports that documented the failures of allotment and described the
rampant poverty among Native Americans. The group also advocated cultural
and religious freedom for Indian tribes.

When Collier took over the Bureau of Indian Affairs (BIA), he immediately initiated a series of programs often called the "Indian New Deal." The Indian Emergency Conservation Work Program, which was part of the Civilian Conservation Corps, employed more than eighty-five thousand Native Americans at a cost of seventy-two million dollars. Along with giving Indians jobs, the program sought to revitalize reservations through agricultural improvements, erosion control, and other infrastructure projects. The Agricultural Adjustment Act, the Soil Conservation Service, the National Youth Administration, and other federal programs also contributed to the Indian New Deal.

The centerpiece of Collier's program was the Wheeler-Howard Act, also known as the Indian Reorganization Act (IRA). Passed in 1934, the IRA ended allotment, reestablished reservations and tribal governments, encouraged conservation of tribal resources, and provided funds for the purchase of new tribal lands. Moreover, under the new act, both unrecognized tribes and individual Indians could petition for federal acknowledgment. The IRA also promoted Indian art and culture and allowed tribes to practice traditional religions, which the federal government had previously discouraged. In keeping to his philosophy of tribal sovereignty, Collier allowed Native Americans to choose whether to accept IRA reforms—181 tribes voted to adopt reorganization, and 71 turned it down.[9]

Some scholars have criticized Collier for being too paternalistic and not understanding the diversity of tribal cultures, but most generally contend that the Indian New Deal was a positive step for Native Americans. The author Stephen Cornell went so far as to call the IRA a watershed in Indian-white relations. Cornell admits that the ultimate goal of the Indian New Deal was still assimilation of Native Americans, though in a less severe way. Nevertheless, the IRA benefited most tribes. According to Cornell, the reforms curbed the power of both the BIA and federal agents and encouraged a cultural renaissance in Indian country. But most important, the IRA led to the formation of numerous tribal political organizations as well as multitribal advocacy groups. In short, the IRA and the Indian New Deal helped tribes pool their resources and mobilize politically. In subsequent years, when Congress would debate policies regarding Native American issues, Indians would actually have a voice, even if it was a muted one. Or as Cornell put it, "While the federal government still called the tune, the political dance was never again the same."[10]

In the mid-1930s, a group of North Carolina Indians tried to earn recognition, and therefore access to federal aid, through Collier's Indian Reorganization Act. The Siouan Tribal Lodge of Robeson County sent Joseph Brooks, one of the group's cofounders, to Washington to act as a lobbyist. The charismatic Brooks quickly established a good relationship with several government officials, including Collier. Influenced by Brooks, the Senate introduced a bill to recognize officially the Robeson Indians as Cherokees. The Senate Committee on Indian Affairs and the acting secretary of the Interior Joseph Dixon attacked the bill, however, arguing that they were not Cherokees and therefore did not have a relationship with the federal government. Elwood P. Morley, a white lawyer from Robeson County, wrote a lengthy letter to the North Carolina senator Josiah Bailey insisting that the Robeson Indians were, in fact, biologically related to the Eastern Band, but he presented little concrete evidence to support this claim. The letter included the names of about six hundred individuals in Robeson County who he believed were Cherokees. Confused, Bailey and others asked the ethnologist John R. Swanton of the Smithsonian Institute to research the heritage of the Native American community. Once again, as with McPherson, the federal government asked an outside expert to determine the origins of these people. Swanton issued a report concluding that they were most likely of Siouan descent. "The evidence available thus seems to indicate that the Indians of Robeson County who have been called Croatan and Cherokee are descended mainly from certain Siouan tribes of which the most prominent were the Cheraw and Keyauwee," Swanton wrote. "Therefore, if the name of any tribe is to be used in connection with this body of six to eight thousand people, that of the Cheraw would, in my opinion, be most appropriate."[11]

Based on this report, several senators initiated a new bill designating the community the Siouan Indians of Robeson County. Hoping that it would lead to recognition, some Robeson Indians supported the new "Siouan" bill. Joseph Brooks, B. J. Graham, and Johnnie P. Bullard traveled to Washington by train to lobby in favor of the bill. Others, however, feared that they would lose control of their children's education. Under the current system, the local community controlled educational policies, including admission. But if the tribe earned recognition, the federal government would take over the local school system. Letters and telegrams both for and against the bill flooded Bailey's office. James E. Chavis, who called himself the secretary of the General Council of the Indians of Robeson County, wrote that his group spoke for the majority of the community, and that they supported the new bill. Clifton Oxendine, a Robeson County Indian, wrote to Bailey that "the majority of the Indians of Robeson County are absolutely opposed to the passing of such a bill by congress . . . this bill isn't backed by our race as a whole but only by a few who do not know exactly what is best for us."[12]

D. F. Lowry led the attack on the bill. Born in 1881, Lowry was a nephew of the famous outlaw Henry Berry Lowry. In 1905 he became the first graduate of the Croatan Normal School and went on to become an influential teacher and minister in Robeson County. Lowry opposed the Siouan bill partially because he wanted to earn recognition as Cherokee. He also believed that Brooks was trying to get the federal government to establish a reservation in Robeson County, something that he opposed. In a letter to Senator Bailey, Lowry contended that Joseph Brooks only had the support of about two thousand of the fifteen thousand Indians in Robeson County and that Brooks had lied to them. "Mr. Brooks told in a public address at the beginnin of this campagne that the money was piled up in bags for distribution as soon as they could get National Recognition at Washington," Lowry wrote. "They were further told by other leaders of groop that each family would get at least twenty acres of land, a mule and wagon and a farm house built there on by the Government and a small appropriation."[13]

Despite initial support from the BIA, the Department of the Interior resisted acknowledging the Indians in Robeson County. Officials feared that other groups in other states would also petition for recognition. In the spring of 1936, the secretary of the Interior concluded that "as the Federal Government is not under any treaty obligated to these Indians, it is not believed that the United States should assume the burden of the education of their children, which has heretofore been looked after by the State of North Carolina."[14] Once again, though they refused to help the Robeson Indians, federal officials did not challenge their identity, but rather their lack of a historical relationship with the government. All certification bills subsequently died in Congress, and the Robeson Native Americans remained unrecognized.

Failing to earn recognition as a tribe, a small group of Robeson Native Americans petitioned the government for acknowledgment as Indians. According to the guidelines of the IRA, individual Indians, as well as tribes, could petition for federal acknowledgment. In the summer of 1936, Joseph Brooks asked the BIA for help, and John Collier responded by sending a three-man committee to Robeson to determine whether the locals were "real" Indians. The committee consisted of Dr. Carl C. Seltzer, a physical anthropologist affiliated with the Peabody Museum at Harvard University; Edward S. McMahon, a probate lawyer; and D'Arcy McNickle, a noted Native American writer who was part Chippewa-Cree. McNickle and McMahon would conduct genealogical and documentary research while Seltzer would physically examine individuals to determine their racial identity.[15]

More than one hundred people paid the two-dollar fee and applied for recognition. Because of the lack of existing written records, McNickle and McMahon contributed very little to the process. The burden of determining Indian identity, therefore, fell to Seltzer. The anthropologist spent most of the month of June in

Robeson testing individuals for Indianness by "measuring" their hair, teeth, eyes, noses, skulls, and other physical features, a process known as anthropometry. Many of the subjects found the examinations demeaning and humiliating, yet they endured the ordeal in order to try to earn recognition. Seltzer, however, concluded that only three of the candidates were at least "one-half" Indian, the minimum requirement for recognition under the IRA. The committee members then left Robeson County and returned to Washington with their results.[16]

Unhappy with the outcome, some Robeson Indians asked the BIA to conduct more research. One year later, in August 1937, Seltzer returned to North Carolina, this time alone. After another series of physical examinations, he certified nineteen more Indians out of a pool of another one hundred. Some others were deemed "borderline" cases. In total, Seltzer declared that twenty-two Robeson County Indians were eligible for benefits under the IRA. From the perspective of the twenty-first century, Seltzer's findings were comically illogical. In several cases, he certified an individual as an "authentic" Indian, then rejected the subject's parents and full siblings. Nevertheless, the BIA and the federal government accepted his results as scientific. Of the two hundred people who applied, the government officially acknowledged only the twenty-two. From the beginning, those who attempted to earn recognition were fighting an uphill battle. "Since it was agreed upon that the burden of proof was on the applicants," the committee stated in 1937, "in all cases where the physical data showed a borderline or a doubtful diagnosis it was considered that the applicant had not satisfied the requirement."[17]

The committee's report and the accompanying documents illustrated how the federal government defined Native American identity. To government officials, Indianness was totally based on biology and physical characteristics. The committee expressed this view in its report. "Our task was made difficult at the outset by the fact that these people did not have a clear understanding of the term Indian," the members wrote to John Collier. "They considered anybody who lived in their community as one of them."[18] The federal government and the Indians of eastern North Carolina also defined "full-blood" and "mixed-blood" differently. "In specifying degree of Indian blood it is evidently their habit to describe as full blood any person whose parents or ancestors have always been members of their community," they wrote in the same report. "And naturally a mixed blood to them is a person some one or more of whose forebears have come into the country from the outside."[19] In other words, the federal government defined Indianness in strictly biological terms, whereas Indians in eastern North Carolina based their identity on community and kinship, which was not limited to ancestry.

Perhaps because he was part Native American, D'Arcy McNickle was sympathetic to the Robeson Indians. Born in 1904, McNickle grew up on the reservation of the Salish and Kutenai tribes. In 1933 John Collier offered McNickle a job at the BIA, where he became a strong proponent of the Indian New Deal. Influenced by his experiences at the BIA, McNickle became increasingly involved in national Indian affairs. He played an important role in the formation of the National Congress of American Indians in 1944 and later helped found the Center for the History of the American Indian at the Newberry Library in Chicago. While visiting Robeson County, McNickle grasped the inherent problems in the way the government defined Indianness. "One realizes after visiting them that a race is something more than a social or political complex," he wrote in 1936. "Here is a people from whom all native language and tradition have disappeared, yet they keep within themselves an unfailing recognition of their link with the past."[20]

Because of Seltzer's report and their failure to earn recognition, most Indians in eastern North Carolina were ineligible for federal aid under the Indian Reorganization Act. Yet Collier, McNickle, and others in the BIA still wanted to help them. Collier asked Interior Department officials to look into the matter. They agreed, and Assistant Commissioner William Zimmerman Jr. sent Fred Baker, the superintendent of the Sisseton Indian Agency in South Dakota, to eastern North Carolina to investigate "the feasibility of setting up a land purchase and work relief project for the rehabilitation of the Siouan Indians of North Carolina."[21] Baker was to report back on the possibility of initiating a program in Robeson under the new Resettlement Administration, which was established in 1935 to give struggling farmers better land. The agent spent several weeks in the area talking to Indians and analyzing the geography, soil, and climate of the area. He also organized meetings at schools and churches in several different communities, perhaps speaking with as many as four thousand local Indians. He concluded that the area was an excellent candidate for a resettlement project. "I do not believe that a better opportunity exists anywhere for the successful carrying out of a rational rural rehabilitation than that which presents itself in Robeson County, North Carolina among this people," he wrote in a letter to John Collier. Furthermore, the Indians in the area really wanted government help. In the same letter, Baker wrote that the local Indians "seemed to regard the advent of the United States government into their affairs as the dawn of a new day; a new hope and a new vision . . . many of the old people could not restrain their feelings; tears filled many eyes and flowed down furrowed cheeks."[22]

Collier, Baker, and the majority of Native Americans in Robeson apparently supported the proposed program, but the Resettlement Administration (RA) had final approval of the project. After reading Baker's report, RA administrators agreed to start a program in the area so that local Indians could establish self-sufficient farms. There was, however, a problem. The RA, which was not part of the BIA, could not legally set up a program exclusively for Native Americans, or any other racial group for that matter. Joseph Brooks, who supported the project, met with the director of the Rural Settlement Division of the RA, Dr. Carl Taylor, to discuss the situation. Taylor ensured Brooks that the Robeson project would unofficially be only for Native Americans, though that fact would never be made public. Consequently, in the mid-1930s, the Resettlement Administration established Pembroke Farms, a nine-thousand-acre tract of contiguous land in Robeson County. The federal government paid for the land to be cleared, a process that cost about thirty dollars per acre. About seventy-five families obtained loans from the regional branch of the Farm Securities Administration (FSA) and purchased small farms that included a modest five-room house. The government also provided livestock, equipment, tools, fertilizer, barns, warehouses, and even a school. The response to Pembroke Farms was lukewarm at best. Many local Native Americans were understandably hesitant to go into debt, even at the low rates offered by the FSA, and about half of the land remained unused.[23]

Because of the fears of debt, the federal government gave the Robeson Native Americans another option. In 1938 the FSA purchased a large tract of land and established Red Banks Mutual Association (RBMA) as an offshoot of Pembroke Farms. The farmers' cooperative included individual homes, barns, sheds, and warehouses. Led by an elected board of directors, the participants borrowed capital together, farmed together, and shared the profits. The FSA also built a community center and school. In 1943 sixteen families were part of the RBMA, which held about seventeen hundred acres on a ninety-nine year lease. Like Pembroke Farms, the co-op met with only mixed success. Many Robeson Indians, who had a tradition of individualism, remained skeptical and avoided Red Banks because of its communal nature. Some also complained that whites, not Indians, ran Red Banks. But it did manage to last for thirty years before finally closing in 1968, making it the longest lasting New Deal program of its type.[24]

In an effort to revive local Indian culture, the Resettlement Administration and Farm Securities Administration also provided funds for the development of a historical pageant in Robeson County. The government hired Ella C. Deloria, the aunt of the noted Indian author Vine Deloria Jr., to write and direct the production. The play's themes partially reflected her own background. Born in 1889, Deloria, a Yankton-Sioux, was the daughter of an Episcopalian minister. She studied with the noted anthropologist Franz Boas before working as a research specialist in ethnology and linguistics for the Department of Anthropology at Columbia University. She is perhaps best known for her novel *Waterlily.* Deloria's script emphasized the supposed connection between the Robeson Indians and the "Lost Colony" and stressed Indian patriotism, Americanism, and Christianity. The whole community got involved in the play, with local Indian college students cast in most of the roles. *A Life Story of a People* was advertised as an "authentic" production of regional Indian history and culture, though characters wore feathered headdresses and Plains Indian regalia. The play, staged in the gym on the Pembroke State campus, ran three nights in December 1940, drew large multiracial crowds, and earned positive reviews from the state's major newspapers. Deloria invited Commissioner Collier to the opening, but, despite expressing interest in the project, he did not attend. During the first week of December 1941, the Robeson Indians again staged *A Life Story,* but the production was subsequently canceled because of World War II.[25]

Indian School Expansion

Despite the economic woes of the 1930s, Native Americans in eastern North Carolina continued building and maintaining their own schools. They also kept asking local and state officials for more financial aid. In Bladen and Columbus counties, for example, the Council of Wide Awake Indians repeatedly asked the local school boards for improvements to their schools. According to legend, one Native American man walked thirty miles on twenty-five separate occasions in the early 1930s to visit the county school superintendent and demand a new school. Finally, in 1933, Bladen County school officials agreed to give them an old abandoned building to use. Indians tore down the structure, carried it back to their community, and rebuilt it into a one-room schoolhouse named the Wide Awake Indian Public School.[26]

Columbus and Bladen Native Americans continued to complain to county officials about the lack of funds and the deplorable condition of the school. In 1941 school administrators responded by designating a small sum for the construction of a new schoolhouse. Once again, however, the local Native American community shouldered the heavy end of the financial burden. Supplying their own labor, they constructed a new four-room brick school that housed grades one through eight.[27]

In Alamance County, the small Indian community known as "Little Texas" also asked the government for its own school. In the early 1900s three small schools that were technically classified as "colored" had served the community. Native American parents did not mind the racial categorization of the schools, though, because they served only their children. But the county school board merged several smaller schools into a new large "colored" school in Pleasant Grove. Native American children were now going to a school where they were in the minority. In the 1930s Indian parents asked the board for their own school because non-Indian students at Pleasant Grove were teasing their children. After county officials rejected their request, Native American parents petitioned the BIA for help under the Indian Reorganization Act. In 1934 the BIA sent the agent Samuel Thompson to "Little Texas" to investigate the community. Though he was considerate, Thompson did not think that the community was eligible for federal assistance. "I do think we ought to know more about these people," he reported after returning. "It's almost certain that . . . the Texas people have some Indian blood, but very little, and they have no documentary evidence."[28]

In Robeson County, the increasing Indian population required educational changes. In 1925 about 3,300 Indian children were enrolled in county schools, and the average daily attendance was about 2,100. By 1935 the total enrollment had grown to 4,600, an increase of 39 percent, and the daily attendance was 3,600, an increase of 76 percent. Not only were more students enrolled, but a much higher percentage was attending school regularly, particularly because of the Depression, as there was little farm work for them to do. This growth necessitated new schools, larger classrooms, and more teachers. County officials responded by expanding educational facilities. By the early 1940s Robeson County had twenty-five Indian-only schools with 5,300 students and more than 140 teachers; twenty-two buses drove Native American students back and forth from home to school each day.[29]

Other Native American communities in North Carolina also improved their schools in the 1930s and 1940s, constructing new buildings, renovating old ones, and hiring better teachers. In Person County, the local Indians opened High Plains School. In Sampson County, Indian veterans demanded the construction of a new agricultural school to teach future farmers modern techniques. Other North Carolina Indian schools expanded their curricula, adding home economics, driver's education, art, health, and other electives. The qualifications of the teachers also improved as administrators hired more college graduates with degrees in education.[30]

Most Indian schools in eastern North Carolina stopped with the eighth grade. Students who wanted to go to high school, or perhaps even college, had to enter North Carolina's biracial system and enroll in black schools. In 1940 a group of parents petitioned the state for funds to construct a Native American high school in eastern North Carolina. The General Assembly approved the request and appropriated ten thousand dollars. Opening in Sampson County in 1942, the Eastern Carolina Indian School (ECIS) was the symbolic peak in the rise of a separate Native American educational system in eastern North Carolina. Indian students from several counties attended the school, often living with local Indian families in Sampson County during the school year. Indian parents had high aspirations for the ECIS, but like so many other Indian schools, it suffered from inadequate funding, lacking both electricity and indoor plumbing. Nevertheless, Native Americans were extremely proud of the ECIS—their children could now attend Indian-only schools from kindergarten through the twelfth grade.[31]

Despite being a source of pride, Native American schools in eastern North Carolina remained, like the ECIS, poorly funded and equipped. The per-pupil expenditure was well below that of white schools, though actually higher than black schools. When visiting Robeson County in the middle of the twentieth century, the noted sociologist Brewton Berry found schools with leaky roofs, broken windows, rotten wood, and crude desks. Textbooks were usually outdated and in poor physical condition, and few schools maintained libraries. A reporter noted children in a Person County Indian school still using an outhouse that had been condemned. Another observer described a North Carolina Indian school where "the windows are poorly spaced and furnish only about one-half of the light needed, dark, dirty walls aggravate this condition. The blackboards are poor and insufficient. The seats are old, and not the proper size. There are no instructional supplies."[32]

The quality of education was obviously inferior to white schools, but, given the financial constraints, the system was somewhat of a success. In the 1930s 53 percent of Indian children in the state attended school, compared to 55 percent of whites and 53 percent of African Americans, a surprisingly close measurement. The median grade level completed for adults over the age of twenty-five that year was 8.1 for whites, 5.1 for blacks, and 4.9 for Indians. Native Americans were still undereducated when compared to others, but their children attended school at about the same rate, and the difference in the education level was small, especially considering all of the other factors that could have retarded Indian education. Although they paid the same local and county taxes that whites paid, Native American parents frequently had to pay additional enrollment fees to send their children to Indian-only schools. And in the early twentieth century, a formal education offered few rewards for Native Americans and other minorities in North Carolina. Most Indians were still farmers, and Jim Crow restricted other economic opportunities.[33]

The growth of Indian-only schools in North Carolina during the 1930s also required more and better-trained teachers. Consequently, the normal school in

Indian schoolchildren of Columbus County, ca. 1940. Photo courtesy of the North Carolina Office of Archives and History, Raleigh NC.

Robeson County expanded and modernized. In the late 1930s Pembroke added a college curriculum and subsequently earned accreditation in 1940 from the Southern Association of Colleges as an institution of higher learning. One year later the newly renamed Pembroke State College for Indians conferred its first baccalaureate degrees. In the 1940s Pembroke State started participating in intercollegiate athletics, playing other small colleges in basketball, baseball, and other sports. At that time Pembroke was the only public four-year college for Indians in the United States. As such, it was a source of tremendous pride for Native Americans in eastern North Carolina.[34]

World War II

Although it did address some of the economic weaknesses in the country, the New Deal did not really end the Great Depression. It took a world war and the accompanying military buildup to bring America out of its greatest economic crisis. World War II was a major turning point for Indians in the United States. Nationally, more than twenty-five thousand served in the military, and forty thousand worked in factories on the home front. After the war many returned to their home communities. Some went willingly, while others went back only after losing their jobs to white veterans. But all of these Indians returned home changed men. Having experienced the outside world and the economic opportunities that others enjoyed, veterans and factory workers refused to accept a subjugated status. Contemporary observers immediately recognized the war's significance for Native Americans. Ella Deloria, who had authored *A Life Story* a few years earlier, wrote in 1944 that "the war has indeed wrought an overnight change in the outlook, horizon, and even the habits of the Indian people—a change that might not have come for many years yet."[35] In recent years, scholars have also noted the significance of World War II for Native Americans. In a comprehensive look at Indians and the war, the historian Alison Bernstein argued that "World War II had a more profound and lasting effect on the course of Indian affairs in this century than any other single event or period."[36]

For Native Americans in eastern North Carolina, World War II also proved to be a turning point. Following Japan's attack on Pearl Harbor in December 1941, many North Carolina Indians heeded FDR's call to arms. Some enlisted; others were drafted. In both cases, racial classification became an issue, as military officials tried to categorize some North Carolina Indians as "colored." During World War II African Americans served in segregated units, whereas Native Americans served with whites. But since Indians in eastern North Carolina were not officially recognized, government officials questioned their racial identity. In 1943, for example, the selective service board drafted six young Indians from Columbus County. The officer tried to list them as "colored," but the young men refused and returned home. The case ended up before a state judge who ruled that the men could serve their country as American Indians. In Alamance County, draft officials listed several young men who claimed to be Indians as "negroes." They refused to serve until their classification was changed to Indian. Indeed, during World War II most Native Americans from North Carolina, as well as other states, served in white units.[37]

Because some probably were classified as "colored," it is difficult to know exactly how many North Carolina Indians participated in World War II. Based on federal records, however, at least one thousand served in either World War II or Korea, though the exact number is most likely higher. According to oral histories, many veterans experienced surprisingly little racism and discrimination in the military. Nor were they relegated to menial tasks as chefs or janitors, like many African Americans were. Some even fought on the front lines, both in Europe and the Pacific. The Lumbee Simeon Oxendine, for example, flew numerous missions for the 360th Bomb Squadron of the Eighth Air Force, also known as "Hell's Angels." At least forty Indians from eastern North Carolina made the ultimate sacrifice, losing their lives while fighting for their country.[38]

North Carolina Indians also participated on the home front, taking advantage of the booming wartime economy to find industrial jobs. Compared to what they were used to earning, these jobs offered good wages. Since most of the factories were in urban areas, many young men moved to cities, both inside and outside of the state. A number of Halifax County Indians went to Detroit, for example, while Robeson Indians migrated north to Baltimore. For many of these Indians—both the soldiers and the workers—it was their first trip outside of the state, and the experience would carry over into the postwar years. As in the military, North Carolina Indians encountered less overt racism than they expected. War and the need for labor had a democratizing effect on many Americans, but this would change when soldiers returned and competition for jobs increased.[39]

After the war Native American veterans returned to North Carolina to a heroes' welcome. In March 1946 more than 350 Indian veterans proudly marched in a Robeson County parade. Many of the young men who had worked in the cities also came back more worldly and self-confident. Upon his return, James Locklear decided to inspire change in the social caste system. "Well I couldn't see myself being a second class citizen," he recalled. "I had tasted . . . what it was like to be a first class citizen. I was with whites and I had heard them talk about their opportunities, opportunities that I didn't have. We discussed those things, me and them [white] boys got very close to each other."[40]

World War II also accelerated the economic transformation in the South, which had begun under the New Deal. The demand for farm products increased in the late 1930s, when the United States sent aid to England, and accelerated in the 1940s, after America officially entered the war. At the same time, the draft and the need for industrial workers on the home front shrank the agricultural labor market and ended the unemployment problem. In the 1940s a labor shortage actually replaced the labor surplus of the 1930s. Large farm owners, who previously had relied on cheap and plentiful labor, now adopted more scientific and capital-intensive methods in order to keep up with demand. The government offered low-interest loans so that farmers could buy new tractors and mechanized cotton pickers. Farmers also used new pesticides and fertilizers to increase productivity. This trend continued after the war as southern farms got bigger and more profitable while the number of small family farms declined rapidly. More than 1.6 million people lived on farms in North Carolina in 1940. That number plummeted to fewer than 500,000 in 1970, despite a significant increase in the state's overall population. From 1940 to 1970, the total number of farms in the state fell from 278,000 to fewer than 120,000. During that same time period, the approximate value of the agricultural output per farm increased from $781 to $33,941, illustrating the trend toward larger and more productive farms. These changes directly affected Native Americans in the state. Whereas before the war, approximately 90 percent of North Carolina Indians worked on farms, by 1980, less than 6 percent still tilled the soil.[41]

While the agricultural sector modernized, parts of the South also industrialized. Two separate but related trends drove this industrialization. First, the federal government pumped billions of dollars into the South's economy during the war, partially by building several large military bases in the region. In North Carolina the Department of Defense established Fort Bragg and Pope Air Force Base. The flow of defense contracts southward continued after the war, with the region receiving increasing shares of the military budget. Second, private companies began to build factories in the 1950s in the South to take advantage of the region's low tax rates, cheap land, and abundance of nonunion labor. As the historians James Cobb and Bruce Schulman demonstrated, a new economy, based on large commercial farming and manufacturing, emerged in the postwar South. From 1929 to 1948 agricultural employment decreased from 35 percent of the total workforce to 20 percent, while the number of workers in the manufacturing sector increased 20 percent. But, as both authors have concluded, the industrialization of the South did not destroy the social, political, and economic traditions of the old "New South," as the benefits of industrialization fell to only a few. Most southerners, particularly minorities, remained poor, and strong institutionalized racism still plagued the region.[42]

Postwar industrialization affected North Carolina as much, if not more, as any other southern state. During and after the war, several Tar Heel politicians actively encouraged industrialization by recruiting companies and convincing them to relocate to North Carolina. In 1948 Governor Kerr Scott pushed through a two-hundred-million-dollar bond to improve highways and roads in the state, which would allow companies to move goods more efficiently. In the 1950s Governor Luther Hodges declared economic modernization his number one goal and played a major role in the creation of the Research Triangle Park, a large corporate campus in the Raleigh, Durham, and Chapel Hill area designed to attract companies in the burgeoning technological field. Scott, Hodges, and other political leaders in the state lured prospective industries with promises of cheap and plentiful nonunion labor. North Carolinians took pride in their economic success, marketing themselves as the most "progressive" of the southern states. For the first half of the twentieth century, agriculture had been the cornerstone of the state's economy, and in 1950 about one-fourth of the state's population still worked on farms. But by 1980 only about 3 percent of the state's labor force worked in the agricultural sector, while one-third worked in manufacturing. In a single generation North Carolina farmers became industrial wage laborers, trading pitchforks and shovels for hard hats and time cards.[43]

These economic changes pushed most eastern North Carolina Native Americans into the industrial wage-labor market. Some took jobs in the new factories opening in the area, such as BF Goodrich and Converse, while others found work in paper mills and chemical plants. The change in eastern North Carolina, which had for years been mostly agricultural, was dramatic. In the 1950s and 1960s, new industries created more than ten thousand jobs in Cumberland County alone. In Columbus County, about one-half of the Indian men worked in the booming construction industry, while Native American women often took jobs in textile mills or as social service workers. In these new jobs, Native Americans interacted much more frequently with people from outside of their home communities.[44]

World War II also offered Native Americans new economic opportunities. In 1944 Congress passed the Servicemen's Readjustment Act, commonly known as the GI Bill. The legislation offered economic assistance to veterans, such as low-interest loans to start businesses and buy homes. The GI Bill also subsidized higher education by paying tuition, fees, and living expenses for up to three years of college. Millions of veterans took advantage of the plan to further their education. Critics, however, complained that the GI Bill benefited white males more than others. The criticism was valid, but the act did help some minorities. Many North Carolina Indians took advantage of the GI Bill to attend college and broaden their economic opportunities. Before the war there were only a handful of Indian professionals in the state, but by 1980, partially because of the Servicemen's Readjustment Act, there were more than thirty-two hundred, including many doctors and lawyers. Historians have concluded that the GI Bill contributed heavily to the growth of the middle class in postwar America; the same can be said for Indians in North Carolina.[45]

The war and the accompanying economic changes also affected the social structure for American Indians in North Carolina. Serving in the armed forces and working in wartime factories broke down barriers between Indians and others in the state. Having fought and worked for their country in a war against fascism and imperialism, Native Americans returned home angered by their second-class status and the continuation of Jim Crow segregation. Despite their patriotism, white store owners still refused to serve them. Indian veterans could not eat in white restaurants, use white water fountains, or drink alcohol in white taverns. When they attended theaters, they had to sit in separate sections. In one specific case, a white barber refused to cut Curt Locklear's hair. Locklear was shocked. "Being gone for three years and living with white boys, I'd sort of forgotten where I'd come from or something," he later recounted in an interview.[46] Over the next few decades, Native Americans in North Carolina, like African Americans, began to challenge the racist caste system in the South, and veterans, who experienced relative equality during the war, often led the way.[47]

World War II also represented a major political turning point for North Carolina Indians. Frustrated at their exclusion from the political process, many questioned the democratic nature of government in their state. Returning veterans, for example, were instrumental in the removal of a bizarre law regarding the selection of the mayor of Pembroke, a small town with a majority of Native American residents. The North Carolina General Assembly, at the urging of prominent Pembroke whites, had passed a law in the early 1900s allowing the governor to appoint the town's mayor. At the time Pembroke was the only town in the state that prohibited its citizens from electing their mayor. Local Indian veterans went to Raleigh in 1947 to challenge the undemocratic nature of such a rule, and under pressure from the town's population, the General Assembly ultimately repealed the law. Since then Pembroke has consistently elected Native American mayors. In other Native American communities in the state, veterans also took the lead in political affairs. In the 1960s and 1970s, Indian activists, both veteran and non, would continue to press for political change, especially regarding the right to vote. Having already proved their willingness to fight for democracy overseas, they now fought for it at home. "First thing I wanted to do [when I got back from the war] was get involved in politics," James Locklear recalled. "I never missed a vote. In 1950 in particular I was one of twelve people that formed an organization to get the blacks and the Indians to vote. We knew education and . . . the ballot box was the way to change things."[48]

On a broader scale, World War II forced many Americans to reexamine their racialist assumptions. The United States had just fought a war against extreme racism abroad, yet racism still existed in much of the country. In this changing atmosphere, African Americans began to organize to challenge the constitutionality of racial segregation. Moreover, in the immediate post–World War II years, the United States entered a new war, a Cold War against the spread of communism in Europe and Asia. In this contest between ideologies, Americans claimed that they stood for freedom, democracy, and equality, but critics quickly pointed out that these values did not even exist within the United States, particularly in the South, where a racial caste system existed. Consequently, the way Americans thought about race began to change. Many, though certainly not all, began to embrace the notion of racial equality. Moreover, in the wake of the Holocaust and Nazi Germany's extreme legal codification of racism, many

Americans became increasingly uncomfortable with biological definitions of race. German methods of determining just who was and who was not Jewish were uncomfortably similar to the way that many Americans defined race. Consequently, the concept of ethnic identity began to replace the concept of racial identity. Whereas race relied exclusively on biology and physical characteristics, as shown by Seltzer's methods of measuring Indianness, ethnicity incorporated culture. Therefore, Indianness, which had previously been a racial classification, now also became an ethnic category. This subtle change would have important consequences for Native Americans in North Carolina during the postwar years.

Conclusion

In the late 1800s Indians living in eastern North Carolina responded to Jim Crow segregation by separating themselves from others. For the first three decades of the twentieth century, Native Americans continued to live in small interrelated farming communities, to worship in their own churches, and to send their children to their own schools. Indian identity was defined internally within these communities, and it was not based on outward appearances, blood quantum, remnants of precontact material culture, or membership in a federally recognized tribe. During the early twentieth century, several Native American groups from eastern North Carolina did attempt, unsuccessfully, to earn government acknowledgment. But at this time federal recognition was primarily about financial need, rather than validation as Indians. In other words, government certification did not define Indianness in eastern North Carolina.

The turbulent forces of the 1930s and 1940s changed America, and changed North Carolina; these changes had consequences for Indians living in the eastern part of the state. The shift from an agrarian to an industrial economy pushed Native Americans off of the land and into factories. Before, most Indians worked as tenant farmers or sharecroppers within their own communities, and there was very little interaction with outsiders. After the war, however, many took wage-labor jobs where they worked alongside others, including whites and blacks. In the wake of the war, some Native Americans, particularly veterans, also became more politically active, demanding inclusion within America's democratic system. World War II also changed the racial climate in the United States, as cultural plurality replaced Social Darwinism in the halls of academia. These ideas trickled down into the general population, as, for the first time, many Americans began to espouse racial equality. These changes began to pull Indians in eastern North Carolina into the "mainstream" of society. Whereas they were previously isolated from others, Native Americans began to interact economically, socially, and politically with others. The United States finally began to move toward a unified country, rather than one divided by skin color. Many of these changes were, of course, positive; but they were still changes, and dramatic ones at that. If Native Americans wanted to maintain their separate identity—or in their terms acculturated but not assimilated—they would have to adopt new "boundaries" to define their Indianness.

CHAPTER THREE

What's in a Name?

I'm real proud of that name [Lumbee]. For a long time we didn't know who we were. Now, at least, we do have a name. – Viola Jacobs (Lumbee)

Prior to World War II, Native Americans living in eastern North Carolina did not base their identity on specific tribal designations. Most called themselves Croatans, or Cherokees, or simply Indians. Neither Croatans nor Cherokees was historically meaningful or accurate—the former was a place, not a people, and there was little connection, other than trade, between the Cherokees in the mountains and the colonial era tribes in the Piedmont and coastal plains. Indian was certainly accurate, but vague and general. Starting in the late 1940s, however, North Carolina Indians resurrected and reconstructed their tribal identities, in some cases even creating new ones. Almost every Indian community in the state either adopted a new tribal name or adapted an old one in the postwar era. These names were usually based on local geographical features or precontact indigenous peoples. Tribal affiliation, consequently, became an important characteristic of Indian identity.

Two interrelated factors drove Native American retribalization in eastern North Carolina. First, as postwar social changes in the United States decreased the racial stigma previously attached to any nonwhite group, more individuals self-identified as Native American. Men and women officially categorized in federal census records as black or white in 1930 became Indians in the 1960s. In 1940 the census listed 334,000 Indians in the United States. By 1960 that number had climbed to 524,000, and by 1980 more than 1.8 million Americans self-identified as Native Americans. This growth in the Native American population was particularly noteworthy in North Carolina. The official American Indian population in the state in 1940 was only 22,500. Twenty years later, however, the population had more than doubled, and by 1980, more than 60,000 North Carolinians described themselves as Native Americans. Natural increase partially explains this growth. As access to health care lowered infant-mortality rates and lengthened life spans, the Indian population grew. But the willingness of Native Americans to assert publicly their identity was the biggest contributor to this growth. In the 1960s the census bureau changed its classification procedures by allowing individuals to choose their own race. Previously, census takers had classified individuals based on their own observations. Also in the postwar era, the children of interracial marriages between Indians and others became more likely to identify themselves as Indians.[1]

The second factor spurring retribalization was the postwar loss of social and economic isolation. As Native Americans moved into the industrial workforce, they interacted more frequently with others, often on a daily basis. Both whites and blacks questioned their identity, arguing that they were not "real" Indians, but rather African Americans or "mixed-bloods" trying to pass themselves off as Native Americans. After all, critics pointed out, they lived in houses, not tepees, dressed in pants and shirts, not buckskins, hunted with rifles, not bows and arrows, and rode in cars, not on horses. They did not even speak a native language. These accusations, based on nineteenth-century cultural caricatures, angered many North Carolina Indians, who responded by strongly emphasizing and asserting their heritage. According to Frederik Barth, minority groups have three options when confronted by members of a dominant group: they can try to pass unnoticed; they can accept their inferior status and try to cope; or they can actively assert their identity. After World War II an increasing number of North Carolina Indians opted for the last choice. One way to do this was to reestablish a strong tribal identity, which, ironically, conformed to the cultural stereotypes held by non-Indians. Nevertheless, modern Indian identity became linked with the concept of "tribe," and during the second half of the twentieth century, North Carolina Native Americans strategically co-opted this stereotype and used it to their advantage to assert their Indianness. In other words, retribalization constituted a new boundary, something that separated Native Americans from others.[2]

Retribalization and the resurgence of Indian identity in eastern North Carolina attracted the attention of people outside of these communities, including members of the media. In the late 1940s and early 1950s, several state newspapers published articles on Native American communities in the state. In 1948 Tom MaCaughelty of the *Durham Morning Herald* wrote an article on the 350 Indians living in a small community in Person County near the Virginia border. In 1949 Bill Sharpe reported in the *Raleigh News and Observer* on several North Carolina Indian communities, including those in Person, Halifax, Bladen, and Robeson counties. Sharpe described them as "lost tribes" and noted that they maintained their identity and social cohesiveness by marrying within their community. In March 1950 the *Greensboro Daily News* ran stories on both the Person County and Bladen County Indians, also describing them as "lost tribes" of several interrelated families.[3]

The term retribalization should not imply that North Carolina Indian communities were not politically and socially organized before the 1940s. Nor should it suggest that they were not real Indians. As discussed previously, in most communities, schools and churches served as informal, but nonetheless important, centers of power. Furthermore, in several communities, Native Americans formed internal political groups, such as the Council of Wide Awake Indians in Columbus County. Outsiders may not have recognized these groups and committees as legitimate and legal government institutions, but local Indians certainly did. Retribalization, therefore, was not an invention of Native American identity; rather, it was a maturation in community organization.

Brown vs. Board

In the immediate postwar years, Native Americans continued to establish new churches and expand their schools. In 1946 Indians living in Person County founded Calvary Baptist Church, while Native Americans in Halifax and Warren counties built Mount Bethel Baptist in 1956. But the role of churches started to change in the 1950s. From the late 1800s until the 1940s, churches had served as important community symbols of Indianness. In eastern North Carolina, to be Native American partly meant being a member of an Indian church. When skeptical whites started challenging their identity in the postwar era, however, Native Americans could hardly point to their churches as symbolic representations of "real Indianness." After all, how could they argue that they were "real" when they based their spirituality on Christianity, rather than traditional native religions? Many whites saw a paradox between Christianity and Indianness, even if Native Americans did not. Churches proved to be satisfactory internal markers of identity during the first half of the twentieth century, when outsiders generally left Indians alone, but after the war, churches did not serve as adequate boundaries, mainly because Indians had to prove their identity to outsiders, not just to themselves.[4]

Likewise, the political and social significance of Indian-only schools started to change after World War II. In the 1930s and 1940s, the National Association for the Advancement of Colored People (NAACP) filed a series of court cases attacking the constitutionality of Jim Crow legislation, especially laws regarding school segregation. In 1952 the Supreme Court began hearing arguments on several school segregation cases collectively referred to as *Brown vs. Board of Education of Topeka, Kansas.* On May 17, 1954, the Supreme Court ruled unanimously that "separate but equal," established by the infamous *Plessy vs. Ferguson* decision in 1896, was unconstitutional. In one of the most momentous decisions in American history, the Court argued that educational segregation was inherently unfair and thus violated the constitutional precept that all are equal under the law. The ruling sent shockwaves across the country, especially the South.[5]

In North Carolina the Brown decision initially met with grudging acceptance. Under the guidance of Governor Luther Hodges, however, this acceptance quickly turned into outright defiance. Hodges and other North Carolina politicians developed a strategy to appease extremists on both sides of the issue and preserve the state's "progressive" image while at the same time maintaining segregation. First, the General Assembly passed legislation stating that local school systems could make the decision whether to integrate, thereby protecting North Carolina from a potential statewide class-action lawsuit from civil rights groups. Local school boards could even choose to close all of their schools rather than integrate. Second, under the Pearsall Act, the state offered financial aid to the parents of white students who wanted to send their children to private schools. With legislation designed to protect the status quo, Hodges embarked on a publicity campaign to encourage African Americans to accept segregation voluntarily, arguing that the system benefited everyone. The historian William Chafe contended that in May 1954, just after the Brown decision, many North Carolinians stood ready to accept the inevitability of integration. The actions of the General Assembly and Governor Hodges, however, revitalized separatism and white supremacy in the state, and officials successfully delayed integration for years. At the same time, though, North Carolina's progressive image remained untarnished, at least when compared with much of the Deep South.[6]

North Carolina Indians initially ignored the Supreme Court's decision. In fact, in some communities, they continued to push for expansion of their school system. In the early 1950s Native Americans in Halifax and Warren counties demanded that the local county boards build a separate school for their children. But the school board rejected their request, arguing that a third school was an unnecessary expense. Most locals continued to characterize the Halifax Indians as African Americans or "mixed-bloods" who should go to "colored" schools.

This attempt to label them black enraged the local Indians. "We are not Negroes and we will not be classed as such," one man told a Raleigh reporter in 1958. "We'd rather have our own little frame school than the most modern school there is [and have to go with blacks]."[7] But local officials remained unconvinced and continued to reject their requests for separate schools.[8]

Unwilling to accept defeat, the local Indians opened a four-room private school in 1957. At that time the school was the only nonreservation, privately financed Native American school in North Carolina—the others all received at least some government aid. Parents of the two hundred students contributed whatever they could afford, both financially and in terms of time and materials, to support the school. Like other Indian schools, however, it suffered from underfunding, and the community could not afford to keep it open. Consequently, local Native American leaders applied to the state government for funds under the Pearsall Act. In an unexpected twist, Native Americans tried to use the act to get government funding for their private school. But North Carolina officials, who did not want to spend money on Indian private schools, rejected the request, in essence admitting that segregation did not in fact mean separate but equal. Indian leaders, though, refused to give up and kept pressuring county officials for their own public school. In 1958 a group of Lumbees testified before the Warren school board in support of the local Indian community. In 1959 the county board finally capitulated and incorporated the Native American school into its county system, even building a better school in 1962.[9]

Despite this victory, the future was becoming increasingly predictable. As the Brown decision fueled the African American civil rights movement in the late 1950s, it appeared that complete desegregation was inevitable. In the future, Indian-only schools would most likely either integrate or close. But, as will be seen, North Carolina Indians, who had fought so hard for so long for their own schools, would not give them up easily.

The Process of Retribalization

With the threat of educational integration looming, Native American communities in North Carolina established formal tribal organizations. The process of retribalization varied from one community to the next, but the overall pattern was consistent. A group of American Indians living in a distinct community would form a social club or group and choose a name based on a historical North Carolina tribe or prominent local geographical feature, such as a nearby river or lake. These social groups evolved into organized community associations governed by "chiefs," boards of directors, or both. These groups, in turn, eventually publicly proclaimed their identity as a Native American tribe. Tribal groups, therefore, evolved out of older community organizations. They were not inventions, fictions, or brand new institutions, but rather reformations and adaptations of older traditions and community practices. Although not new, retribalization was, however, a change—and a significant one at that.

A few examples of retribalization will illustrate the process. In the late 1940s a group of Indians in northeastern North Carolina formed the Haliwarnash Croatan Indian Club. The cumbersome title combined the name of the three counties (Halifax, Warren, and Nash) where most of the members lived. A few years later the group simplified its name to the Haliwa Indian Club, dropping both the "nash" suffix and the historical reference to Croatan. The small Native American community, probably no more than a few hundred at the time, began publicly referring to themselves as the Haliwa Indians in the 1950s. Local whites, however, continued to doubt their heritage and refused to acknowledge their Indianness. A debate over racial classification in the local hospital typified the controversy. During the first half of the twentieth century, county and state hospital administrators divided all newborns into two categories: white and colored. Native Americans in Halifax and Warren had challenged this system for years. After the war the newly renamed Haliwas filed a lawsuit in state court to change their birth certificates from "colored" to Indian. In 1965 the state judge Ballard Gay ruled in favor of the Haliwas and ordered officials to change the racial designations on fifty-five birth certificates. The case represented a landmark victory for the fledgling tribe and helped affirm the new name. The Haliwas later added the suffix Saponi, which meant "Red Earth People," to their official name, a reference that connected them to a specific precontact North Carolina tribe. The Haliwa-Saponis claimed descendancy from several indigenous peoples, including the Tuscaroras, Nansemonds, and Tuteloes, as well as the Saponis.[10]

More than any other individual, W. R. Talking Eagle Richardson led the retribalization movement among the Haliwas. After returning to North Carolina from Philadelphia in 1955, Richardson emerged as the leader of the Haliwas when the community elected him its first chief. A large and imposing figure, Richardson was a very effective chief who wore a business suit to a professional conference on one day and an elaborate headdress and Plains-style regalia to a powwow the next. Richardson was an engaging personality and would often give talks promoting Haliwa history and culture to white civic groups. In 1981, for example, he spoke at a luncheon of the Rocky Mount chapter of the Daughters of the American Revolution. Decked out in full Indian regalia, Richardson recounted the Haliwas' past, connecting the modern tribe to the colonial Tuscaroras. Richardson died in April 2001 at the age of eighty-six, only a few days after the tribe's thirty-fifth annual powwow. "As a boy sitting in meetings I can remember him talking about how the name [Haliwa] represented the two counties," Greg Richardson (no relation), a Haliwa and head of the North Carolina Commission of Indian Affairs, fondly recalled. "He talked about how back in time, the tribe would pick out a name based on the land or the river they lived near. He said our people were separated by two counties and the name was a way to join our people together."[11]

The Coharies further exemplified retribalization in postwar North Carolina. In Sampson County a few hundred Native Americans lived in a small community in the late 1940s, when a local group formed the Cherokee Clan of Sampson County. The name lasted for two decades even though no historical connection existed between the Sampson Indians and either the Eastern Band in western North Carolina or the Cherokee Nation in Oklahoma. The name was nevertheless attractive—the Cherokees were well known to most Indians and whites, both inside and outside of North Carolina. In an effort to establish their own unique identity, the group renamed itself the Sampson County Indian Association in 1969, but the name lacked popular appeal. James Brewington, an influential member of the group, suggested that they adopt the name Coharie, which came from a nearby river, which in turn may have been named after James Cohary, a Tuscarora Indian who received a land grant in the area from King George in the 1700s. The group agreed and changed their name to the Coharie Tribal Development Association.[12]

The Waccamaw-Sioux of Columbus and Bladen counties also went through a similar process. In the late 1940s James Evan Alexander, a white journalist from California, accidentally "stumbled" upon a "lost tribe" of Native Americans living in the swamps of Columbus County. Alexander moved in with one of the Indian families, and in return for room and board, he agreed to research the history of Buckhead and Ricefield, two small Native American communities. Basing his conclusions on geography and land grants from the 1700s, Alexander contended that the local Indians were the descendants of the Waccamaws and Cape Fears, two Siouan-speaking tribes who had lived near present-day Wilmington during the precontact and colonial eras.[13]

Alexander encouraged the community of about seventy families to petition the federal government for recognition under the 1934 Indian Reorganization Act. In 1949 Alexander and representatives of the community appeared before a congressional committee. R. T. Freeman, one of the group's leaders, testified that he spoke for the Council of Wide Awake Indians, Waccamaw Tribe of the Siouan Nation. Although the Wide Awake council had been around for

*W. R. Talking Eagle Richardson in 1972. Richardson served as chief of
the Haliwa-Saponis from 1955 to 1999 and was instrumental in the founding
of the North Carolina Commission of Indian Affairs. Photo reprinted
by permission of the* News and Observer, *Raleigh NC, N.73–9.304.*

decades, according to the anthropologist Patricia Lerch, who has conducted
extensive research on the community, this was the first official modern reference
to the tribal name "Waccamaw Sioux." Influenced by the group's testimony,
Congressmen Norris Poulson introduced legislation in February 1950 officially
acknowledging the Waccamaws. Fearing that the bill would open the door to
other tribes, BIA and Department of the Interior officials opposed recognizing
the group. Though the quest for certification failed, the tribal name Waccamaw
stuck. In the following years the group formalized its internal political structure,
elected a chief and a tribal council, and incorporated as a nonprofit institution
under state law.[14]

Influenced by the Haliwas, the Coharies, and the Waccamaws, other American Indian communities in eastern North Carolina also formed new tribal organizations. In the 1970s Native Americans living in Hertford, Bertie, and Gates counties formed the Meherrin Indian Tribe, adopting their name, which literally meant "People of the Muddy River," from a local river and a precolonial era tribe. In the mid-1980s American Indians living in Orange and Alamance counties organized the Eno-Occaneechi Indian Association. In 1984 Forest Hazel, who was part Native American but not a native of the area, organized a meeting of local Native Americans in Alamance County. In recent years Hazel had become increasingly interested in the Indian history of the area. Based on his research, Hazel became convinced that many of the local residents were the direct descendants of the Siouan tribes, such as the Enos and the Occaneechis, that had lived in the area during the colonial era. At the meeting the group formed the Eno-Occaneechi Indian Association (EOIA). In the next few years, the EOIA incorporated under state law, enrolled local Native Americans, elected leaders, and held regular meetings.[15]

The Lumbees

Although all the groups listed above attracted attention, the renaming of the Lumbee Indians in Robeson County was the most publicized example of retribalization in the postwar era, primarily because of their large population. In the 1940s the Robeson Indians, who numbered around twenty-five thousand, were still officially known as Cherokees, at least according to the state government. But many members of the community did not like or accept the name. The quest for a new identity revived when returning Indian veterans and others became increasingly unhappy with their lack of a unique name. In the early 1950s D. F. Lowry co-organized the Lumbee Brotherhood, drawing the name from the Lumber River, which runs through Robeson County. Lowry and others in the group contended that the Indians currently living in Robeson County most likely descended from several different colonial-era tribes, a theory that many historians supported. Because their ancestors were a fusion of various tribes, the Brotherhood argued that the local Indian community should adopt a new name. "We haven't any right to be called any one of the various tribal names," Lowry wrote in the periodical *The State* in 1952, "but should take the geographical name, which is Lumbee Indians, because we were discovered on the Lumber River."[16] The "Lumbee" movement gained momentum, and in 1951 local representatives introduced legislation in the North Carolina General Assembly to change the community's official designation to the Lumbee Indians of Robeson County. The bill failed at first because many state legislators were unsure of its support within Robeson, and indeed there was internal resistance to the name change. Some local Indians mocked their neighbors, calling them "Lumber" Indians, and argued that the new name was "silly." One such critic complained that some local Indians wanted to "name an ancient people by a name [Lumbee] that didn't exist until recently."[17]

After the first bill failed, the group advocating the new name embarked on a publicity campaign to convince other Robeson Indians as well as white legislators to support the change. Lowry and others drew up a petition to hold a referendum in the county to determine the level of support for the new name. Two choices appeared on the ballot: Robeson Indians could vote to change their title to the Lumbee Indians of Robeson County, or they could vote to remain the Cherokee Indians of Robeson County, a name that few liked. In February 1952 Robeson Indians voted twenty-one hundred to thirty-five for the proposed name change.[18] Fewer than 10 percent of the local Indian population participated in the election. Lack of interest and a long tradition of not voting in elections—both by force and by choice—contributed to the low turnout. Nevertheless, state representatives reintroduced legislation in 1953 to change the designation of the Robeson Indians, the Senate Committee offered a favorable report on the act, and the General Assembly passed the bill. According to the state government of North Carolina, the Robeson Natives' official name became the Lumbee Indians of Robeson County. But the future of the name remained somewhat in doubt. After all, the Robeson Indians had adopted and discarded several names earlier in the 1900s. Moreover, based on the voter turnout, only a minority was firmly committed to the name.[19]

Shortly after the North Carolina General Assembly officially changed their name, the Lumbees managed to earn limited acknowledgment from the federal government. Congressmen from North Carolina introduced legislation recognizing the Lumbees, and in 1956, both the House and the Senate passed the bill. At first the Lumbees celebrated the victory, but it quickly became apparent that the new bill was a mixed blessing.

The 1956 Lumbee Act was written during a time when the federal government was actually trying to end its historical government-to-government relationship with Native American tribes. In the mid-1940s an odd alliance of conservative and liberal politicians began attacking federal Indian policy. They were especially critical of the reforms initiated by John Collier during the 1930s. Conservatives argued that the reservation system was both expensive and socialistic, the latter an especially harsh criticism as America moved into another era of strident anticommunism. Liberals, by contrast, compared reservations to segregation in the South, contending that communal land ownership prevented Native Americans from escaping poverty and assimilating into the mainstream. To critics on the left, reservations, like Jim Crow segregation, were outdated relics of the nineteenth century. Consequently, a bipartisan coalition of congressmen advocated a new policy designed to dissolve reservations and get the federal government out of the "Indian business." Termination, as the policy came to be called, had three objectives: (1) break up reservations by assigning individual Indians and families their own piece of land; (2) settle all outstanding land disputes between tribes and the government; and (3) encourage Native Americans to move into urban areas where they could find new jobs and assimilate into American society.[20]

As part of its new Termination policy, the federal government created the Indian Claims Commission (ICC) in 1946 to settle all outstanding land and treaty disputes. Native American tribes that had a grievance could make a claim against the United States through the ICC. If the case was deemed valid, the ICC would then decide what and how much to award the tribe. The commission was originally chartered for only ten years, but by 1951, 852 separate claims had been filed by disgruntled Native American tribes—the government's long history of land dispossession had finally caught up with it.[21]

The next step in Termination was urban relocation. The federal government encouraged Native Americans to leave their reservations and move into cities where they could find industrial wage-labor jobs. During the 1940s the number of Indians living in metropolitan areas nationwide doubled as many young men looked for work in new war-related industries. In the 1950s the Bureau of Indian Affairs tried to accelerate Indian urbanization by encouraging individuals to relocate. Under the Voluntary Relocation Program, the BIA spent millions of dollars trying to get Native Americans to move into urban areas, and from 1945 to 1957, more than one hundred thousand did so. The results were mixed. Some prospered and acquired long-term employment, but others experienced harsh discrimination and found the impersonal nature of urban life alienating. Though estimates vary, somewhere between one-third and one-half of those who relocated subsequently returned to their home communities and reservations. The Relocation Program died in the 1960s, but the trend of Indian urbanization continued. In 1950 only about 13 percent of Native Americans lived in urban areas; by 1990 that number had increased to more than 50 percent.[22]

The ultimate goal of Termination was tribal dissolution. A special committee divided all federally recognized tribes into three categories: those most ready to assimilate; those that would soon be ready; and those that would not be ready for a while. From 1954 to 1961 Congress began proceedings to terminate its government-to-government relationship with more than sixty tribes specified as ready for assimilation. The results were often disastrous. Several government studies conducted in the 1960s detailed the failure of Termination, including the Kennedy Report, which described the educational problems that Indian children encountered. Perhaps most famously, the case of the Menominees in Wisconsin illustrated the failure of Termination as a policy. In the 1950s the federal government dissolved the tribe's reservation. Termination failed to prepare the tribe for incorporation into the Wisconsin economic and political system. The Menominees opened a few businesses, but these quickly fell on hard times because of debt, and tribal members fell into despair. Like the Menominees, other terminated tribes experienced increased rates of poverty and unemployment. In the 1960s the federal government realized the failures of Termination, and the policy mercifully faded under the Kennedy and Johnson administrations.[23]

With Termination, the federal government was once again trying to deal with the "Indian problem" by extinguishing Native American tribal identity. Some authors, however, contend that the policy actually had a very different effect. The threat of Termination united Native Americans across the country in a way that they had never been united before. They overcame tribal rivalries and internal disputes within tribes to fight a common enemy. Consequently, Termination reinforced tribal identity and encouraged an emerging supratribal or pan-Indian identity. Pan-Indianism did not simply replace tribalism, but rather enlarged Native American identity. The Indian Reorganization Act of the 1930s may have provided the means for Native American tribes to organize politically, but Termination provided the motivation. Individually, tribes had very little power, but collectively they could voice their opinions more effectively. Previous attempts to forge pan-Indian alliances had failed, but this one proved more successful. The best example of this was the formation of the National Congress of American Indians (NCAI). In 1944 a group of disgruntled BIA employees, worried about the looming threat of Termination, called for a pan-Indian meeting. Representatives from about fifty tribes from across the country gathered in Denver to discuss Native American affairs, particularly Termination. They subsequently formed the NCAI, a congress of American Indian tribes. The NCAI quickly became the primary advocacy group for American Indians, advising tribes regarding federal policies and lobbying the federal government on their behalf. According to Stephen Cornell, the policy of Termination "provided Indians with a critical issue around which to mobilize and it persuaded many of the value—indeed, the necessity—of united action and of organizational structures through which to act."[24]

Congress wrote and passed the 1956 Lumbee Act during the peak of the Termination campaign. Consequently, the bill recognized the Lumbees in name only and did not establish a relationship between the tribe and the federal government. The act also failed to offer any financial benefits. According to the last paragraph of the bill, "nothing in this Act shall make such Indian eligible for any services performed by the United States for Indians because of their status as Indians, and none of the statutes of the United States which affect Indians because of their status as Indians shall be applicable to the Lumbee Indians."[25] The concluding clause used the term "Indian" six times, an obvious acknowledgment of Native American identity. At the same time, however, the legislation denied the Lumbees the accompanying rights and privileges. In effect, the 1956 legislation simultaneously recognized and terminated the tribe.[26]

Despite these legislative victories, skeptics, both Indian and non, continued to question Lumbee tribal identity. Ironically, the Ku Klux Klan (KKK) unintentionally helped the Lumbees legitimize their new name, especially outside of Robeson County. During the 1950s racial tensions blazed in the county as Indians, blacks, and whites competed economically and interacted socially more frequently than in previous decades. Moreover, the Brown decision of 1954 further stoked the flames of racial hatred as all groups in the county anticipated the coming integration of the public school system. This, of course, meant that black, white, and Indian schoolchildren might be learning and playing together, a fact that scared many. On January 13, 1958, members of the Klan burned a cross in the yard of a Lumbee woman who was dating a white man. Later that evening they burned another cross in the yard of a Native American family that had moved into an all-white neighborhood. The message was clear—racial intermixing would not be tolerated in Robeson County.[27]

The next day KKK leaders publicly announced plans to hold a large rally near the town of Maxton in Robeson County on the following Saturday night. Well aware of the upcoming event, local Native Americans planned to retaliate rather than quietly submit to racial terrorism. Afraid of potential violence, the Maxton police chief requested help from both the state police and the Federal Bureau of Investigation. When Saturday finally arrived the rally was the talk of the county. Just after sunset about seventy armed Klansmen, led by the notorious Reverend James "Catfish" Cole, gathered in a large field near Maxton. They set up floodlights, a microphone, and a small stage complete with a large white banner with the letters KKK emblazoned across it. Around seven o'clock several hundred Indians, most of whom were also armed, showed up and surrounded the stage. As the two groups exchanged insults, someone, allegedly a Native American, fired. During the next few minutes, the crack of gunshots filled the cold January air in rural southeastern North Carolina. Heavily outnumbered, most of the Klansmen quickly fled, some even abandoning their wives and children. Waiting nearby, the local and state police quickly moved in with machine guns and tear gas and broke up the rally before anyone was seriously hurt. Eventually, tempers settled. A few Indians even helped push Cole's car out of a ditch where his wife had driven it; Cole was still hiding somewhere in the nearby swamp. As the situation calmed down, the sheriff told the victorious Indians to go home to their families, prodding them by suggesting that, if they hurried, they could make it back in time for *Gunsmoke*.[28]

Native American veterans, fresh from their victories overseas, dominated the crowd that broke up the rally. Based on their recollections, their military experience influenced their decision to stand up to the Klan. After hearing about the planned rally, "most of the veterans . . . got their guns, and they started for Maxton," the Lumbee William Sampson recalled.[29] The veteran James Locklear was also there. "I had a [German] P38 that I brought from overseas. That was my weapon that night," he remembered in a later interview, perhaps relishing the irony of using a Nazi pistol against the Ku Klux Klan. "And I was going there right in the inner circle but the light was shot out and that's what we call the stopping of it, that's when everybody started scattering."[30]

The "Indian uprising of Robeson County," as one author and eyewitness designated it, made national news and marked a turning point in Lumbee history and identity.[31] The popular weekly magazine *Newsweek* described the event much as one would a battle between cowboys and Indians in the nineteenth century. According to the reporter, "They [the Lumbees] gave the United States the first war-whooping, gun-toting, Indian raid it had seen in fifty years and more—even though it was ended by something as prosaic as two tear-gas bombs."[32] The veteran Simeon Oxendine garnered local and national recognition for capturing the large KKK banner. Across the country, Indians and non-Indians alike heard and read about the Lumbees' dramatic victory over the Klan. Two folk singers, Pete Seeger and Malvina Reynolds, recorded songs about the event. The media attention legitimized Lumbee identity, especially since their new tribal name was repeatedly mentioned by television and print media. The incident still holds special importance for the Lumbees, who recently moved to construct a commemorative historical marker at the site. "Catfish" Cole, who was sentenced to two years in jail for inciting a riot, had predicted a different long-term outcome for the rally. After his conviction, he proclaimed that "the action of the court in Robeson County has done more to prove in three and one-half days than I have done by my preaching in eight years that this country is fast falling into communism and dictatorship."[33]

The importance of an accepted and recognized tribal name should not be underestimated. Guy Johnson, the noted North Carolina sociologist, stressed the significance of a name in the establishment of group identity. Traveling in Robeson County in the 1930s and 1940s, Johnson noticed that many Indians were upset at their lack of acceptance by local whites and made a connection to the absence of a historical name. Later, writing in the 1950s, Johnson addressed the consequence of the name Lumbee and its connection to public recognition. "Thus power and progress contributed to the acquisition of a 'good name' at last," Johnson wrote. "The new name in turn has contributed to further progress and to a much higher sense of identity and self-esteem than these people had ever known before."[34]

Criticism

Retribalization acquired its share of skeptics, both inside and outside of North Carolina. Whites and other Native Americans criticized Indian communities for efforts to reshape and reform their tribal identity. Most focused on racial issues, characterizing many as blacks trying to hide their ancestry. Cynical whites often called Native Americans derogatory names, including "Brass Ankles," "Moors," "Turks," and "issues." Guy Johnson spoke with many whites in Robeson County who openly questioned the identity of the Lumbees. They joked about the name Lumbee, calling them "Lumber" Indians, and questioned their authenticity. Many critics just assumed that the Lumbees were pretending to be Native Americans in order to qualify for government handouts, an odd argument since few Indians in eastern North Carolina received government aid.[35]

Academicians and authors also challenged the identity of Native Americans in eastern North Carolina. In the 1950s the sociologist Brewton Berry insinuated that most were merely peoples of mixed ancestry who really wanted to be white. A series of articles published in the journal *American Anthropologist* in the early 1970s agreed with Berry, characterizing North Carolina Indians as "marginalized people" or "racial isolates" trying to avoid being classified as black because of segregation. According to critics, these communities of "middle peoples" chose to emphasize their Indian heritage to avoid being labeled black. When North Carolina finally integrated its public institutions and facilities, the argument went, these "little races" would simply disappear along with Jim Crow. Some members of these communities agreed with the critics, questioning the legitimacy of the new tribal groups. "Whatever his mind wants him to be, that's what a person be," one Halifax woman told a Raleigh reporter in 1972. "I'm a colored woman, myself. Not black, because as you can plainly see, I'm not black. And I'm not Haliwa, because that's just something somebody made up."[36] Others, more concerned about the future than the past, contended that the issue of tribal identity obscured the real problems facing contemporary Native Americans. "I don't see why people are more interested in where we came from than what we are today," one Indian man told Guy Johnson.[37]

North Carolina Indians responded to these criticisms by trying to prove their authenticity. One way to do this was to establish membership criteria that, like schools and churches, incorporated biological definitions of identity. If critics questioned their Indianness on racial grounds, they would defend their identity using racial criteria. The Haliwas, for example, required potential tribal enrollees to trace their ancestry back to a core group of Halifax County Indian families using particular source documents, including federal census records from the late 1800s. The Tribal Enrollment Committee reviewed every application and made the final determination, much the same way school and church committees defined Indianness. But the qualifications were not strictly based on biology. Under special circumstances, such as the adoption of children, individuals failing to meet the criteria could still become enrolled members of the Haliwas. The tribe also maintained the power to expel enrolled members who severed social ties to the community. In eastern North Carolina community membership still trumped blood quantum. Other North Carolina tribes established similar requirements, as tribal membership committees replaced church and school committees as the primary arbiters of Native American identity.[38]

Conclusion

In focusing on federal policy, most historians have described the immediate post–World War II years as a dark period for Native Americans. Obviously, Termination was a setback. For some tribes, like the Menominees, the new policy led to unemployment, poverty, and other problems. Moreover, the ideological drive behind Termination, which was based on the destruction of Indian communities, threatened the future of tribal identity. In *Native Americans in the Twentieth Century*, James S. Olson and Raymond Wilson characterized the postwar years as a time when "compensation [the ICC], termination, and relocation programs from 1946 joined the allotment, education, and citizenship programs from 1887 to 1934 among the bankrupt efforts of the assimilationists to solve the 'Indian Problem.' "[39] But as other historians are starting to realize, the examination of federal policies only scratches the surface of the broader changes for American Indians following the war. Terminationists, like previous assimilationists, failed to appreciate the strength and resiliency of Indian culture and identity. Furthermore, as Alison Bernstein has shown, it is difficult to generalize about the postwar experience of all American Indians. For some tribes, such as the Eastern Band of Cherokees in western North Carolina, the threat of Termination loomed over much of the 1950s. But for other Native Americans, Termination was obviously not a direct concern. In fact, while the federal government was trying to detribalize the Cherokees and other Native American peoples, the Indians in eastern North Carolina were in the process of retribalizing.

The dramatic changes of the middle of the twentieth century forced Native Americans in eastern North Carolina to reshape their conceptions of Indianness. The shift from agrarianism to industrialization in the state pushed Indians into the wage-labor market; political changes seemed to indicate that Indians may become part of the democratic process; and the Brown decision challenged racial segregation in schoolrooms, as well as elsewhere in society. As a result of these changes, Native Americans in eastern North Carolina began interacting much more frequently with others, some of whom challenged their identity. Angered by this attack, American Indians responded by aggressively asserting their identity. One way to do this was to form tribal organizations. In the postwar era, Native Americans across eastern North Carolina founded social groups. They adopted names based on geographical features or colonial-era tribes, such as the Haliwas in Halifax and Warren counties, the Coharies in Sampson County, the Waccamaws in Columbus and Warren counties, and the Lumbees in Robeson County. Particularly in their cases, the broader social, political, and economic changes effected by the war were much more significant than specific federal policies.[40]

CHAPTER FOUR

Protests and Powwows

We have fought for almost a century to build our schools and to give our children the educational opportunities they need and this one move could wipe out all of our progress. – American Indian parent, 1970

If Robeson County Indians want to wear feathers that is their business. – Bruce Barton (Lumbee), 1973

In 1961 the Lumbee Helen Maynor scheduled a preconference for North Carolina Native American leaders in Robeson County in preparation for a large multitribal meeting in Chicago. Shortly after the meeting Maynor, the Haliwa chief W. R. Richardson, and several others traveled to Chicago to participate in the conference. More than seven hundred Indians representing five dozen tribes gathered in the Windy City to define a broad pan-Indian political agenda. "What we ask of America is not charity, not paternalism, even when benevolent," conference organizers pronounced in their Declaration of Indian Purpose, drafted by D'Arcy McNickle. "We ask only that the nature of our situation be recognized and made the basis of policy and action."[1] The Chicago Conference was significant for several reasons, but two in particular are noteworthy. First, it symbolically kicked off the Indian rights movement of the 1960s and 1970s; and second, Native American leaders from the West and the East met to discuss their problems as a unified group. To many Native Americans, this meeting marked a turning point in political activism, and Native Americans from eastern North Carolina were there as active participants.[2]

Native American Activism

The 1960s were turbulent times in American history. Racial strife, political assassinations, and the escalation of the Cold War shattered the postwar prosperity that, at least on the surface, seemed to define the 1950s. Feeding off of the Supreme Court's Brown decision, minority groups rallied behind the election of John F. Kennedy, who appeared to be sympathetic to their cause, to agitate for change. In the South, African Americans fought for social and political equality, while in the Southwest, Hispanics organized for empowerment.

Influenced by these minority movements, American Indians also demanded political, social, and economic inclusion. The 1961 conference ignited a series of other meetings that led to the formation of several multitribal organizations. Shortly after the conference ended, a group of young college students, led by Clyde Warrior, Mary Natani, and Mel Thom, established the National Indian Youth Council (NIYC). The NIYC attracted attention for its involvement in the fishing-rights protests in the Pacific Northwest in the 1960s. In November 1969 a group of Native Americans led by Richard Oakes and Adam Fortunate Eagle formed Indians of All Tribes and seized the abandoned prison on Alcatraz Island. The group organized a conference on the island and invited Native Americans from across the country to participate. The occupation lasted seventeen months before federal agents forcibly evicted the last holdouts in June 1971.[3]

Of all the new groups, however, the American Indian Movement (AIM) became the most visible. Formed in 1968 by young Indians in Minneapolis, AIM was virtually synonymous, at least in the eyes of the mainstream media, with national Indian activism. AIM organized numerous protests to focus attention on the historical injustices committed against their ancestors, such as the dispossession of Native American land. In perhaps their most well known demonstration, AIM members, along with a group of Oglala Sioux, occupied a trading post in February 1973 at Wounded Knee on the Sioux reservation in South Dakota, the site of the infamous 1890 tragedy. The two-month standoff between AIM and law enforcement officials led to the death of several Indians and two federal agents. The actions of AIM and other groups forced many Americans to reconsider the past exploitation of Native Americans, and, more important, the current situation on many reservations.

The budding national Native American movement inspired Indians in North Carolina. Along with Maynor and Richardson, other Indians from the state participated in these events. The Lumbee Ruth Woods, for example, went to San Francisco in late 1969 for the Conference of All Tribes at Alcatraz. The

Waccamaw-Siouan chief W. J. Freeman frequently drove to Washington in the 1960s to participate in pan-Indian gatherings, taking his daughter Priscilla and others along with him. Indian activism in North Carolina was, however, somewhat different. Although certainly influenced by national affairs, activism in the state was more localized and, in general, more tempered and conservative. The first issue Native Americans rallied around was school integration, but rather than support federal desegregation efforts, North Carolina Indians defended their community schools.[4]

The Fight over Integration

For a decade after the Brown decision, segregated schools remained the norm in North Carolina, and Native Americans, unlike African Americans, were satisfied with the educational status quo. In 1964, however, a new Civil Rights Act threatened the future of Indian-only public schools. Pushed through by President Lyndon Johnson following the assassination of John Kennedy, the landmark legislation outlawed discrimination in public facilities and in the workforce and gave the attorney general the authority to file lawsuits in order to facilitate integration. Over the next few years, federal officials would use the legislation to order the desegregation of all schools.

Indians in eastern North Carolina united to challenge federally mandated integration. They argued that desegregation threatened their culture and would ultimately lead to complete assimilation. Moreover, Indian children would be bused all over the state and sent to schools where they would constitute a very small minority in relation to whites and blacks. In short, to many Indians, integration threatened identity. "We don't want to be assimilated," Lew Barton, summing up the fears of many, defiantly stated in 1971. "We'd like to maintain our identity. [Integration] wouldn't be tantamount to wiping the Indians out, but it would be close."[5]

The largest group of Native Americans in the state also protested the loudest. In the late 1960s federal officials tried to force the integration of Lumbee schools in Robeson County by threatening to withhold federal education funds. In the fall of 1970, the federal government ordered Robeson County officials to end segregation. That fall a group of Lumbees defiantly resisted a federal integration order by organizing a protest at a local school. Indian students literally "sat in" their old schools and refused to attend their new ones. The protest lasted months, as five hundred Native American students illegally attended their old schools for the entire academic year. "We have fought for almost a century to build our schools and to give our children the educational opportunities they need and this one move [integration] could wipe out all of our progress," one parent explained.[6]

In late 1970 the Lumbees filed a lawsuit in the U.S. Eastern District Court in Fayetteville that directly challenged the legality of forced desegregation. The suit claimed that the federal government placed an unreasonable share of the burden on Native Americans and asked that they be exempt from the pupil assignment plan, which forced children to bypass community schools and travel great distances to attend integrated ones. The Lumbees also argued that the Brown decision and subsequent federal legislation were primarily designed to help African Americans in the South, and that integration would actually hurt Indians, making it clear that they chose segregation, rather than having it forced upon them by the state government. According to the Lumbees, blacks wanted to attend white schools, which were vastly superior. Therefore, Native Americans, who did not want to integrate, should be exempt from federal desegregation guidelines. The suit ultimately failed.[7]

Federal and state officials once again tried to integrate Indian schools in the fall of 1971 by enrolling African Americans in Prospect School, which had previously been Indian-only, and busing Native Americans to other county schools. In protest, thirty-five angry parents, some of them brandishing hatchets, blocked the door at Prospect and refused to let non-Indians, including teachers, enter the building. County officials called the police and closed the school in order to avoid a violent confrontation. Authorities subsequently arrested and convicted several of the protesters for inciting a riot. Other parents, not wanting to go so far as violence, silently boycotted integration by simply keeping their children at home. During the late 1960s and early 1970s, similar, though perhaps less dramatic, demonstrations occurred throughout eastern North Carolina. Unlike African Americans, Native Americans fought to preserve segregation, an institution that allowed them to define themselves socially and culturally.[8]

Despite this resistance, federal civil rights laws forced either the closing or integration of all Native American schools in the state by 1973. High Plains Indian School in Person County was one of the first to shut down in 1961, followed by the East Carolina Indian School in Sampson County in 1965, and the Halifax high school in 1967. The immediate results of desegregation reinforced the fears of its Native American critics. County administrators forcibly bused Indian children long distances to schools where they constituted a small minority. In Columbus County, Indian children had to travel thirty-four miles round-trip to school each day. After their arrival, Indians faced teasing from other students, teachers, and administrators in their new schools. On his first day at an integrated school, Daystar Dial and other Native American students were greeted by their principal. "First of all," he said, "I do not want ya'll running on campus like a pack of wild Indians." The principal later apologized, but Dial remained frightened and worried. "I was sure it [integration] was going to be hell," he later recalled. [9]

Facing such animosity, many Indian students simply gave up and quit. Across the state, dropout rates for Native American teenagers climbed dramatically. Most quit because of the racism that they encountered, or as one woman put it, "because of prejudice, because they never paid you any attention if you were an Indian." [10] Others persevered, though not without problems. Regina Mills, a Haliwa-Saponi from Hollister, had to switch to an integrated high school for her senior year in 1966. Although the transition was difficult for Mills, she graduated in June 1967. "It all adds up to an identity problem," James Revels told a reporter in 1975. "TV and history books picture us as in bells and feathers, whooping about and scalping people. That's how the white man expects us to be when we get to school. It's a constant fight to prove otherwise, to keep a decent opinion of ourselves when we see whites looking at us with contempt." [11]

Saving Old Main

While federal officials were pushing the integration of Indian public elementary and secondary schools in eastern North Carolina, Pembroke State College also underwent a transformation during the postwar years. The college opened its doors to whites in 1953 and blacks in 1954, making it one of the first schools in the South to integrate completely. With open admissions and the influx of veterans taking advantage of the GI Bill, enrollment skyrocketed, increasing from 150 students in 1956 to more than 750 in 1962. In 1972 the General Assembly consolidated the state's university system and made Pembroke State University part of the University of North Carolina system. But this growth had important side effects. Because of the subsequent increase in white and black students, American Indians became a minority in a school originally built exclusively for them. In fact, while the total number of students continued to grow in the 1970s, the number of Native Americans enrolled at the university remained steady at about 300. [12]

Upset at the "de-Indianization" of the college, local American Indians found a concrete campus symbol to rally behind. In 1970 Pembroke administrators requested funds to construct a new auditorium on the site of Old Main, which had rapidly deteriorated and was in need of major renovations. A group of Robeson Indians formed the "Save Old Main" commission and argued that the

Old Main as it appeared after the fire in November 1973. Courtesy of
the North Carolina Office of Archives and History, Raleigh NC, N.73–10.338.

building constituted a social and cultural symbol, a reminder of a time when the
school belonged to them. As the issue figuratively smoldered, Old Main literally
burned in March 1973 when a suspicious fire gutted the structure, apparently the
work of arsonists. As tensions mounted, Governor Jim Holshouser intervened
and promised to help restore the historic building. In 1972 the Lumbees had
supported Holshouser in his successful run for the governorship. In 1979 Old
Main finally reopened. At the rededication ceremony, Janie Maynor Locklear,
a leader in the Save Old Main campaign, declared that the reopening was "the
fulfillment of a dream, the answer to a thousand prayers and a high moment in
the history of a proud people."[13]

Despite saving Old Main, North Carolina Indians were losing control of
their college. By the early 1970s the majority of faculty and staff—as well as
students—was, in fact, non-Indian. With consolidation into the UNC system,
most major decisions were now made by the all-white Board of Governors.
In 1979 English E. Jones, a Lumbee, retired from Pembroke State after a long
tenure as chancellor. Jones was very popular in the community and played an
integral role in the growth of the college. The UNC president and the governors
chose a white man over two Native American candidates to succeed Jones. Local
Indians expressed outrage and charged that race played the determining role

in the selection. Indians in eastern North Carolina now faced the prospect of losing control of their college, much like they lost control of their elementary and secondary schools.[14]

Advancing the Cause

In the mid-to-late 1960s, the African American civil rights movement started to change. During the 1950s black activism was largely localized, depending on grassroots protests such as the Montgomery Bus Boycott. But in the 1960s blacks organized more widely. The Congress of Racial Equality (CORE), the Southern Christian Leadership Conference (SCLC), and the Student Non-violent Coordinating Committee (SNCC) joined the National Association for the Advancement of Colored People (NAACP) in the fight for civil rights. Furthermore, the movement turned more radical. Young blacks, upset by the slow pace of change, advocated confrontation and aggression rather than peaceful resistance and passiveness. This change was illustrated by the emergence of Malcolm X, a charismatic black Muslim leader, and the popularity of the phrase "black power."[15]

Influenced by African American demonstrators, North Carolina Indians also organized and demanded political inclusion. In Robeson County an informal group of Indians known as "the Movement" formed to "advance the cause," primarily by demanding suffrage. White politicians in North Carolina dominated local, county, and state government, even in areas where minorities constituted the majority. Poll taxes and literacy clauses designed primarily to keep African Americans away from the voting booth had also disfranchised Native Americans during the twentieth century. According to state law, potential voters had to read and interpret sections of the U.S. Constitution in order to register in North Carolina. In one case a white county official told a potential North Carolina Indian voter that he needed to recite the entire Constitution from memory in order to register. When these methods failed, whites turned to violence and extortion to keep minority groups away from the voting box and perpetuate their control of all levels of government.[16]

Federal legislation offered hope in the late 1960s. North Carolina Indians may have resisted federal legislation regarding schools, but they welcomed new voting laws. In 1965 Congress passed a Voting Rights Act that gave federal authorities the right to supervise registration. Consequently, civil rights workers and Native American activists organized a voter registration campaign in eastern North Carolina. Several Robeson County Indians formed the Lumbee Citizens' Council in 1966 to educate and register voters. The council later changed its name to Hope, Inc., fearing that the old name too closely resembled the White

Citizens' Councils, state and local organizations formed by whites to protect segregation in the South.[17]

In their fight for the right to vote, the Lumbees received help from an unlikely source. The SCLC sent monetary aid and support personnel to Robeson County in the late 1960s to assist the local Indian activists. In 1968 Native Americans and African Americans in the county tried to work together to elect nonwhites to office. According to the authors and anthropologists Karen Blu and Gerald Sider, both of whom were living in Robeson at the time, this alliance marked a turning point. Previously, the Lumbees and other North Carolina Indians resisted openly associating with African Americans. By the late 1960s, however, a political alliance seemed strategically wise. Together, blacks and Indians accounted for more than 60 percent of Robeson County's population. More important, because of the voter registration movement, the number of registered blacks and Indians was about the same as the number of whites. Fearing an electoral disaster, whites in the county successfully rallied to quash the alliance, which elected only one minority candidate to office in 1968. Whites still controlled powerful local positions in the county and used economic scare tactics to either keep Indians from voting or force them to vote for white candidates. A young female Indian political activist experienced the pressure firsthand. "Don't go to that damn house," one white landowner told her as she tried to meet with an Indian family regarding the upcoming election. "They live on my damn farm and they vote the way I say vote."[18]

In *Lumbee Indian Histories*, Sider further explained how whites kept Indians from winning elections. According to the author, voter fraud was rampant in Robeson prior to the 1970s. Votes were literally "delivered" on election day, when party officials would pay individuals to vote for certain candidates. Votes were cheap in poverty-stricken Robeson, perhaps costing as little as one dollar. Intimidation was also common in the county. When a potential voter entered the polling place, usually a classroom in a local school, he or she had to sign the registration book then manually fill out a ballot at a separate table and give it to the election official, who then placed the ballot in a box. Prior to the electronic booth, it was easy for county officials to look at the ballot and see whom the person had voted for, a fact that they made very clear to the voter. Furthermore, outright cheating was not uncommon. In 1968 one official told Sider that it was easy for him simply to discard the votes of Indians and African Americans. Those ballots were never even counted.[19]

The Robeson Indians finally scored an important political victory in 1975. Even after integration, most white children went to city schools while most Indian children went to rural schools. Robeson officials, with the permission of the state government, instituted a rule that allowed city residents to vote for both city and county school boards. The Lumbees called this "double-voting," as some parents, mostly whites, could vote in two elections. The General Assembly gave the county a lump sum to distribute to the various schools in Robeson based on needs. If whites controlled both boards, they dictated school policy, as well as the allocation of funds throughout the county. Local Native Americans challenged the legality of double-voting by filing a lawsuit against the North Carolina State Board of Elections. In 1975 the U.S. Circuit Court of Appeals declared double-voting unconstitutional, thus ending the practice. The change allowed Lumbees to elect several Indians to the Robeson County School Board during the 1970s and 1980s, returning some degree of control over educational issues in their community.[20]

Other than the defeat of double-voting, North Carolina Indians enjoyed few political successes in the 1960s and 1970s. Nevertheless, Karen Blu argued that the "movement" was significant. Because of the Indian-black coalition, being nonwhite became an important part of Native American identity, whereas previously the primary focus had been on being nonblack, a subtle but important distinction. The alliance was loose and often strained but also changed the way that Indians defined themselves. Most important, Native Americans actually registered to vote; in Robeson County alone, the number of Indian voters increased more than 25 percent between 1966 and 1972. Native Americans still constituted a minority, but state and local officials, including a few governors, began meeting with tribal leaders in the 1970s. In 1972 the Republican gubernatorial candidate Jim Holshouser actively campaigned in Robeson County. The local Indians responded by turning out and voting for Holshouser, helping him become the first Republican governor in the state since the end of Reconstruction. Consequently, when the Robeson Indians wanted help, such as with Old Main, Holshouser listened. The political investment would pay even greater dividends in the 1980s and 1990s.[21]

The Tuscaroras

Partially in response to federally mandated integration, a new tribe emerged in Robeson County. In 1970 a group of Indian parents in Robeson formed the Eastern Carolina Tuscarora Indian Organization (ECTIO). Although many were related to Lumbees, the ECTIO rejected the name. They argued that they were not Lumbees, but rather the descendants of the Tuscaroras, an Iroquoian-speaking tribe that inhabited North Carolina during the colonial era. "Call us anything, but don't call us Lumbee," one Tuscarora man told a reporter. "The word Lumbee has no historical significance, it came right out of the bottom of the river."[22]

Although the Tuscaroras first emerged in the early 1970s, the split within the Robeson Indian community regarding identity was not new. In fact, Gerald Sider contends that the formation of the Tuscaroras was symbolic of a broader, and older, ideological rift. According to Sider, the pursuit of tribal sovereignty and the protection of identity under the modern system of state domination presented Native Americans in North Carolina with only two options. First, they could accommodate, or choose to deal with state structures and work within the political system. This would allow Indians to acquire some rights and benefits but would also make them dependent on the state. Second, Indians could choose to challenge the system by avoiding active engagement in state structures, an appealing option, but a difficult one, especially given the poverty in many Native American communities. In the 1970s the Tuscaroras came to symbolize the second option, those who opted to confront, rather than work within, state structures. But this division in the Robeson County community was nothing new, as illustrated by the same types of arguments and disagreements in the 1930s regarding federal recognition and the adoption of a new name.[23]

In his broader examination of Native American politics and sovereignty, Stephen Cornell reached similar conclusions, though he used different terms. According to Cornell, the competing factions within Indian societies over issues can be divided into two general groups, though the author admits this is somewhat of a simplification. "Realists" advocate working within the structures of the dominant society, whereas "radicals" oppose such action. Again, these types of splits within Native American groups were not new. Cornell compares them to past divisions between so-called "conservatives" and "progressives," or even "full-bloods" and "mixed-bloods." Both radicals and realists have the same goals: they want to protect their people and their sovereignty. Where they differ is in the approach. Radicals look to protect cultural traditions, while realists propose survival through successful adaptation.[24]

Traditionally, most authors contend that tribal factionalism has hurt Native Americans. More recently, others have challenged this. All peoples and societies, not just Native Americans, exhibit internal divisions. Therefore, the argument that internal dissent has hurt Indians, but not others, is culturally biased. In fact, the term factionalism itself, which carries a negative connotation, is usually used to describe Indian societies but not others. Indians have "factions," but other peoples and societies have competing groups or parties. In examining Indian politics in Robeson County, both Sider and Blu concluded that internal dissent actually helped the community, fostering competition and creative energy. Tuscaroras and Lumbees have the same goals—the promotion of sovereignty and the protection of identity—just different methods of achieving them. Moreover, this dissent often overshadows an underlying unity. Whenever threatened by outsiders, as with the KKK incident in the 1950s, the Indians of Robeson County came together to repel that threat.[25]

In the early 1970s the Tuscaroras, who were located mostly in and around the Prospect community in Robeson County, became the most politically militant Indian group in North Carolina. The school issue in Robeson had attracted much national media attention. Consequently, AIM established an office in Robeson County in 1972 and sent several representatives to help organize the community. Most Lumbees ignored the activists, but the Tuscaroras were more receptive to their message. The Tuscaroras were generally younger, poorer, and more rural than other Indians in Robeson. They were also more culturally conservative and advocated a return to traditional Indian ways. In October 1972 several Tuscaroras accompanied AIM representatives on their trip to Washington DC to participate in the "Trail of Broken Treaties," a protest march scheduled to coincide with the presidential election. Although not planned, the demonstration ended with the occupation of the BIA office building. Determined to find proof of corruption within the agency, the protesters stole thousands of documents and fled the capital.[26]

Shortly after the BIA protest and occupation, the Tuscaroras split over internal issues, a process that would repeat itself in future years. In late 1972 the Tuscaroras held an election to choose an official leader. Elias Rogers, a moderate activist, faced Howard Brooks, who was more radical in his rhetoric and methods. Rogers won the election with about two-thirds of the vote. Undaunted, Brooks took his followers, left the Tuscaroras, and formed a new group, called the Tuscarora Council.[27]

With the support of AIM, Tuscarora activism peaked under Brooks during the first half of 1973. For several weeks in February and March, suspicious fires destroyed dozens of white-owned buildings in Robeson County. Although never proven, most suspected young Tuscaroras of arson. During the first week of March, Brooks and his supporters paraded around Robeson for several nights celebrating AIM's occupation of Wounded Knee in South Dakota. They broke several store windows and smashed a few automobile windshields, but there were no casualties or major damage. In April 1973 Brooks, wearing a warbonnet and carrying a ceremonial lance, led a contingent of about seventy-five Tuscaroras and a few African Americans, including Golden Frinks of the SCLC, to the state capital, Raleigh. They demanded to meet with both the executive director of the North Carolina Commission of Indian Affairs and the governor.

The group camped outside the capitol building, handing out fliers to passersby that asked for basic human rights, the return of Indian land, and freedom from police harassment. "We are no longer afraid," the flier read. "We can say what we want, and our demand is just: We want Indian power in Robeson County."[28] Arguing that he did not represent a legitimate tribe, both the NCCIA and the governor refused to meet with Brooks and swore out a complaint against him for holding a rally without a permit and damaging state property. Brooks and his followers returned to Robeson County angry at their apparent snub.[29]

As the Tuscaroras radicalized, the potential for violence and bloodshed increased. In the spring Brooks planned a rally at Prospect School, but the local board refused to issue him a permit. Outraged, Brooks and other Tuscaroras protested anyway. The demonstration, later dubbed the Prospect Riot, ended in violence and the arrest of several Indians, including Brooks. In April the Robeson sheriff arrested two young Tuscaroras and a representative of AIM for starting a fire that destroyed Joe's Cash Store, a white-owned business. The sheriff also charged them with shooting into the home of Carnell Locklear, one of the leaders of the moderate and competing group of Tuscaroras. Also in April, federal agents found thousands of BIA documents stolen from Washington in a house in Maxton, North Carolina. Dock Locklear, the owner of the house, arrived after the authorities had entered his home and, declaring the search unconstitutional, chased the agents out with a shotgun. After a brief but tense standoff, the FBI arrested Dock Locklear and Keever Locklear, both Tuscaroras, and the AIM member William Sargent for possession of stolen property. An all-white jury ultimately found that the federal agents had tampered with the evidence and acquitted Sargent and both Locklears.[30]

After the turmoil of 1973, Tuscarora activism waned. There were about three thousand Tuscaroras in Robeson County, but, unable to agree on an agenda, they continued to split into smaller competing factions. By the mid-1980s five separate groups existed in eastern North Carolina: the Eastern Carolina Tuscarora Indian Organization, the Hatteras Tuscarora Tribe, the Drowning Creek Tuscaroras, the Tuscarora Tribe of North Carolina, and the Tuscarora Nation of North Carolina. Nevertheless, the Tuscaroras remained an important part of the story in Robeson County and represented an alternate definition of Indian identity. They could have enrolled as Lumbees but chose not to, preferring instead to maintain their own unique tribal identity.[31]

Although the Tuscaroras and AIM attracted much media attention in the 1970s, the African American civil rights movement apparently influenced more Native Americans in eastern North Carolina. Most Indian leaders preferred moderate activism and rejected radical confrontation. Many were great admirers of Martin Luther King Jr., a fellow Southern Christian who advocated peaceful resistance. Culturally and religiously conservative, North Carolina Indians shied away from militant actions or confrontations. Some even criticized activists and "outside Indians" for trying to tell others how to be "real" Indians. "They [AIM members] don't have anything to offer us because we've been out of teepees a long time," one Indian man told an interviewer in 1972. "I think they should go back to Wounded Knee or Pine Ridge or wherever they came from."[32]

Economic Development

Much like Roosevelt's New Deal, Lyndon Johnson's Great Society affected Native Americans in North Carolina. The 1950s had been a decade of steady economic growth in the country, but not all Americans benefited from the prosperity. In 1962 Michael Harrington's *The Other America* demonstrated the disparities in wealth between the rich and the poor in the United States, a stinging criticism for a supposedly classless society. After his overwhelming electoral avalanche in 1964, Johnson pushed through a blizzard of legislation to help the poor that rivaled the New Deal in its historical significance. The Economic Opportunity Act provided job training for the poor, aid to migrant workers, and loans to rural workers and small businesses. Volunteers in Service to America (VISTA) attacked illiteracy, while the Elementary and Secondary Act supplied underfunded schools and established Headstart programs in poor areas. Through the Department of Housing and Urban Development (HUD), Johnson attacked the shortage of decent low-rent housing in many cities. Medicare and Medicaid provided health care to the poor and elderly. Ever the optimist, Johnson envisioned a "Great Society" where all Americans had the opportunity to succeed or fail based on merit, not happenstance.[33]

Johnson's programs benefited many Native Americans. VISTA sent representatives to reservations to teach Indians to read and write. HUD provided funds for low-cost housing, and Headstart and the Education Act helped Native American schools. Other federal programs provided funds for job training, day care, counseling, and other services. In the 1970s the federal government continued to establish programs to help Native Americans, passing the Indian Education Act, the Indian Health Care Act, and the Indian Child Welfare Act. The increase in available funds was dramatic—between 1950 and 1980, total federal spending on Native Americans went from $174,000 to $2,000,000 (both figures in 1982 dollars). Indian groups and organizations were eligible for this aid if they could prove need and navigate through the bureaucratic red tape.[34]

As Johnson pursued his grand vision, Native Americans in eastern North

Carolina remained poor. According to the 1970 census, approximately one-half of Native Americans, as opposed to less than 20 percent of whites, lived below the official poverty line in the state. Several studies conducted in the late 1960s and early 1970s also noted the widespread impoverishment and unemployment within Indian communities. In Halifax County, for example, many Haliwas lacked indoor plumbing and frequently shared outhouses with other families. In the early 1970s the American Indian Policy Review Commission, a task force partly charged with examining the situation among nonrecognized Indian communities, found that more than one-half of Robeson County Indians lived in substandard housing and that one-third were infected with intestinal parasites. Studies conducted by the North Carolina Commission of Indian Affairs and the North Carolina Civil Rights Advisory Committee reached similar conclusions.[35]

To take advantage of Johnson's programs, North Carolina Native Americans formed economic development organizations. In 1968 Bruce Jones, Horace Locklear, Ronald Revels, Ruth Woods, and Rod Locklear, among others, formed the Regional Development Association in Robeson County, a nonprofit corporation to help local Indians economically. Their goal was to "analyze and develop solutions for the health, education, economic, and general welfare of rural and urban Indians in and around Robeson County."[36] In 1970, at the suggestion of a member of the U.S. Department of Commerce, the group added Lumbee to their name to signify their Indian heritage. The Lumbee Regional Development Association (LRDA) subsequently elected an executive director and board of directors and successfully applied for funds from the OEO, HUD, and the Department of Labor. In 1971, with a budget of $440,000, the LRDA managed five programs in the county exclusively for Indians. During the 1970s the LRDA continued to grow, and by 1980 it operated with a budget of more than $4,000,000, including grants from federal, state, and private agencies. Although initially formed as a nontribal community program, the LRDA quickly became the primary economic and political voice of the Lumbees, a fact that would cause controversy in the late 1990s.[37]

In other areas of the state, Native Americans adopted similar strategies. In the 1960s Indians in Columbus and Bladen counties formed the Waccamaw Improvement Club to petition for federal aid, attract outside investment, and increase self-sufficiency. In 1972 a group led by Clifton Freeman incorporated the Waccamaw Sioux Development Association (WSDA), which eventually became the official governing body of the tribe. The WSDA received funds from the federal government for education, low-cost housing, and job training. Recognizing the increasing need for families to have two incomes, the WSDA established a tribal day-care center in 1974. In 1969 Native Americans in Sampson County formed the Coharie Tribal Development Association (CTDA) and applied for government assistance for health care, education, and job training. These and other North Carolina Indian groups also received funds for community food programs and training for employment as masons, carpenters, and nurses.[38]

Urban Indians

The various tribal development associations were effective in helping rural Indian communities. Since the end of World War II, however, a growing number of North Carolina Indians had migrated into urban areas to find jobs. They moved into cities within North Carolina, such as Greensboro, Fayetteville, and Charlotte, as well as cities outside of the state, including Baltimore, Philadelphia, and Detroit. In 1930 only about 130 American Indians lived in urban areas in North Carolina, but by 1980 almost 15,000 Native Americans had moved into cities, where they entered a strange and confusing world. Most of the men took low-paying blue-collar jobs as welders, roofers, carpenters, mechanics, or truck drivers, while young women found work in the apparel industry. Rather then permanently settling in one place, some frequently moved, looking for better work. "I would come home . . . stay maybe a week or two weeks, then I would leave again," the Lumbee William Sampson recalled. "I first went to Baltimore then I left Baltimore and went to Detroit. I left Detroit and went to Ohio. Everywhere I went I wasn't happy so I finally came back to Robeson County."[39] Urban Indians often clustered into the same neighborhoods within cities in order to offer support and reassurance. "We are very clannish," explained one Native American who had moved to Greensboro in the 1970s. "If you find one Indian living in a certain district, you'll often find a group of Indians."[40]

The Lumbee migration to Baltimore was particularly noteworthy. Robeson County Native Americans first moved to the Maryland city during the 1940s. After the war a steady stream continued to flow both ways along Interstate 95, a major north-south highway that runs through both eastern North Carolina and Baltimore. The Lumbees earned a reputation for their willingness to work dangerous "height" jobs, such as bridge construction and maintenance on skyscrapers. In 1970 about thirty-five hundred Indians lived in a small community near the corner of East Baltimore Street and Broadway known as "the reservation." Local whites frequently challenged their identity, arguing that they were not "real" Indians. Baltimore Lumbees, like other eastern North Carolina Indians, did not fit the typical white stereotype of Native Americans. To assert their identity, Baltimore Lumbees often strategically conformed to white notions of Indianness, growing their hair long and wearing Plains-style regalia, a phenomenon that would also occur in North Carolina, as well as other areas of the country.[41]

Urban Indians struggled with the economic changes. Native Americans and other Southerners referred to wage-labor jobs as "shift work," as factories and plants operated three eight-hour shifts per day. Many had a hard time adapting to the new regimen, with its strict rules, boring routines, authoritarian managers, and exacting time constraints. Native American workers also experienced discrimination, both in trying to find a job and within the workplace. White employers characterized them as lazy and undisciplined and hesitated to hire them. When they did find employment, Indians filled the most menial and degrading positions and earned less than their white counterparts. Moreover, the chances of promotion were slim. "An Indian works up to a certain position then watches as other people pass him by and get raises," one disgruntled Native American told a Greensboro reporter in 1975. "It doesn't matter how good or how fast the Indian is. Indians are only allowed to reach a certain level."[42]

In order to adjust to the changes, North Carolina "city Indians" formed urban intertribal associations. Native Americans in the Fayetteville area established the Cumberland County Association of Indian People (CCAIP) in 1965. In Greensboro a group led by Lonnie and Ruth Revels organized the Guilford Native American Association (GNAA) in 1975. Indians in the Metrolina area, the ten-county metropolitan region surrounding Charlotte, formed the Metrolina Native American Association (MNAA) in 1976. A board of directors, elected annually by the members of the association, governed each urban group. Native Americans originally from outside North Carolina could also join these associations if they belonged to either a federal- or state-recognized tribe. The urban groups also received grants and financial aid from both public and private sources to help their constituents. All of these organizations emphasized economic issues, offering job-training programs, day care for working parents, job placement services, and assistance for those suffering severe poverty. "But it doesn't stop there," according to Jerry Brewer, former president of the GNAA. "If an Indian needs assistance in applying for welfare or if he can't read or write and wants help with his employment application, we'll be there. We [the GNAA] want to help our people work on bettering themselves, and whatever that takes, we'll do it."[43]

The formation of urban Indian organizations and centers was not unique to North Carolina. In the postwar era Native Americans living in cities across the country established intertribal groups to foster unity, protect cultural identity, and deal with the problems of urban life in modern America. By the 1970s Indian centers in Chicago, Milwaukee, Los Angeles, and other metropolitan areas offered a variety of services, such as day care and job training. Nationally, these associations and centers helped thousands of Indians adjust to life in the city.[44]

The NCCIA

To further address their economic, political, and social needs, Native Americans in North Carolina looked to the state government for additional help. In the late 1960s W. R. Richardson (Haliwa), Clifton Freeman (Waccamaw), Early Maynor (Lumbee), and James Brewington (Coharie) approached Governor Robert Scott and state legislators about establishing an office specifically to deal with Indian issues. Their timing was perfect. North Carolina was becoming a two-party state for the first time since Reconstruction. As more Native Americans registered, their political influence increased. Not wanting to alienate thousands of potential Indian voters, the governor and the legislature acquiesced, and in 1971 the General Assembly appropriated twenty-five thousand dollars for the creation of the North Carolina Commission of Indian Affairs (NCCIA). The NCCIA consisted of representatives from the state-recognized tribes. At the time the Lumbees, Waccamaws, Haliwas, Coharies, Cherokees, and Person County Indians were certified. Initially a separate agency, the NCCIA became part of the state Department of Administration in 1977. According to Senate Bill 642:

> The purposes of the Commission shall be to deal fairly and effectively with Indian affairs: to bring local, state, and federal resources into focus for the implementation or continuation of meaningful programs for Indian citizens of the State of North Carolina; to provide aid and protection for Indians as needs are demonstrated; to prevent undue hardships; to assist Indian communities in social and economic development; and to promote recognition of and the right of Indians to pursue cultural and religious traditions considered by them to be sacred and meaningful to Native Americans.[45]

The NCCIA initially focused most of its attention on the economic problems plaguing Indian communities. Acting as an intermediary between federal agencies and the various Indian groups and organizations in the state, the NCCIA navigated through the complicated and time-consuming red tape of federal bureaucracy to secure funds for non–federally recognized North Carolina Indians. In 1976 HUD designated the NCCIA a public housing agency, which allowed the commission to receive funds for the development of low-rent housing in poor areas. The NCCIA also received a grant under the Comprehensive Employment and Training Act (CETA) to train poorly skilled Indians for the changing workplace. With the backing of the NCCIA, the General Assembly allocated

$500,000 in the mid-1970s to the Haliwas, Waccamaws, and Coharies for the construction of new community centers and tribal housing. In 1975 members of the NCCIA organized a one-day conference for members of various tribes and communities to come together in fellowship and discuss common problems. It was such a success that the Indian Unity Conference became a yearly event. By 1976 the North Carolina Commission of Indian Affairs had expanded from seven employees to more than thirty and operated with a budget of more than $1.6 million.[46]

The establishment of the NCCIA was a watershed for Native Americans in North Carolina. The very existence of the commission officially acknowledged that the Tar Heel state contained a large Indian population. Native Americans from various communities in the state interacted frequently through the commission, which allowed them to organize more effectively. And perhaps most important, Native Americans finally had an official forum for addressing their concerns and grievances. More than any other organization or association, the NCCIA played a vital role in the advancement of pan-Indian identity in eastern North Carolina, at least for the groups who enjoyed state acknowledgment.[47]

Despite its success, the creation of the NCCIA generated controversy. Critics argued that the commission divided North Carolina's Indian peoples into those with state recognition, which carried certain privileges, and those without. Moreover, the NCCIA controlled the recognition of other groups. Those seeking certification criticized the NCCIA's commissioners, arguing that they protected their own personal agendas, rather than acting objectively. Other critics argued that the NCCIA was too political and that members served only their friends and relatives. In 1975 one Coharie man wrote a letter to the governor contending that the policies of the NCCIA splintered Indian people in his community and the state. The commission, he complained, consisted of individuals who protected their own interests, not those of the state's Native Americans.[48]

Cultural Revival

During the political and social turmoil of the late 1960s, many Americans began to question the democratic nature of their country. A century after the Civil War, African Americans remained second-class citizens; although America was the most prosperous nation in the world, millions remained impoverished; and half a world away, thousands of young Americans were fighting an undeclared and increasingly unpopular war. To critics of federal policies, the government was becoming the enemy, rather than the protector, of the common man.

As a by-product of this new cynicism, Native Americans came to symbolize government corruption and exploitation. Furthermore, the Vietnam War, described by some as a war of imperialism, directed attention to the injustices of European and American colonialism. Consequently, popular and scholarly interest in Native American history and culture increased. Indian writers, such as N. Scott Momaday, James Welch, and Gerald Vizenor, earned national acclaim. Momaday, a Kiowa, won the Pulitzer Prize in literature in 1968 for his novel *House Made of Dawn*, which explored the travails of a Native American veteran in postwar American society. Vine Deloria Jr.'s nonfiction work *Custer Died for Your Sins* attracted national attention in 1969 for its scathing critique of Indian-white relations in American history. Dee Brown's *Bury My Heart at Wounded Knee*, a popular history of the Plains Indian wars, became a best seller in the early 1970s. Native American paintings, crafts, sculptures, artifacts, and relics, some quite expensive, filled gift boutiques and the homes of affluent non-Indians. Much of this renaissance focused on the Great Plains tribes of the nineteenth century, a way of life that was based on the horse, ironically a European import, and limited to a specific geographic area during a particular historical time. In reality, very few Native Americans actually shared the cultural tradition of the nineteenth-century Plains Indians, but that did not seem to matter to Americans fascinated with indigenous culture in the early 1970s.

This renewed interest in all things Indian influenced individuals and groups throughout all levels of American society. Native American culture affected mainstream fashion trends, especially on college campuses, where white students wore traditional Indian clothing and jewelry. Arguing that commercialization destroyed spirituality, New Agers appropriated, or more accurately altered and adapted, some of the spiritual beliefs of America's first inhabitants. Environmentalists, looking to get back in touch with Mother Earth, idealized Indian culture and history and hearkened back to a time when Native Americans supposedly lived in harmony with nature. To some eco-activists, the plight of American Indians was a metaphor for the age of industrialization and the rape of the planet. In a popular 1970s television campaign attacking litter, a Native American man dressed in Plains regalia wept at the sight of trash along a highway. Environmentalists frequently quoted from Chief Seattle's famous speech, in which, in explaining Indian philosophy, he observed, "We are part of the earth and it is part of us," a catchphrase that found its way onto T-shirts and bumper stickers. According to the author Fergus Bordewich, a white documentary filmmaker actually wrote the speech in 1972, which others falsely attributed to Seattle. Moreover, the slogan was a gross oversimplification. According to Bordewich, "It no more represents universal native attitudes toward the earth than the Confucius of fortune cookies does the ambiguities of Chinese civilization."[49] Moreover, many of the people who deified indigenous culture rarely engaged modern Native Americans; in Philip Deloria's terms, they "played Indian" to escape and critique modern society.[50]

In *The Ecological Indian: Myth and History*, Shepard Krech III attacked the mythology of the American Indian as protector of the environment. According to Krech, Native Americans, like all humans, interacted with and altered their environment, at times even overexploiting it. Acting as a judge, Krech examined several case studies to determine if Native Americans were really environmentalists. For example, did Native American practices contribute to the overhunting of certain animals? Although the results were mixed, his interpretations regarding indigenous peoples were more complex than those of previous scholars, who often argued that Indians were either primitive savages who did not correctly use the land or environmentalists living in perfect harmony with nature. Too often, Krech contended, presentists have used American Indians to push their own political agenda. Interpretations of Indian culture were, therefore, oversimplified, false, and even dehumanizing to Native Americans.[51]

The publication of *The Ecological Indian* sparked an intense debate within the fields of Native American studies and environmental history. Supporters praised Krech for challenging the one-dimensional interpretation of Native Americans as the perfect environmentalists. By doing so, Krech allowed Native Americans to become real people, rather than caricatures. Some reviewers lauded *The Ecological Indian* as a groundbreaking book. Alfred Crosby wrote that Krech "rescues Native Americans from the editorializings of their erstwhile advocates in a book that I see as holding its own as the standard single volume on the Native American and the environment for twenty and more years to come."[52] In his review of the book, Clyde Ellis contends that Krech "challenges the trope of the Noble Indian and forces us to reconsider the intellectual, political, and cultural baggage that comes with it."[53]

Others, however, have not been as complimentary. Critics attacked *The Ecological Indian* for being methodologically flawed, relying on overgeneralizations founded on just a few test cases. Moreover, they contend that his conclusions are based on documents written by Europeans and white Americans, both of whom were culturally biased. According to one reviewer, Krech's thesis was "a construction of generalizations about people, time and space. He bases his analysis on a thin wedge of evidence. . . . The bias of the documentary evidence is not questioned, which I find very disturbing."[54] Others claimed that Krech went too far in overturning the myth of the Indian as the perfect environmentalist. According to Louis S. Warren, "In his effort to undermine a myth of Noble Savagery in which all Indians live in mystical harmony with the land,

Krech comes perilously close to endorsing an old version of the Savage myth, in which Indians were gluttonous, cruel, and generally incapable of restraining their appetites."[55]

Unfortunately, this debate was as much about modern politics as it was about history. Critics of industrial capitalism often used Native Americans as symbols of a romantic past. Indians supposedly represented nature. Their story, therefore, was an allegory for the evils of modern industrialization. This, of course, was unfair and historically misleading. Equally unfair, however, critics of Native American sovereignty used—actually misused—Krech's work to attack Indian control of valuable natural resources on reservation land. This is why some Native Americans have characterized Krech's work as "anti-Indian" or even racist. Richard White addressed this dilemma in his review of *The Ecological Indian* in *The New Republic*. On the one hand, the stereotype of an ecological Indian gave contemporary Native Americans a feeling of moral superiority over whites, who, allegedly, had needlessly exploited their environment. On the other hand, according to White, this image of the environmentally superior Native American "imprisons Indians, since virtually anything that Indians do that goes against the stereotype . . . gets them denounced as un-Indian. Thus it becomes un-Indian to seek development to relieve the often crushing poverty of modern reservations and Indian communities."[56]

The motion picture industry also contributed to the cultural makeover of Native Americans. In the late 1960s and 1970s, directors made westerns that portrayed American Indians as innocent victims rather than hostile savages. Arthur Penn's *Little Big Man*, released in 1969, typified the trend. In the film, Dustin Hoffman stars as the last living survivor of the Battle of Little Big Horn, where George Armstrong Custer made his ill-fated attack. *Little Big Man* reversed the traditional stereotypes of Hollywood westerns, with Native Americans becoming good guys and the cavalry donning the traditional black hats. Unfortunately, although better than previous characterizations of Indians, Hollywood's revisionism in the late 1960s was often overly romantic and treated Native Americans as passive victims of white imperialism, an interpretation that was almost as one-dimensional as the "blood-thirsty savage."[57]

Influenced by these national trends, many North Carolina Indians became more interested in their history. They also made a more intense effort to both preserve and exhibit their Indian cultural traditions. They did this in two distinctive, though certainly related, ways. First, they looked inward for the cultural traditions within their own communities that had survived into the late twentieth century. Some Haliwa men, for example, still carved soapstone and wood. In Columbus and Bladen counties, Waccamaw women wove baskets and sewed quilts. In Robeson County, Lumbees still used traditional herbal cures and medicinal plants, treating ulcers with calmus root, kidney stones with huckleberry leaves, and baby thrash with sage. Other Lumbees did bead- and leatherwork. Second, North Carolina Indians looked to broader pan-Indian cultural traditions, particularly those based on Plains culture, such as clothing and feathered headdresses, and southeastern Indian culture, which made more sense geographically.[58]

In the 1970s tribal communities in North Carolina initiated programs to preserve old traditions and teach new ones. In 1973 the Haliwas received a federal education grant to teach beadwork, pottery, basketry, and other "Indian" arts and crafts. The tribe also organized the Red Earth Youth Council, in which children sang, made tribal regalia, and wove baskets. In the early 1970s a group of Robeson Indians developed plans to open an alternative school, called the Henry Berry Lowry College, to teach people how to "be Indian." The college was an outgrowth of the Longhouse Movement, wherein Robeson Indians, mostly Tuscaroras, held cultural awareness classes on Saturdays in which children learned Indian songs, dances, and oral traditions. In Sampson County the Coharie Tribal Council introduced an arts and crafts enrichment program, while in Columbus County the Waccamaw day-care center regularly ran cultural classes, teaching skills such as shellwork and pottery. Teachers in these classes drew upon a wide variety of Native American customs, including pan-Indian themes. That is, they did not focus exclusively on the traditional culture of North Carolina's first inhabitants. These efforts to recover, protect, and express Indian culture generally succeeded; in the 1970s basket making, quilting, beadwork, leatherwork, and pottery, among others, thrived.[59]

In the late 1960s the Lumbees revived the historical drama, defunct since the start of World War II. Influenced by the success of the Eastern Band of Cherokees and their summer play *Unto These Hills*, a group formed Robeson County Historical Drama, Inc. (RCHD) and asked the noted North Carolina playwright Paul Green, who had written the popular drama *The Lost Colony* performed each summer in Manteo, to author a new script. Green declined but recommended the North Carolina Central University professor Randolph Umberger, who accepted the offer. Delays and other problems postponed the production for several years, but in 1976 the new play, *Strike at the Wind*, finally debuted in Pembroke and received positive reviews in several state newspapers. That same year construction started on a new thirteen-hundred-seat amphitheater, which ultimately became the permanent home of the play. Featuring the renegade hero Henry Berry Lowry, *Strike* enjoyed immediate financial success and became an annual event; it was even performed at the 1982 World's Fair in Knoxville, Tennessee.[60]

Of all the outward manifestations of the Native American cultural revival in North Carolina, the contemporary tribal powwow was easily the most visible and significant. Community celebrations and festivals were not new to American Indians in the state. In the early twentieth century, Native American communities regularly held large gatherings, including church picnics, end of school festivals, and large family homecomings. Although all of these festivities included some reference to and manifestation of Native American culture and heritage, they were primarily internal community events, rather than external public assertions or exhibitions of Indianness. In the late 1960s, however, North Carolina Indians organized new festivals with a more outward expression of Native American identity.

The Haliwa-Saponis of Halifax and Warren counties staged the first modern powwow in eastern North Carolina in April 1967. After a Christian prayer and the "Star Spangled Banner," the Haliwa chief and tribal elders entered wearing traditional Plains regalia, complete with feathered headdresses and warbonnets. The event was a success, and over the next few years, the Haliwa powwow expanded in both size and significance. In 1973 the North Carolina governor Jim Holshouser, as well as representatives from the Cherokees, Lumbees, Seminoles, Creeks, Narragansetts, Mattaponis, and Chickahominies, attended the event, which drew about five thousand visitors, including many non-Indians. Holshouser, who did not smoke, symbolically shared a peace pipe with Chief W. R. Richardson. The following year Haliwa officials unfurled the first tribal flag, which was red and yellow with corn and tobacco emblems and had two dates stitched on it—1953, when the Haliwas first organized, and 1965, when they earned state recognition. The annual powwow became the primary unifying force in the community. "This is what holds our people together," said one Haliwa. "More people come home for this than Christmas."[61]

Feeding off of the Haliwas' success, other Indian communities in the state also staged powwows. In 1970 the Lumbees expanded their tradition of homecoming to include a cultural celebration. The event, which was held during the first week of July, included an opening parade, a dance, and a Princess Pageant. In Columbus County, Priscilla Freeman, the chief's daughter, led a group that organized the first modern Waccamaw-Sioux powwow in 1970. The anthropologist Patricia Lerch argued that the annual festivals were vital to their emerging identity as Waccamaws. After the closing of Indian schools, powwows became a new representation of identity for the tribe, a way of publicly asserting their Indianness. According to Lerch, "The Waccamaw have adopted the powwow

Haliwa powwow dancers at their 1968 powwow. Note the use of Plains Indian regalia. Courtesy of the North Carolina Office of Archives and History, Raleigh NC, N.69.6.513.

complex with its pan-Indian features as a way to communicate their presence to their neighbors but, as in the past, they have chosen to do so through the explicit expression of their image of themselves as Indian people."[62]

The North Carolina cultural renaissance was part of a broader national trend in the 1960s and 1970s. Across the country Native American culture flourished. Consequently, the growing popularity of powwows and the emergence of a generalized national Indian identity became popular topics for authors and scholars. The historian Alvin Josephy contended that federal policies, improvements in education, the demand for political inclusion, and improved technologies, especially in transportation and communication, all contributed to the rise of modern pan-Indianism. Hazel Hertzberg and others reached similar conclusions. In a detailed examination of Indian ethnic renewal, Joane Nagel asserted that federal Indian policy, changes in post–World War II American ethnic politics, and the Red Power movement of the 1960s and 1970s were the most vital forces in the Indian cultural renaissance. Nagel contended that "the American Indian ethnic renewal arose, in part, as an unintended consequence of assimilationist federal Indian policies that forced schooling and English on tribal children, encouraged urban relocation of Indian adults, and funded reservation and urban organizations and programs."[63] In other words, Nagel argued that federal policies, such as the Dawes Act, the Boarding School program, and Termination, unwittingly sowed the seeds of the cultural rebirth, which eventually blossomed into the Red Power movement and the Indian cultural renaissance of the 1960s.[64]

This postwar cultural rediscovery was not limited to American Indians. Indeed, other minority groups experienced a similar phenomenon. For example, the civil rights movement renewed African Americans' interest in their history and heritage. Black activists wore traditional African clothing and jewelry, gave their children African names, and demanded that schools and universities incorporate African studies into their curriculums. The similarities between the Indian and African cultural revivals were striking. Both started as political movements before also becoming social and cultural ones. Both were based on "pancultural" themes, despite the fact that, traditionally, there was no such thing as "African" or "Indian" culture, but rather many different ones. The African American movement was heavily influenced by Swahili/Tanzanian culture, whereas the Native American revival was obviously influenced by the lifestyle of the Plains tribes. And, finally, both gained mainstream and critical acceptance. African art, dance, jewelry, literature, music, and dress became accepted, even celebrated, by many middle-class Americans. In *Pan Africanism in the African Diaspora*, Ronald Walters concluded that African culture became a vital component of modern black identity in the United States. Furthermore, Walters argued that "there [was] still a predominant African dimension to the identity of the Black man and woman in the Diaspora today that overwhelms the other dimensions of birth, physical make-up, language, and even nationality."[65]

Conclusion

In the years following World War II, Native American communities in eastern North Carolina retribalized, forming new tribal groups, adopting new names, and electing new leaders. This in turn led to more changes. Some Native Americans, influenced by the African American civil rights movement, became more active in politics, particularly in their efforts to secure suffrage. In Robeson County blacks and Indians even formed a political alliance to try to elect nonwhites to county offices. At the same time, others fought against integration, fearing that the loss of Indian schools may lead to the loss of identity. Re-tribalization and political activism energized Native American communities in eastern North Carolina. Indians actively celebrated their history and culture. Consequently, a Native American renaissance spread across the state, much as it did elsewhere in the country. This renaissance was characterized by a blend of pan-Indian cultural themes, best illustrated by the contemporary powwow movement.

The Great Depression, the New Deal, and World War II transformed the country. North Carolina, in particular, modernized quickly between 1920 and 1960. As Indians became more integrated into American society, they needed new strategies for asserting their Indianness to others. As a result, the way that Indians marked and protected their identity also changed. Tribal membership, community activism, and participation in cultural celebrations all became vi-tal components of Indian identity. Moreover, beyond tribal identity, a new pan-Indian or supratribal consciousness was also emerging in eastern North Carolina. In Native Americans' attempt to secure their place in a changing world, however, one key component was still missing—official government recognition.

CHAPTER FIVE

Consolidation and the Search for Validation

Give us a fish and we'll eat for a day. Teach us to fish, and we'll eat every day. That's what we're trying to do—teach our people to fish. – Ruth Revels (Lumbee), 1987

In 1983 the North Carolina government announced plans for a yearlong cele-bration in 1986 to mark the four hundredth anniversary of the settlement of Roanoke Island, the first English colony in America. Although Native American leaders wanted to participate in the festivities, none was asked to serve on the planning committee. Furthermore, the whole celebration seemed to ignore, or at least diminish, Native Americans' role in the region's history. After all, the event implied that the English were the first people—or at least the first civilized people—to inhabit the land that would subsequently become North Carolina. As a consolation, in a speech at the annual Indian Unity Conference, Governor Jim Martin declared 1986 "The Year of the Native American" in North Carolina. In addition, November officially became "Indian Heritage Month" in the state, a time when schoolchildren would applaud Native American history and culture by dressing up like Indians and reenacting the first Thanksgiving. Martin's announcement was partly a token gesture; yet, at the same time, it was symbolic of another trend. During the previous two decades, Native Americans had moved into the state's political and economic mainstream. Consequently, for perhaps the first time, they had become North Carolinians.[1]

During the 1960s and 1970s, North Carolina Indians had demanded political and economic inclusion. At the same time, broader trends, such as desegrega-tion and the emergence of a new industrial wage-labor economy in the South, brought other changes. After the turmoil of the previous twenty years, the 1980s and 1990s were a time of consolidation and adjustment for Native Americans in the state. They occasionally struggled with these changes, but in the long run, they successfully adapted to modern life while at the same time protecting their Native American identity. Therefore, while they became North Carolinians, they also remained Indians. In the 1990s Native Americans in the state would use their new political and economic power to pursue the ultimate endorsement of Indianness, full federal acknowledgment.

Life after Integration

The closing of Indian-only schools and the integration of white and black schools represented the biggest change for Native Americans in North Carolina. By the early 1980s more than twenty-one thousand Indian children were enrolled in state public schools. During the early years of integration, the graduation rate for Indians had decreased significantly. But in the late 1970s, the graduation rate for Native Americans gradually increased, though it still remained well behind that of whites. According to the 1980 census, 57 percent of Indians in North Carolina aged eighteen to twenty-four were high school graduates compared to 75 percent of whites. In retrospect, many Native Americans concluded that integration was ultimately necessary and provided their children with better educational opportunities, even as they fondly reflected on the Indian-only schools of yesteryear. "In the beginning, the Indian people had worked hard for their school, and I think we had, not the largest, but one of the cleanest schools in the county," one Sampson Native American recalled. "But as time went by we realized that this was something that had to be done and very shortly we accepted the fact that it was necessary and we did have to go with the system."[2]

Other Native Americans, however, were not as sure. Some questioned whether integration had in fact benefited their communities. After the closing of the Columbus County Indian school, one Waccamaw woman found that fewer children and teenagers participated in community cultural events. She contended that the closing of their schools contributed to a loss of social cohesiveness and that non-Indian schools deemphasized certain values, such as respect for local elders, that their community schools had encouraged. Native American children, who were small minorities in their new schools, were also less likely to assert their heritage, perhaps even choosing to mask it. The change was rapid and dramatic—within less than a generation, most Indian communities in eastern North Carolina had gone from relative educational autonomy to a total lack of control over their children's schooling.[3]

The closing of Indian schools also effected a change in the political and social dynamics within Native American communities. For decades schools had functioned as one of the two political centers in Indian communities (the other was the church). Though they lacked any legal political power under state law, school administrators, teachers, and "blood committee" members acted as leaders. The closing of schools, therefore, left a social and political power vacuum in many communities. New organizations, such as tribal councils and economic development associations, filled this political void, eventually becoming official governing bodies in most communities. Moreover, schools had also served as social gathering places for neighborhood events such as picnics, reunions, and celebrations. Churches would continue to play a significant role in local social activities, but Native Americans would also look to other outlets, such as powwows. In fact, according to Patricia Lerch, it was no coincidence that the Waccamaws and other North Carolina Indians revived powwows during the peak of school integration in the late 1960s. And finally, schools had served as concrete markers of identity. Prior to the 1970s Indian children went to Indian schools, and communities pointed to these schools as evidence of their Indianness. But because of integration, new ethnic and cultural boundaries would be needed.[4]

Even after they closed, Indian schools, or at least their actual structures, retained a special place in many communities. The buildings continued to serve a variety of purposes. In 1987 the Haliwa-Saponis organized "Preserve Haliwa Now" to raise funds and save their old school from destruction. The tribe purchased the building, which now houses tribal offices, and the surrounding land for forty-five thousand dollars. They held their annual powwow on the campus, while a renovated central room hosted weddings, reunions, and other events. In Sampson County the Eastern Carolina Indian School initially became a technical institute before later being converted into the Coharie tribal headquarters. Other former schools in Native American communities, such as the old Waccamaw school, also served as tribal offices, museums, and day-care centers. For better or worse, the days of Native American schools were gone, but the memory of these important institutions lingered.[5]

Pan-Indianism

Fueled by the cultural revival of the early 1970s, a more general Indian identity had emerged in North Carolina by the 1980s. Native Americans took advantage of this pan-Indianism by forming and joining several intertribal organizations to fight for Indian rights. The process actually started in the late 1960s when non–federally recognized tribes and urban American Indians east of the Mississippi River organized the Coalition of Eastern Native Americans (CENA). Two North Carolina Indians, Helen Schierbeck and W. J. Strickland, helped organize a conference that led to the creation of CENA. Several federally acknowledged tribes briefly joined the association but later withdrew, signifying the sometimes tense relationship between recognized and nonrecognized Indians in the East. CENA, formed to provide services to its members and to act as an information network, folded after only a few years because of financial problems. Nevertheless, according to the historian Helen Rountree, the short-lived coalition was historically significant because it fostered intertribal unity among nonrecognized groups and showed eastern Native Americans that they were not alone in their experiences, especially in dealing with discrimination and racism.[6]

In the 1970s North Carolina Indians continued to participate in larger multitribal organizations. In 1972 the National Congress of American Indians, the largest Native American advocacy group, accepted a representative from the Lumbees. Since the 1950s individual Lumbees had established a relationship with the NCAI, but here the congress was recognizing them as a tribe. In the next couple of years, delegates to the NCAI even elected a few Lumbees to serve in positions of power within the organization. In 1974, however, tensions increased between the Lumbees and several other tribes in the NCAI. At that time the Lumbees were petitioning the federal government for official certification. Consequently, a bill was introduced in the U.S. Congress to recognize the Lumbees. Indian leaders from around the country sent letters and telegrams to federal officials opposing the bill and questioning the Lumbees' tribal identity. In a letter to Congressman Lloyd Meeds, a leader of the Florida Miccosukees wrote that "information received [by him] indicates no identifiable tribal or cultural history among the Lumbee people within the states of North Carolina and Maryland."[7] The Eastern Cherokees, worried about the prospect of overextending federal funds, also worked against Lumbee recognition. "[They] have no treaties, no Federal trust land base, no historical tribal organization, and literally thousands of persons claiming to be Lumbee Indians—who are in fact of no Indian lineage whatsoever," a Cherokee leader wrote to a congressman in the 1970s. "Passage of this legislation [recognizing the Lumbees] would . . . dilute Federal services to historically recognized tribes and open the gates to other multi-racial groups to obtain funds and services rightfully owed to the historically recognized Indian groups."[8]

To the Lumbees' surprise, the NCAI became their most vocal critic. At the 1974 annual meeting, a Navajo-Chippewa representative introduced a resolution opposing Lumbee recognition, arguing that "the claim by the Lumbee people of

North Carolina to be 'Native Americans' within the meaning generally given to the term by Congress . . . is the subject of substantial doubt and controversy." The Lumbees learned about the proposition only the night before the vote to approve it. "That's like slapping you in the face and kicking you in the ass at the same time," one Robeson Indian remarked. The chairman of the Rosebud Sioux Tribe expressed the primary economic concern of many in the NCAI. According to him, "The issue is greater than you think. We have from 40,000 to 79,000 persons waiting to make an onslaught on Congress—people suddenly coming out of the woodwork. How many do we allow to become Indians, while we diminish our resources every day."[9] The NCAI approved the resolution fifty-nine to three. Without the support of the powerful Indian group, the Lumbee recognition bill subsequently died.[10]

The rebuke from the NCAI stung the Lumbees. Moreover, one year later the NCAI excluded the Lumbees from their annual meeting and petitioned the federal government to stop giving the Robeson Indians financial aid, including monies from OEO and the Department of Health, Education, and Welfare (HEW). In 1979 a new director, who was more sympathetic toward the Lumbees because of personal connections, was chosen to lead the NCAI. The next year the congress readmitted the Lumbees, and the relationship improved, though differences with some tribes remained a problem.[11]

In the 1980s North Carolina Indians organized within the state. In 1981 the Cherokees, Haliwa-Saponis, Coharies, Meherrins, and Waccamaw-Siouans formed the United Tribes of North Carolina (UTNC) to perform functions that were beyond the reach of the NCCIA. In the 1990s the UTNC assumed responsibility for running the annual Indian Unity Conference (IUC), which had grown into a large multi-day gathering. The yearly conferences attracted a wide variety of visitors as North Carolina Indians tried to develop strategies to protect their culture and improve their standard of living. Workshops covered everything from economic development plans to traditional arts and crafts. In March 2000 the city of Fayetteville hosted the Twenty-fifth Indian Unity Conference. More than six hundred people participated in the four-day event, which included a variety of cultural programs, guest speakers, and seminars on important issues.[12]

The gathering of hundreds of Native Americans at the annual IUC led to the creation of more specialized intertribal groups and conferences in the state. In the early 1980s young Native Americans organized the first North Carolina Indian Youth Conference (NCIYC) in Pembroke. At the three-day gathering, members from various tribes held workshops on traditional culture, organized a powwow, and held seminars on self-awareness and legal issues. In 1986 college students established the North Carolina Native American Council on Higher Education (NCNACHE) to provide a forum on the state's various campuses and to improve the recruitment and retention of Indian college students. Also in the mid-1980s, older Native Americans formed the North Carolina Indian Senior Citizens' Conference to focus attention on the housing and health-care needs of the elderly.[13]

Intertribal organization paid off for North Carolina Indians. By working together, they dramatically increased their political power and presence in the state. Moreover, with suffrage secured, Native Americans could influence elections. In the 1980s Indian leaders began winning elections and holding powerful positions in local, county, and even state governments. In 1989 Governor Jim Martin appointed Dexter Brooks to the North Carolina Superior Court, making him the first Indian to hold such a position. In 1994 Glen Maynor became the first Indian sheriff in Robeson County, and Joanne Locklear was elected the first Native American clerk of court. Pantribal organization also allowed Indians to pursue agendas important to them. In the 1980s, for example, Native Americans persuaded the North Carolina General Assembly to pass two bills regarding procedures for dealing with Indian artifacts: the Archaeological Resources Protection Act and the Unmarked Burial and Unmarked Skeletal Remains Protection Act. The bills required archaeologists to consult with tribal leaders and the North Carolina Commission of Indian Affairs about the handling and disposition of human remains and artifacts. Eventually, the federal government established national guidelines when President George H. W. Bush signed the Native American Graves Protection and Repatriation Act in 1989.[14]

For many North Carolina Indians, economic issues remained the primary focus. In the 1980s Indian tribes in the state started their own businesses to attack the unemployment and poverty so common in many of their communities. Both the Waccamaws and the Coharies, for example, opened tribal catfish farms to create jobs and bring money into the local economy. In Fayetteville the Cumberland County Association of Indian People established a furniture design and production company. In Greensboro the Guilford Native American Association opened Rising Star, an Indian-themed greeting card company, and an apparel-packaging plant that employed forty local Indians. In the 1990s the former Lumbee activist Harvey Godwin opened Two Hawks, a placement agency in Robeson County that helped Indians find jobs in a variety of fields, from construction companies to high-tech firms. Tribal economic assistance extended beyond communally owned businesses. Following the lead of the Waccamaws, a few communities, including the Haliwas and Coharies, established tribal day-care centers that allowed women to seek work. The Lumbee

Regional Development Association, the Waccamaw Sioux Development Association, and other tribal economic organizations also remained very active. These groups continued to attack poverty and offer employment assistance within their communities. During the 1980s and 1990s the LRDA distributed millions of dollars' worth of food to thousands of needy Indian families in Robeson and surrounding counties through the Community Services Project, a government-financed relief program.[15]

To further promote economic growth, two dozen business owners got together in 1990 and formed the North Carolina Indian Business Association (NCIBA). Encouraging Indians to do business with other Indians, the NCIBA created a statewide business directory listing more than 850 Native American–owned enterprises. The NCIBA also inspired entrepreneurs to diversify their companies. In the early 1990s about one-third of all Indian-owned businesses in the state were connected with the construction industry and often competed against one another for the same contracts. The NCIBA wanted Indian businesses to cooperate with one another and compete with outsiders.[16]

The North Carolina Commission of Indian Affairs contributed to the economic changes in Indian communities during the 1980s and 1990s. In 1984 the NCCIA initiated an Economic Development Program (EDP) to offer technical assistance and financial advice to Indian business owners. Administrators of the EDP worked closely with the NCIBA by organizing seminars and workshops for entrepreneurs. The Educational Talent Search (ETS) initiative sought to reduce the high school dropout rate and increase the number of Indians enrolling in college by recruiting promising youth between the ages of eleven and twenty-seven. Program representatives visited schools, sponsored tours of local universities, and conducted financial aid workshops, teaching both parents and children how to get loans, scholarships, and grants for higher education. In the 1990s the U.S. Department of Education subsidized the ETS, allocating more than two hundred thousand dollars in 1999 alone. A substance abuse program tried to reduce the rates of alcoholism and drug addiction among Indians, a serious problem in many communities. The Community Services operation offered transportation and delivered meals for the homebound and the elderly. Monies from the federally funded Job Training Partnership Act (JTPA) provided skills instruction and work opportunities for the unemployed. North Carolina Indians did not look at these programs as handouts or charity, but rather as opportunities to lift themselves out of poverty and dependence.[17]

By the 1990s economic progress was readily apparent in many Native American communities. Across the state, Indian enterprises prospered. For example, in Halifax County, Haliwas owned more than fifty businesses, including restaurants, grocery stores, floral shops, garages, and real estate agencies. Although many Native Americans were still blue-collar workers, an increasing number moved into white-collar positions. The 1990 census looked in detail at American Indians in five Tribal Designated Statistical Areas (TDSAS), one each for the Coharies, Haliwa-Saponis, Lumbees, Meherrins, and Waccamaw-Sioux. According to the data, in 1989 11 percent of Indians in those designated areas worked in managerial and professional fields. A generation or two earlier, that percentage was near zero. Of the rest, 13.8 percent were in sales and administrative support, 10.6 percent in the service sector, 22.9 percent in repair and precision production, and 37.2 percent were in manual labor occupations such as operators, fabricators, and laborers. Remarkably, less than 5 percent worked in agricultural or forestry-related fields, a dramatic transformation from the pre–World War II era. The news was not all good, however; 23 percent of families still lived below the poverty line, a rate much higher than the state average.[18]

The biggest concrete example of Indian economic progress could be found in the town of Pembroke. In the 1960s and 1970s, many Lumbees became very frustrated by the constant discrimination that they encountered in white-owned banks and other financial institutions. Starting businesses and other entrepreneurial enterprises often required capital. In Robeson, as elsewhere, it was difficult for Native Americans to establish credit. Consequently, a group of Lumbees organized more than six hundred investors, 80 percent of whom were Indian, and founded the Lumbee Bank, the first Indian-owned financial institution in the United States. The venture was an immediate success. During the 1980s the bank grew, serving the needs of Indians, blacks, and whites in Robeson County. By the 1990s the Lumbee Bank controlled a dozen branches and loan proceeds of more than forty million dollars.[19]

As the Lumbee Bank illustrated, North Carolina Indians wanted economic self-sufficiency. The legacy of the sharecropping and tenant system was not just a fading historical memory. After decades of economic dependence on others, Native Americans wanted at least a modicum of control over their economic future. At the same time, however, many argued that, because of historical injustices, it was the government's responsibility to help Native Americans get the tools to compete in modern society. They did not want "handouts," but rather "help-ups." The Lumbee Ruth Revels summed up this view by paraphrasing an old proverb. "Give us a fish and we'll eat for a day," she told a reporter in 1987. "[But] teach us to fish, and we'll eat every day. That's what we're trying to do—teach our people to fish."[20] And for the first time in decades, if not centuries, North Carolina Indians appeared ready and able to bait their hooks. Despite decades of oppression, discrimination, and exploitation, Native Americans became increasingly optimistic about their future. "I see greater things for the Waccamaw-Siouans," Shirley Freeman, whose brothers owned their own business, told an interviewer in the 1990s. "I see [us] not dependent. We can be self-supporting."[21]

The Renaissance Flourishes

The cultural renaissance that blossomed in the 1960s and 1970s continued to flower in the 1980s and 1990s. In the 1970s the Lumbee artist Lloyd Oxendine, among others, had sparked initial interest in North Carolina Indian art. In the 1980s other state Indian artists, such as Patricia Richardson (Coharie) and Arnold Richardson (Haliwa), also attracted attention for their work. By the 1990s several state museums frequently held exhibits by Indians. Some local artists even attracted national attention. The Smithsonian Institute in Washington DC featured the work of the Haliwa Senora Lynch. Karen Lynch-Harley earned recognition for her work using a variety of mediums, including oil, egg tempera, watercolor, charcoal, and clay. Much of this art reflected two central themes: the retention of Indianness in modern America and the difficulties of living in two cultural worlds.[22]

In the Piedmont section of North Carolina, the city of Greensboro, which is in Guilford County, became a major supporter of Native American art. In 1990 the city council created the Greensboro Cultural Center, which subsequently established the Guilford Native American Art Gallery. In the 1990s the gallery became a primary venue for the display of North Carolina Indian art. In 1998 the Guilford gallery hosted an exhibit by the Haliwa artist C. M. Dreamweaver Cooper titled Singing the Blues, Painting the Reds. In 1999 it displayed an exhibit titled Recollections: Lumbee Heritage, a collection of photos taken from 1870 to 1945. In the summer of 2002, it exhibited Walking in the Spirit Circle, a selection of about sixty pieces by Native Americans in the state, and Crying to the Great Spirit, a collection of paintings by the Lumbee James Locklear. Other exhibits have included a wide variety of art forms, such as quilts, baskets, pottery, carvings, and sculptures, from all recognized tribes in the state. The city and the center also host a Native American Cultural Festival each November to coincide with Indian Heritage Month.[23]

Native American art became so fashionable in the 1980s that controversy arose regarding authenticity. Indians complained that some artists were posing as Native Americans in order to sell their goods at a higher price. The debate over artistic authenticity occasionally plunged into the quicksand of "blood quantum" arguments, where artists with a higher degree of ancestry claimed to be more Indian, and therefore more real. In 1990 Congress passed the Indian

Arts and Crafts Act, in essence legally defining authenticity. In general, a certified Indian artist or craftsperson must be a member of a state- or federally recognized tribe or must be sanctioned and approved by a state- or federally recognized tribe. Those certified can market their art as made by a "real Native American." Noncertified artists and craft makers who market their products as Native American face stiff fines for false advertisement. The issue of authenticity continues to stir debate in North Carolina and elsewhere.

In the 1980s and 1990s, North Carolina tribes formed a variety of groups and organizations to celebrate, revive, and protect their cultural practices. In 1988 the Tuscaroras established a drum and dance society. In the early 1990s John Blackfeather Jeffries cofounded the Traditional Occaneechi Heritage Association (TOHA), a nonprofit open-membership group in Alamance and Orange counties. The TOHA received several grants from outside sources to finance research into its members' history, including a total of $370,000 from the Administration for Native Americans. TOHA also got funding to revive Indian languages indigenous to the area. Jeffries played a key role in the cultural revival of the Native Americans in the Alamance County area, teaching himself traditional cultural practices, such as flint making, and then teaching others. He was a key figure in the construction of a replica of an eighteenth-century Indian village on a wooded five-acre lot on the banks of the Eno River. The site would include several huts, a sweat lodge, and a protective palisade fence, all common to Indian villages in the 1700s. In November 2001 the Occaneechis staged a living history reenactment at their village, selling various crafts and serving traditional foods prepared in a cooking pit. The TOHA also gave public lectures and presentations on local American Indian history and culture. In the 1990s other communities established similar groups.[24]

The two trends of cultural revival and pan-Indian organization inevitably merged in North Carolina. In the 1980s several tribes and urban organizations developed plans for a $50 million North Carolina Indian Cultural Center to be built in Robeson County near Interstate 95, a major north-south highway that millions of potential tourists used when driving from the Northeast to Florida. The NCCIA appropriated $550,000 in 1985 to purchase a five-hundred-acre site for the center, which would include a museum, outdoor exhibits, a reproduction of a nineteenth-century American Indian village, a hotel, and recreational facilities. Unfortunately, the development of the facility stalled because of internal division on the steering committee and a shortage of funds. At the turn of the twenty-first century, the future of the cultural center remained somewhat in doubt, but state Indian leaders were still determined to establish it as a regional and national tourist attraction.[25]

Across the state the tribal powwow remained the dominant symbol in the resurgence of Native American culture. By the 1990s the annual powwow schedule, which ran from early spring to late fall, was almost completely full. But the role of the tribal powwow had evolved since its reincarnation in the late 1960s. In "Powwows, Parades, and Social Drama," the anthropologist Patricia Lerch noted the changes in the Waccamaw powwow between 1970 and 1991. According to Lerch, the early Waccamaw powwows resembled a large family gathering, attracting only local Native Americans. The drummers played for free and the dancers danced for fun. The overall theme celebrated the revival of Indian culture. The 1991 powwow, however, was noticeably different. It was open to the public and drew hundreds of non-Indians. The drummers were paid for their services and contestants danced for cash prizes, as well as for fun.[26]

Similar changes occurred at other tribal powwows in the state. With the closing of Indian schools, powwows quickly became the primary method of publicly exhibiting Indianness. Moreover, what started as rather small gatherings of local Indians became large events attracting thousands of visitors, most of whom were not Native Americans. Vendors set up tents around the dance grounds to sell a variety of Native American goods to curious tourists. At any given powwow, shoppers could find traditional Indian clothing, feathered headdresses, handmade jewelry, pottery, woven baskets, leather products, wood works, books, compact discs, paintings, and a range of other goods, even velvet portraits of Elvis and John Wayne. Concession stands offered drinks and an assortment of Indian foods, such as fry bread. Visitors and participants wore T-shirts with pro-Indian slogans, and cars were decorated with similar bumper stickers. North Carolina Indians added a wide variety of events to their tribal powwows in the 1980s and 1990s, such as wrestling, pony racing, princess pageants, parades, softball, gospel sings, disco dancing, volleyball, baseball, basketball, golf, cakewalks, three-legged races, and sack races to the core activities of dancing and feasting.[27]

Despite other changes, the cornerstone of the modern powwow remained dancing. Native American dancers made their own regalia using natural, not manufactured, items. If the outfit was purchased, it was considered a costume, which implied imitation rather than participation. There were two basic Indian dance styles: traditional and fancy. Fancy dancing involved elaborate and colorful outfits, was faster, and included more athletic movements; younger dancers preferred it. Traditional dancing was slower, more refined, and the regalia more basic and traditional, often imitating nature. Traditional female dancers wore tan buckskin dresses covering their legs, carried feathered fans, and draped shawls over their arms. Competitions became increasingly popular

Young male fancy dancer at the 2001 Occaneechi powwow. Young Native Americans often prefer the fancy style of Indian dance, which is usually faster and more athletic than traditional dance. The regalia worn is usually elaborate and colorful. Photo from the author's collection.

and important parts of the powwow in the 1990s, but dancing nevertheless retained its cultural significance. "We're telling history every time we dance," according to one Native American man. "We dance to honor our ancestors, to show respect for the elders, and to show respect for everybody and everything. After all, everything is here for a reason, the grass, the trees—we respect it all."[28]

Powwows and cultural festivals became so popular in North Carolina that urban Indian associations and non-Indian groups and organizations began hosting them. The urban associations in Raleigh, Charlotte, and Fayetteville sponsored yearly festivals. The North Carolina School of Science and Mathematics in Durham established a powwow to attract Indian students to the highly selective high school. Durham Technical Community College invited all of the North Carolina tribes to participate in its annual Indian cultural celebration. First held in the 1970s, the Guilford Native American Association (GNAA) powwow in Greensboro became one of the most well known and well attended Indian cultural events in the Southeast. The 2001 GNAA powwow offered more than twelve thousand dollars in prizes for dancers. Across the state, the number

Male traditional dancer at the 2001 Occaneechi powwow. Some Indians
prefer the traditional style of dancing, which is slow and refined.
The regalia often mimics nature. Photo from the author's collection.

of Native American festivals seemed to multiply each year. By the late 1990s
it was possible for Indians to participate in some cultural event almost every
weekend from April to September.[29]

For most Indian communities in the state, powwows and other cultural
events became economic endeavors. Tourists, both Indian and non-Indian,
visited the festivities and pumped money into the local economy. Some tribes
charged admission, usually between two and five dollars per person. But some
critics questioned the growing commercialism of Native American festivals in
the state. Arguing that money, rather than cultural pride, fueled the circuit,
skeptics criticized contemporary powwows, noting that many activities had
little to do with Indian culture. Supporters of modern powwows responded
by contending that critics continued to define Indianness based on eighteenth-
and nineteenth-century typecasts. But the participants themselves often emphasized certain stereotypes in these celebrations, as Plains Indian culture
consumed the atmosphere at many North Carolina powwows. This decision
to stress pan-Indianism was at least partly strategic—some North Carolina
Indians conformed to white conceptions of identity in order to win approval
and acceptance. Furthermore, the growing presence of non-Indians, who began
to outnumber Native Americans at many powwows, caused concern. "[White]

Haliwa fancy dancers at the Tar River Festival in Rocky Mount, 1999. Photo courtesy of David Weaver of the Rocky Mount Telegram, *Rocky Mount* NC.

hobbyists come to our pow wows to dance in our sacred circles and wear our regalia as if it were Halloween costumes," complained one Occaneechi man. "They are making a mockery of our Indian traditions."[30]

The controversy over the changing role of powwows was not unique to North Carolina Indians. Other tribes in other states have also worried about the commercialization of cultural events. In a recent article, Robert DesJarlait examined the changing role of powwows in Native American communities. Although competitive dancing predated contact with Europeans, the contemporary contest powwow, where Indians dance for prizes, emerged in the 1960s. As a result, according to DesJarlait, powwows quickly became the primary representation of modern pan-Indianism. In the 1990s critics began to fear that the commercialization of powwows was dividing Native American communities. DesJarlait, however, disagreed. He contends that "the result of the contest powwow has not been to divide different tribal cultures but to bring different cultures together."[31]

Ultimately, contemporary powwows allowed North Carolina Native Americans to present themselves positively to others in the state. Too often, the

Female fancy dancer at the Tar River Festival in Rocky Mount, 1999. Photo courtesy of David Weaver of the Rocky Mount Telegram, *Rocky Mount* NC.

media emphasized the poverty, disease, and economic problems plaguing many Indian communities. These difficulties certainly merited attention, but Native Americans also wanted others to note their progress. Powwows allowed Indians to showcase themselves to outsiders while emphasizing their achievements. In doing so, Native Americans shaped their powwows to attract non-Indians. "If we just do a normal powwow," one Waccamaw woman admitted, "there wouldn't be anybody but us."[32]

Although powwows became the primary external symbols of modern Indian identity, they were also battlegrounds in the fight over the meaning of Indianness. According to Mark Mattern, modern powwows managed internal tension in many Indian communities. Therefore, Indian identity was not only asserted and exhibited at these events but also negotiated and contested. These negotiations took a variety of forms: who should be the master of ceremony, what to include on the program, whom to honor, whom to invite, who can dance, and so forth. "Powwows," Mattern argued, "are constituents of identity and a unifying force in contemporary Indian life, but they are also arenas of conflict and disagreement in which power plays an important role and which Indians implicitly and explicitly debate their identity and mutual commitments."[33] Every powwow, therefore, was another chapter in the continuing story of Indian cultural renewal in North Carolina. At the core of this movement was the public assertion of identity, especially to whites. Even at non-Indian events across the state, such as the annual Tar River Festival in Rocky Mount and the Eno River Festival near Durham, Indian performers frequently sang, danced, and told stories for white audiences. While helping to preserve cultural traditions, these efforts were also designed to get whites to accept their identity.[34]

Lumbee English

Despite their best efforts, skeptics still questioned the identity of many North Carolina Indians. Critics who challenged their identity frequently pointed to the lack of an indigenous language as proof that they were fakes. Real Native Americans, they argued, spoke "Indian," not English. In recent years some tribes have attempted to address this criticism. The Occaneechis, for example, established a relationship with Meredith College in Raleigh to study, and hopefully revive, their traditional Siouan language. In Robeson County the Lumbees adopted a different approach to the language question. They contended that they, in fact, did speak an Indian language, or at least a unique dialect.[35]

A linguist at North Carolina State University agreed with the Lumbees. Professor Walt Wolfram, who has conducted extensive research on the community, argued that Lumbee speech patterns were, indeed, distinctive. Prior to the arrival of Europeans, present-day Robeson County was centrally located between numerous tribes who spoke a variety of Algonkian, Siouan, and Iroquoian dialects. According to Wolfram, all of these traditional languages influenced the current English spoken by the Lumbees. Consequently, Lumbee speech was a mixture of Old English and various Native American dialects. Based on his research, Wolfram concluded that Lumbee English was unique, easily recognizable by non-Indian residents of Robeson County, and a vital element of their identity. A couple of characteristics made the dialect exceptional. First, the Lumbees used a singular vocabulary, for example calling sling shots "juvembers," coffee with sugar "ellick," and a bad omen a "toten." Second, Lumbees employed creative sentence constructions, such as the frequent use of the verb "be" in perfect constructions; Lumbees said "I'm been there" and "we're been there" instead of "I've been there" and "we've been there."[36]

According to Wolfram, Lumbee English placed the community in what he termed "double-jeopardy." Their adoption of English, which occurred in the eighteenth century, fueled criticism that they were not real Indians and hindered efforts to earn federal recognition. After all, critics argued, if they did not have a tribal language, then they were not a tribe. At the same time, white schoolteachers dismissed the Lumbee dialect as simply poor English. Consequently, their speech was neither "Indian" nor "white," at least according to outsiders. Nevertheless, Wolfram's studies concluded that Lumbee English was important to their Indianness. In his research, he showed that whites, blacks, and Indians from Robeson County easily recognized the Lumbee dialect. In other words, speech was a key component of Lumbee identity, at least within their own community. In one experiment, Wolfram asked individuals to identify the race of the speaker on several taped interviews. In Robeson County whites, blacks, and Indians correctly identified Lumbees based on the way that they talked more than 80 percent of the time. In studies conducted outside of the county, however, whites and blacks, who had never heard Lumbees talk, frequently misidentified them as whites. For their part, Lumbees insisted that they spoke a distinctive language that signified their identity. "That's how we recognize who we are, not by looking at someone," one Lumbee told Wolfram. "We know who we are by our language. If we're anywhere in the country and hear ourselves speak, we know exactly who we are."[37]

More "Trouble in Robeson County"

Despite the political, social, and economic gains of the 1980s, North Carolina Native Americans still faced numerous problems in their communities, including poverty, unemployment, and discrimination. In the 1980s Indians usually tried to voice their displeasure through their new supratribal organizations and associations, most notably the NCCIA. They also expressed themselves via the voting booth, using, rather than fighting, the political system. But occasionally, some felt the need to resort to protests to remind others of their continuing problems. Often, these new demonstrations were relatively small and orderly and attacked symbolic remnants of historical injustices. In the early 1980s, for example, the IUC attracted media attention by demanding that the state change the name of one of its highways. In the early 1960s the North Carolina Department of Transportation (NCDOT) had designated a stretch of Highway 74 "Andrew Jackson Highway." The road ran along the southern border of the state from Wilmington through several counties containing substantial Indian populations all the way to the town of Cherokee in the western mountains of the state. Protesters wanted NCDOT to rename the stretch "Native American Highway," or some variation of that theme. The initial movement waned, but in the 1990s another group, led by Robert Chavis, revived the protest. Chavis was influenced by contemporary events. "I saw what the Cuban-Americans did with Elian Gonzalez and what blacks did in South Carolina with the Confederate flag, and it looked like a good time to bring things up," he told a reporter. "I sense a little more empathy for the minority."[38] To many white southerners, Andrew Jackson was a frontier hero and one of the most popular American presidents. North Carolinians were especially proud of "Old Hickory," arguing with South Carolinians over the exact location of his birthplace, which was somewhere along the border between the two states. American Indians, however, felt quite different. Jackson was the primary architect of Indian removal in the 1820s and 1830s, when the federal army forced thousands of southern Indians, including the majority of Cherokees, to leave their homelands and move to the West. Chavis summed up the feelings of many Native Americans regarding the former president: "Jackson is no hero to us. He's like Hitler. He's a killer." The protest ultimately failed, and the road remained Andrew Jackson highway.[39]

Some acts of resistance were more desperate. In 1988 radical activism and violence briefly returned to Robeson County, and once again Tuscaroras were leading the way. On the morning of February 1, Eddie Hatcher and Timothy Jacobs stormed the offices of the *Robesonian*, a white-owned newspaper in Lumberton. Armed with shotguns, the two Tuscaroras barricaded themselves inside along with seventeen hostages, including Bob Horne, the paper's editor. "We do not want the death of any hostage," Hatcher ominously told the police as they surrounded the building. "However, we are prepared, if necessary, to enforce the action we have demanded. Should we meet death, we shall not meet it alone."[40]

Racism and discrimination motivated the two Tuscaroras to take confrontational action. Specifically, Hatcher and Jacobs complained about the Robeson Sheriff's Department. Recently, a white deputy had shot and killed a young Indian male during a traffic stop. In another case, a black prisoner who suffered from chronic asthma died in his jail cell from lack of medical attention. After brief internal inquiries, both deaths were ruled accidental. There had also been several other mysterious and unsolved murders in the county during the 1980s; many of the victims were Native Americans. And finally, Hatcher and Jacobs charged that the sheriff's department was connected with the illegal drug trade. In the 1980s Robeson County had earned a reputation as a major drug distribution area for narcotics, especially cocaine.[41]

That cool February morning, North Carolinians across the state listened to the radio and watched television for hours as tensions increased between the authorities and the two Tuscaroras. Not trusting the local police, Hatcher and Jacobs demanded to negotiate with state officials. Governor Jim Martin sent his chief of staff, Phillip Kirk, to Lumberton to deal with the situation. Kirk promised the two men that he would form a state task force to look into their allegations. After several hours Hatcher and Jacobs started to release prisoners, first the women, followed by African Americans and, finally, all others, including Horne. Ten hours after charging the newspaper, Hatcher and Jacobs surrendered to agents from the Federal Bureau of Investigation.[42]

Many in Robeson County, including several prominent whites, sympathized with Hatcher and Jacobs. Even Horne expressed understanding. Most, though, did not agree with their methods, wishing that the two men would have attempted other means first. Hatcher and Jacobs were tried in federal court under the new domestic terrorist act. In October 1988 a jury of nine blacks and three whites acquitted them. State authorities quickly rearrested Hatcher and Jacobs and charged them with kidnapping. Jacobs pleaded guilty and served two years of a six-year sentence before making parole. Hatcher fled after making bail but was eventually caught in San Francisco after unsuccessfully seeking asylum at the Soviet consulate. In February 1990 a state jury sentenced Hatcher to eighteen years in jail. After being paroled in 1995, Hatcher was arrested for murder and sentenced to a life term.[43]

Only a few weeks after Hatcher and Jacobs stormed the *Robesonian*, violence again erupted in Robeson County. In March Julian Pierce, a prominent Native American attorney, was shot and killed. Because Pierce was running for Superior Court judge, local Indians initially suspected his white opponent, the local district attorney, had ordered his assassination. The murder, however, turned out to be the by-product of a domestic feud. A young man who had been dating Pierce's girlfriend's daughter apparently killed the lawyer for obtaining trespassing warrants against him. He shot himself before police could arrest him. Nevertheless, Pierce's death increased interracial tension in the county. Once again, these events focused national media attention on the Indians of Robeson County. In May 1988 *US News and World Report* ran a story titled "There's Trouble in Robeson County." In the fall Pierce posthumously won the election by more than two thousand votes, but his opponent took office anyway.[44]

The Pursuit of Recognition

Prior to the 1970s few Native American tribes actively pursued federal acknowledgment. In the 1950s and 1960s, government recognition carried few real advantages. Federal certification allowed tribes to establish a government-to-government relationship with the United States and to place land in trust. The BIA also offered acknowledged tribes a few financial programs, but the benefits were minimal. Moreover, no one knew exactly how to characterize the relationship between recognized Indians and the federal government. On paper, the two entered into a relatively friendly alliance between governments; in reality, the United States treated American Indians like wards. And in the postwar years, the federal government had actually tried to terminate that relationship. Consequently, in the 1950s and 1960s, very few tribes pursued acknowledgment.[45]

Several factors increased the number of American Indian groups applying for federal certification in the 1970s. First, the broader social changes of the post–World War II years began reducing the stigma of being labeled a minority. Nonrecognized Indians in the South internally celebrated their identity within their own communities before the war, but, because of the intense racism in the region, downplayed it when among outsiders. By the 1970s, however, being Indian was not necessarily a negative; in fact, it was almost fashionable. Second, a change in federal Indian policy opened the door to acknowledgment. In the 1950s and 1960s, Termination prevented new tribes from earning certification. But by the 1970s Termination was deemed a failure, and the federal government let the policy mercifully die. And finally, Native Americans also saw a new financial incentive to recognition. Starting with LBJ's "Great Society" legislation in the mid-to-late 1960s, the government increased spending on Native Americans, especially in education, health care, and housing. All Indians could participate in some of these programs, such as Head Start, the Education Assistance Act, and the Indian Health-Care Act. Other programs, mostly those administered by the BIA, served only federal tribes. In either case, recognized tribes enjoyed a clear advantage over other Native Americans—since their identity was already established, they did not have to demonstrate that they were Indians. Unrecognized tribes, such as many of those in the South, still needed to prove themselves, and various government agencies often defined Indianness differently, complicating the process even more.[46]

In addition to access to funds, federal acknowledgment also meant an increase in tribal sovereignty, or control over internal political, social, and economic affairs. The definition of tribal sovereignty, broadly defined as the right of an Indian group to govern its own affairs, changed during the 1900s in correlation to federal Indian policy. After 1975 tribal sovereignty expanded under the Indian Self-Determination Act. In general, federally recognized tribes defined their own membership, passed tribal laws, established courts, levied taxes, allocated federal monies, and regulated the use of natural resources on their lands. Reservations, technically held in trusteeship by the national government, were subject to federal laws but exempt from state regulatory laws. In the 1970s and 1980s, a series of court cases tried to define more accurately the real meaning of tribal sovereignty; nevertheless, it remained complicated and confusing, even to legal experts. Literally thousands of court rulings, statutes, regulations, and treaties defined the relationship between American Indians and the federal government, and the actual meaning of sovereignty shifted with the prevailing political winds.[47]

Because of these changes, the number of tribes petitioning for federal certification skyrocketed in the 1970s. To address the backlog of applications, the BIA took it upon itself to establish guidelines for recognition. Before 1978 federal law demanded that Native American tribes meet only two basic requirements in order to earn acknowledgment. First, the tribe had to be a separate and distinct political entity. Second, the government had to have an established official relationship at some point with the petitioning tribe, such as a former treaty. Therefore, Congress and the president, not the BIA, officially recognized tribes. In 1978 the BIA created the Branch of Acknowledgment and Research (BAR), which, in turn, developed specific criteria for earning recognition. Commonly known as the Federal Acknowledgment Process (FAP), the new guidelines required tribes to submit a petition to the BIA that documented and proved each of the following criteria: (1) continuous tribal existence since historical times; (2) a separate homeland; (3) a tribal government that maintained political influence over members; (4) a governing document that outlined membership requirements; (5) members were not associated with other tribes; (6) the group was never the subject of federal termination legislation; and (7) an official tribal roll. A subcommittee within the BIA would rule on each petition.[48]

Native Americans complained that the BIA's new guidelines were unfair and required the use of experts to research and document their history, an expensive and time-consuming endeavor given the dearth of written records. Many Indian tribes could not afford to hire outsiders to do research that might take years. This was especially true for Indians in the Southeast, most of whom lacked treaties and other written proof of their existence. "The region's [Southeast] only documentation was done by whites," the Haliwa Greg Richardson explained. "Finding documentation by Indians is next to impossible."[49] When asked by a U.S. senator what was wrong with the FAP process, one Tuscarora woman from North Carolina bluntly answered that tribes tried to avoid it "because it is slow, because it is cumbersome, because it is desperately, desperately expensive."[50] Other Native Americans argued that the guidelines reinforced white stereotypes of Indianness. The criteria assumed that tribal identity was continuous and demanded that Indian groups trace their existence back to "historical times," a vague temporal requirement. Tribal identity had always been fluid, as communities and groups formed and reformed several times, a process that dated back centuries before the arrival of Europeans. In response to criticisms, the BIA redefined the guidelines in 1994, requiring petitioning tribes to trace their historical connection back only one hundred years and prove that they lived in a separate "community" rather than a distinct homeland. But the bar for federal acknowledgment remained high, and many Indian communities lacked the tools, or in some cases the qualifications, to get over it.[51]

In the late 1970s the North Carolina Commission of Indian Affairs also streamlined its procedure for state recognition. Previously, North Carolina had already acknowledged the Lumbees, the Person County Indians, the Haliwa-Saponis, the Coharies, and the Waccamaw-Sioux. The first three were recognized by the General Assembly, while the Coharies and Waccamaws were certified by the NCCIA in 1971. The NCCIA had also previously recognized three urban associations as Indian organizations: the Metrolina Native American Association, the Guilford Native American Association, and the Cumberland County Association of Indian People. In 1979 the state Indian commission established specific guidelines for recognizing Native American tribes and organizations. The NCCIA defined a tribe as a population of related Indian people who lived in a distinct community and could trace their existence back two hundred years to indigenous tribes within present-day North Carolina. In addition, a petitioning tribe had to meet five of the following eight specifications: (1) a traditional North Carolina Indian name; (2) kinship with other recognized tribes; (3) official records (birth certificates, death certificates, church and school records, etc.) that recognized them as Indians; (4) the support of state and federal authorities; (5) anthropological or historical accounts of their history and culture; (6) the support of other recognized tribes; (7) other documents or proof of their history, culture, and so forth; and (8) the reception of grants designated for Native Americans only. An Indian organization was described as a group of Indian people made up primarily of members of either state- or federally recognized tribes. Therefore, if Native Americans from different recognized tribes were living in a city, they could form an Indian group, such as the Metrolina Native American Association in Charlotte. An NCCIA subcommittee consisting of representatives from the state's recognized tribes oversaw the application process and ruled on each petition.[52]

Some critics argued that the new state guidelines, like the federal ones, were unfair. They contended that the process required expensive research and prevented legitimate Indian groups from earning state recognition. Many North Carolina Indian communities lacked the financial and educational capital to complete such an arduous undertaking. Moreover, the procedure was established by tribes that did not have to go through the process. From 1979 to 2004 only one tribe, the Meherrins in 1986, and one urban group, the Triangle Native American Society in 2000, applied successfully. Recently, as will be discussed below, the Occaneechis of Alamance County earned state recognition, though they did so through court order. "If any of these tribes [those recognized before 1979] had to go through this process or the same sort of guidelines that are out now, none of them would make it," one critic complained in 2000. "I think it's a little ludicrous to interpret the criteria in a way that the same people [who made them and interpreted them] wouldn't meet them."[53]

Supporters, by contrast, pointed to the need for strict requirements in order to legitimize the process. NCCIA officials agreed that the criteria were tough but argued that if the standards were too low, state recognition would be meaningless. A legal representative of the NCCIA bluntly summarized this view. "You just don't go out and gather up a bunch of Indians and say 'Let's be Joe's Indian tribe, and let's go get recognized,' " he told a reporter in 2001 when discussing the merits of a particular petition.[54] Many Indians and others shared these concerns. If the criteria were too lenient, any group could apply for recognition and take advantage of programs designed to help struggling and disadvantaged Native Americans. According to one member of the NCCIA, "Everybody says they're Indian these days because there's a benefit."[55]

Despite the costs and difficulties, several North Carolina groups applied for state recognition in the 1980s and 1990s, including the Meherrins and Occaneechis. The Occaneechi case was particularly interesting and illustrated the significance and contentiousness of the issue. In 1984 the Occaneechis contacted the North Carolina Commission of Indian Affairs regarding state-recognition procedures. Community leaders subsequently began working on a petition for state certification based on the guidelines. In early 1990 the Occaneechis submitted their application under the name Occaneechi Band of the Saponi Nation (OBSN). The NCCIA Recognition Committee rejected the OBSN petition in 1995 by a vote of fourteen to one. The committee ruled that the Occaneechis, who had a tribal roll of more than four hundred, met only three of the eight requirements—they had a traditional North Carolina name, historical and anthropological accounts that described them as Indians, and official records that documented their identity. But, according to the committee, the Occaneechis failed to meet the other five, and most important, they could not establish a two-hundred-year link to a particular indigenous North Carolina tribe, a requirement that must be met in order to earn recognition. The Occaneechis appealed the committee's decision, but the full NCCIA voted in 1997 to uphold the initial finding.[56]

Believing that they had a strong case, the Occaneechis claimed that they were being treated unfairly by the NCCIA. OBSN leaders argued that the current commissioners did not want to recognize new groups because it would diminish their political power and financial resources. Moreover, they contended that the NCCIA had not interpreted the standards fairly, especially when compared to the Meherrins, who had been acknowledged a decade earlier. Recognizing the Meherrins and not the Occaneechis was, according to one tribal representative, "a clear indication these people [committee members] keep moving the scale. The treatment the Meherrin received was totally different."[57] He had a point. Based on the NCCIA's criteria, the Occaneechi case was not overwhelming, but neither was the Meherrins'; and neither group made a definitive genealogical connection to a colonial-era tribe.[58]

The members of the Recognition Committee saw the situation very differently. NCCIA representatives argued that disunity and factionalism prevented the Occaneechis from earning recognition. In the late 1980s a split developed within the Occaneechi community, as another group planned to apply separately for acknowledgment. The Occaneechis would be better served, NCCIA officials asserted, if they would learn to work together. Otherwise, the commission was unable to know which group really represented the people. Other critics simply doubted the tribal identity of the Occaneechis. "Their Indianness is obvious, we don't doubt that," admitted one member of the Recognition Committee. "But in my estimation, the Occaneechi-Saponi could be called an organization with a non-profit status, not a tribe."[59] The executive director of the United South and Eastern Tribes put it more bluntly. "You don't make Indians . . . and you don't make tribes," he said in 1998 directly referring to the OBSN. "Recognition is the legitimacy of something that has always been there. If you let everybody in, that would devalue everybody who has truly been part of a tribe."[60]

Undeterred, the Occaneechis filed a lawsuit in the North Carolina court system claiming that they had been treated unfairly by the NCCIA. In 1998 the administrative law judge Dolores Smith ruled in their favor, arguing that the group had met the minimum requirements and should be recognized. The NCCIA appealed the decision, and in 1999 the Orange County Superior Court judge Henry V. Burnette overturned Smith's verdict. The OBSN then appealed that ruling, sending the case to the North Carolina Court of Appeals, which ruled in favor of the Occaneechis. The NCCIA filed another appeal, but the court rejected it in November 2001, apparently ending the case. The Occaneechis would become the eighth tribe recognized by North Carolina.[61]

The Occaneechis' victory may, ironically, weaken the ability of Native Americans to define their own identity, at least within North Carolina. After 1971 the NCCIA, which was largely controlled by Native Americans, officially defined tribal identity in the state. But if other groups applied for recognition and failed, they too might choose to take their case to the courts, where non-Indian judges would ultimately determine Indianness, a practice that would decrease the power of the NCCIA. The Occaneechis, of course, maintain that the NCCIA's unfair treatment of the tribe left them no other recourse. In fact, one Indian activist contended that the commissioners lacked the qualifications to handle recognition. "One of the problems with the process is that those folks on the commission may have been well-intentioned, but they're not trained to evaluate that sort of history," he told a reporter in 2001. "Just because you're Indian doesn't mean you know the history of Indians. It's not easy to read a genealogy chart unless you have dealt with a lot of them."[62]

Despite the significance of state recognition, the true brass ring of Indian identity was full federal acknowledgment, which meant a separate relationship with the U.S. government and access to funds and programs. In some cases, such as with the Eastern Band of Cherokees, federal recognition also allowed for the establishment of legalized gambling. But most important, acknowledgment equaled official government validation. Several North Carolina tribes, including the Lumbees, Haliwa-Saponis, Meherrins, Waccamaw-Sioux, Person County Indians, Coharies, Occaneechis, and Tuscaroras, petitioned for federal recognition in the postwar era. Thus far, with the important exception of the 1956 Lumbee Act, which recognized the Lumbees as Indians but denied them federal services, all have failed.

Prior to the establishment of the FAP guidelines, a small group of Tuscaroras managed to earn limited federal recognition through the U.S. court system. In 1973 the Eastern Carolina Tuscarora Indian Organization (ECTIO) filed a lawsuit against the Department of the Interior to gain rights for the descendants of those individuals who were determined to be at least one-half "Indian blood" by the physical anthropologist Dr. Carl C. Seltzer in the 1930s. The suit was filed by the ECTIO on behalf of Lawrence Maynor, who was actually one of the original twenty-two certified by Seltzer. Through the lawsuit, the Tuscaroras were trying to gain access to federal money for education, health care, and housing. Officials from the Department of the Interior contended that the 1956 Lumbee Act had terminated the rights of those recognized by Seltzer. The Tuscaroras responded that the original twenty-two were recognized as individual Indians, not members of any tribe, through the Indian Reorganization Act of 1934. Moreover, the tribal name Lumbee did not even exist in the 1930s. In 1975 the U.S. Court of Appeals ruled that Maynor and other surviving members of the original twenty-two were eligible for benefits, but excluded their family members and future heirs. Despite this limited acknowledgment, the Department of the Interior continued to withhold aid to the Tuscaroras, including Maynor.[63]

A few years later the Tuscaroras were among the first to petition for federal acknowledgment under the new 1979 guidelines. With the help of Lumbee River Legal Services and the anthropologist Wesly White, the Tuscaroras submitted their application in 1984. Arguing that the group appeared to be a collection of individual Indians but not a formal tribe, the BIA rejected their petition. According to the BIA, the federal government recognized tribes, not individuals. Moreover, historical injustices had been committed against tribes, not individuals. Therefore, only tribal groups, not individual Indians, were eligible for federal acknowledgment. The defeat divided the Tuscaroras, who, over the next few years, split into competing groups, which further impeded their pursuit of certification. To overcome this divisiveness, three competing subgroups of Tuscaroras created a coalition in 1989 called the Tuscarora Tribe of North Carolina and filed another petition for federal recognition. Again, the BIA rejected them. Again, the Tuscaroras became divided. In the late 1990s four different Tuscarora groups sought federal recognition: The Tuscarora Nation East of the Mountains, The Tuscarora Tribe of North Carolina, The Tuscarora Nation of the Kau-ta-noh, and The Tuscarora Nation. Elijah Locklear, vice chief of the Tuscarora Tribe of North Carolina, admitted that internal bickering hindered their efforts to earn recognition. "There is jealousy, and that's what has kept us apart," he told a Durham reporter in 2000.[64]

The Lumbees' pursuit of federal recognition attracted the most attention, both from the popular media and scholars. Over the past century Robeson County Native Americans have sought acknowledgment several different times under several different names. In the 1980s the Lumbees made their most concerted, time-consuming, and expensive effort to earn federal recognition. In a 1984 referendum, the Lumbee people authorized the Lumbee Regional Development Association to act as the governing body of the Indian community. The LRDA subsequently established an enrollment office and membership criteria, sponsored homecoming activities and other cultural events, ran the tribal day cares, and negotiated economic contracts. In conjunction with Lumbee River

Legal Services (LRLS), the LRDA also worked on an application for federal certification. The two groups spent seven years and $1.5 million compiling a massive two-volume petition that included thousands of supporting documents and a tribal roll of more than thirty-six thousand names. The LRDA and LRLS also enlisted the aid of ten anthropologists, six historians, and several genealogists. The petition closely followed the organization outlined by the 1979 guidelines and devoted a complete section to each of the seven criteria. The petition made a strong case but suffered from two glaring weaknesses. First, the LRDA failed to prove that it, or any other group, historically governed the community, a requirement for federal recognition. Second, and perhaps most significant, the aforementioned 1956 Lumbee Act recognized the community as Indians but prevented them from being eligible for federal programs designated for acknowledged tribes. Specifically citing the 1956 act as precedent, the BIA concluded that the Lumbees were ineligible to continue through the FAP process.[65]

Broken but not defeated, the Lumbees regrouped and developed a new strategy. Rather than working through the BIA, tribal leaders tried to earn recognition directly from Congress. Lumbee leaders convinced the local representative Charlie Rose and the North Carolina senator Terry Sanford to introduce a recognition bill in the House and Senate, respectively. Several other North Carolina representatives cosponsored the bill in the House, but the other senator from the state, Jesse Helms, conspicuously left his name off of the Senate bill. If passed, the new legislation would amend the language of the 1956 act by making the Lumbees eligible for benefits provided to federally recognized Indians.[66]

In August 1991 the House Committee on Interior and Insular Affairs and the Senate Select Committee on Indian Affairs met in a joint session to hear arguments on the Lumbee Recognition Act. At the hearing several Lumbees testified in favor of the bill, as did the anthropologist Jack Campisi, the primary author of the Lumbee petition that had failed in 1989. The governor of North Carolina, Jim Martin, sent a representative to express his support of the bill. Campisi and other witnesses argued that the Lumbees needed legislative recognition because the 1956 act placed the tribe in a unique "catch-22." In 1989 the associate solicitor of Indian Affairs for the Department of the Interior had ruled that the 1956 act precluded the Lumbees from proceeding through the BIA administrative process. Yet critics, both Indian and non, contended that tribes could be certified only through the acknowledgment process, which was established more than twenty years after 1956. The Lumbees were bureaucratically trapped with nowhere to go. Therefore, the Lumbees should be allowed to bypass the FAP process and appeal directly to Congress. Campisi also pointed out that the Lumbees had petitioned for recognition ten times between the 1880s and the

1950s, and not once had Congress denied their Indianness. Yet they remained unrecognized because of administrative details and political motivations. "I am convinced that there is a bias against the Lumbees and that every document presented by the tribe in support of its request is treated with suspicion," he told the committee at the hearing.[67] A few federally recognized tribes, including the Mashantucket Pequots of Connecticut and the Menominees of Wisconsin, also declared their support for the Lumbees.[68]

The BIA, the Department of the Interior, and other federal tribes, however, opposed the Lumbee Act. Representatives from the Interior Department cited two arguments when testifying against the legislation. First, they maintained that the Lumbees should have to go through the BIA's certification process; recognizing the Lumbees legislatively could open the door to other, less-qualified tribes. Of course, the BIA had already determined that the Lumbees were not eligible because of the 1956 bill. Second, Lumbee acknowledgment would cost the federal government one hundred million dollars per year. Several federal tribes, including the Eastern Band of Cherokees and the Sault Ste. Marie Chippewas, also voiced their opposition to the bill, echoing the arguments of the Interior officials. The House passed the bill by a vote of 263 to 154, but Jesse Helms filibustered the Lumbee bill in the Senate, where it died in 1994.[69]

In recent years several authors have analyzed why the Lumbees' quest for recognition has thus far failed. In a 1995 article, Anne Merline McCulloch and David E. Wilkins pointed to several factors. First, the authors argued that the Lumbees lacked the stereotypical social cohesion that all Indian tribes supposedly shared. All Indian societies, indeed all societies, exhibit some evidence of internal division. Yet, according to stereotypes, Native American tribes are completely unified. The Lumbees, of course, were not, as illustrated by the formation of several splinter groups in Robeson County. Nor for that matter were other communities, both Indian and non. Rightly or wrongly, critics pointed to this internal division among the Lumbees as evidence that they lacked unity and therefore were not really a tribe. Second, as numerous critics pointed out, federal services for the tribe could cost tens of millions of dollars a year. Such a dilution of funds would seriously affect the benefits received by other tribes. Moreover, BIA funding shrank in the 1980s when the Reagan administration reduced the agency's budget from $3.5 billion to $1 billion. In addition, if recognized, the forty thousand Lumbees would immediately become one of the most powerful Indian groups in the country. Consequently, the BIA and other federal tribes fought Lumbee acknowledgment. And finally, the authors contended that the general public failed to support the Lumbees primarily because of the perception that they were doing well economically, especially when compared to other tribes.[70]

Some critics, including other Indians, also argued that the Lumbees, who might well be of Native descent, were not a formal tribe because they lacked a distinctive history and tribal government. The Lumbees could easily disprove the first complaint—they obviously had a history. The second charge, however, was more problematic. Historically, the Lumbees did not have what many outsiders would consider a formal tribal government, at least according to the typical definition, which usually meant a "chief" and a "council." But they did have community governmental traditions. Dating well back into the 1800s, certain families, and prominent individuals from those families, played major roles within local Native American communities. Furthermore, for most of the twentieth century, the Lumbee political system was centered in community churches and schools. Unfortunately, though, these political structures did not conform to white stereotypes of tribal institutions.

In response to this criticism, the Lumbees redesigned their formal political structure. In the 1990s a group established the Lumbee Tribe of Cheraw Indians (LTCI). Calling for the adoption of an official constitution and the election of a tribal council, the LTCI charged that the LRDA acted without the popular consent of the Indian community and sued in state court for the right to control the tribe. One LTCI representative contended that "the [LRDA] was a bunch of self-appointed people who were recognized by the [state] government, but they were never directly elected."[71] Responding to the criticism, the LRDA refused to recognize the LTCI, claiming sole authority over Lumbee political and economic affairs and downplaying the internal division. "It's not unusual to have these kinds of debates in Indian communities," the executive director of the LRDA told a Durham journalist in 1994. "Outsiders look at it as Lumbees not being united. The white race is not united. The Indian people have a right to debate their differences."[72] Nevertheless, the friction between the LRDA and the LTCI intensified while the case snaked its way through the North Carolina court system.[73]

In the late 1990s the State Superior Court judge Howard Manning heard the arguments between the two groups competing for official control of the Lumbees. Manning ruled in January 1999 that neither group legally governed the tribe and established a thirty-nine member commission, dubbed the Lumbee Self-Determination Commission, to end the debate and form a new elected body. As part of Manning's decision, the Lumbees held an election in November 2000 to establish a twenty-three-member tribal council. The newly elected representatives took office in December and wrote a governing document that called for the creation of executive, legislative, and judicial branches; the first two would be determined by popular election, while the latter would be appointed by the tribal chairperson. In November 2001, tribal members approved the constitution in a referendum by a vote of 2,237 to 412. The Preamble of the Lumbee Constitution explicitly stated the goals of the new government: "In accordance with the inherent powers of self-governance of the Lumbee Tribe of North Carolina, the Tribe adopts this Constitution for the purposes of establishing a tribal government structure, preserving for all time the Lumbee way of life and community, promoting the educational, cultural, and economic well-being of Lumbee people, and securing justice and freedom for the Lumbee people."[74]

The election and the adoption of a new tribal constitution initially appeared to solve the question of internal legal authority, but the debate over the outcome continued. Critics contended that many of the new officials lacked the experience to run tribal political and economic affairs, especially the complicated issue of fund dispersal. Others, however, argued that the new system was much more fair and democratic. According to the Lumbee Jerry McNeill, who actually lost the 2000 race for tribal chairman, "This new government will be much more of a voice of the people."[75]

The Politics of Blood

The debate over federal recognition inevitably led to arguments over "blood quantum," or the degree of Indian ancestry expressed as a fraction of one's biological heritage. This debate over quantum was somewhat ironic given the postwar repudiation of Social Darwinism. Moreover, it was historically anachronistic—Europeans, not Indians, introduced the concepts of blood and biology as key components of cultural identity. Traditionally, Native Americans based identity not on race, but rather on community and kinship, which was not solely defined by biology. Therefore, one could in theory be of European or African descent and still be Indian. In the twentieth century, though, many Native Americans accepted the use of biology in order to limit the size of their tribes and keep out "weekend Indians" and those looking for special benefits. Some Native Americans also adopted quantum as a measurement of cultural authenticity—those with higher percentages were deemed to be somehow "more Indian."[76]

In a 2001 article, Karen Blu argued that racialist theories regarding Indianness assumed added significance in the late 1990s. As more Indian communities pursued federal certification, biological definitions of race and culture reemerged under the guise of gene theory, which sounded more scientific and less racist than blood. But in many ways, gene theory hearkened back to the late-nineteenth and early-twentieth-century ideology of Social Darwinism, which argued that people carried certain traits that determined their personality and other characteristics. This debate over the meaning of Indian identity was as much economic as it was social and cultural. Because of the shrinking pool of resources, federally recognized tribes often demanded strict definitions of Indian identity based on race—the more tribes that earned recognition, and the more enrolled members of those tribes, the fewer the rewards and benefits for those already certified.[77]

The use of biology in defining Indian and tribal identity was, and continues to be, controversial. Many North Carolina Indians fully supported employing racial definitions of tribal membership. To them, Indianness was primarily biological, and strict guidelines kept out "poseurs" and "wannabes." To others, though, biological definitions were problematic at best and racist at worst. One North Carolina Indian expressed it this way: "When people ask how much Indian blood I have, I ask them, 'What degree of Caucasian blood are you?' That usually stops them."[78] Perhaps, but the debate surrounding the use of quantum to define identity was much more complex. Physical appearance, or looking Indian, and biology partially defined status and authenticity within many Native American communities.[79]

Comparatively, American Indians in eastern North Carolina have relied less on blood quantum than have other Indians in defining identity. Most tribes required potential members only to trace their ancestry back to certain families; the actual percentage of "blood" was less important. The decision to rely on kinship over quantum was partially driven by reality—very few Native Americans in eastern North Carolina were "full-bloods." But this practice also seemed more consistent with traditional Native American definitions of community, which were based on kinship ties, not race. At the same time, the open membership criteria invited criticism from both the federal government and other acknowledged tribes, who often argued that many North Carolina Indians lacked sufficient quantum to be federally recognized.[80]

Conclusion

The 1960s and 1970s were a time of tremendous change for Native Americans in eastern North Carolina. Wage-labor factory jobs replaced farming as the economic lifeblood of the region. The government had either closed or integrated Native American schools, and complete desegregation of all public facilities soon followed. Political changes, particularly the Voting Rights Act, allowed Indians to participate in the electoral process, igniting Indian activism across the country. North Carolina was no different. In the late 1960s and 1970s, Native Americans in the state stood up for their rights as both Natives and Americans.

In the wake of these changes, the 1980s and 1990s were a period of acclimation for North Carolina Indians, a time to adjust to the developments of the previous two decades. The transition was often difficult. School integration, for example, presented a large obstacle for many. One year a ten-year-old Indian boy or girl was in a small classroom with teachers and students that he or she knew. The next year, that same student was bused to a much larger school where he or she was surrounded by strangers. Native Americans also had to learn how to participate in the political system. Having been excluded since the nineteenth century, many were ignorant of the intricacies of American democracy. At the same time, Indians had to adjust to the economic changes. No longer would they arise and go to work in the nearby fields with family members and then return home in the evenings, rarely interacting with outsiders. Now they woke up and commuted to factories where they worked for eight to ten hours a day beside strangers.

Native Americans in eastern North Carolina responded to these changes in numerous ways. They formed pan-Indian or supratribal groups to facilitate the transition. Business groups helped Indians move into the new industrial economy, while political groups formed to give Indians a united voice in government. Now that Indians could vote, white politicians had to pay attention to their complaints (or at least pretend to) or risk losing a close election. Through these organizations, Native Americans were learning how to survive in their new environment. More than anything, they wanted autonomy and self-sufficiency, the ability to take care of themselves, a goal that had eluded them since the 1800s.

But perhaps the biggest development of the 1980s and 1990s was the aggressive pursuit of official government acknowledgment. Some Indian communities in the state applied for state recognition through the NCCIA, while others chased the big prize, full federal recognition. Despite all of the successes of the 1970s, North Carolina Indians remained, at least according to the U.S. government, uncertified. When the BIA established the FAP process in the late 1970s, North Carolina Indians immediately started the application process. Recognition partly meant access to federal funds, but it was mostly about cultural pride. To many Indians in the state, federal certification was like a government stamp of approval, unequivocal proof of their identity. Their pursuit of acknowledgment quickly ran into stiff resistance, from the BIA, from politicians, and from other Indians. Driven by the postwar economic, social, and political changes, a new definition of Indian identity was taking shape, and official government acknowledgment was a major component of that new definition.

Conclusion
Keeping the Circle Strong

Keeping the circle represents generation after generation. . . . Keeping tradition alive, visiting with each other is all a part of the circle. – Senora Lynch (Haliwa-Saponi), 1998

In 2004, more than four hundred years after the "Lost Colonists" landed at Roanoke Island, one hundred thousand people in North Carolina identified as Native Americans. Although dispersed all over the state, the Indian population remained concentrated in several areas. In the mountains more than ten thousand resided on the Cherokee reservation. In the southeastern part of the state, about sixty-three thousand lived in Bladen, Columbus, Cumberland, Hoke, Robeson, Sampson, and Scotland counties. Another seven thousand lived in the upper central counties of Alamance, Guilford, Halifax, Hertford, Orange, Person, and Warren. In addition, several thousand now resided in urban areas. The majority of these Native Americans were affiliated with one of the state's recognized tribes. There were about thirteen thousand Cherokees, twelve hundred Coharies, thirty-five hundred Haliwas, fifty thousand Lumbees, six hundred Meherrins, one thousand Occaneechis, four hundred Person County Indians, and three thousand Waccamaws. A few smaller groups, such as the Hattadares and the Cherokee Indians of Hoke County, were seeking state recognition, as were a few thousand Tuscaroras in Robeson County. In addition, several thousand other Indians in North Carolina were either affiliated with tribes from outside the state or were not members of any group.[1]

A New Millennium

Despite the progress of the 1980s and 1990s, contemporary North Carolina Native Americans still faced economic problems. At the turn of the twenty-first century, the median income for Indians was nine thousand dollars less than that of whites in the state. About one-fifth of Native American families lived below the poverty line, compared to less than 9 percent of whites, and their unemployment rate was almost double the state average. There was some good news, however; the gap between Indians and others in the state was slowly shrinking. In the 1990s most Indians were still blue-collar workers—almost 40 percent were employed in the construction industry alone—but more than 15 percent worked in professional jobs, and that number was increasing yearly. In 2003 the North Carolina Indian Economic Development Initiative and the University of North Carolina Kenan-Flager Business School collaborated to study ways to promote economic growth for Native Americans in the state. After decades of poverty and deprivation, Native Americans appeared to be turning a corner.[2]

By the early 2000s the North Carolina Commission of Indian Affairs was firmly entrenched as a significant part of the state government. Operating with an annual budget of about five million dollars, the NCCIA consisted of representatives from the eight state-recognized tribes and four urban associations. Five non-Indian state officials, an appointee from both the lieutenant governor and the speaker of the house, and ex officio representatives from the North Carolina Native American Youth Organization and the North Carolina Native American Council on Higher Education also sat on the commission. The Eastern Band of Cherokees officially joined the NCCIA in the 1970s, but, more concerned with federal policies, they were never very active, occasionally leaving their seat vacant. Each tribe and urban group elected its own representative and set the term of office, usually between one and three years. Along with its primary economic objectives, the NCCIA actively entered the political field, issuing a statement in 2001 calling for a temporary moratorium on state executions because a disproportionate percentage of individuals on death row were Native Americans. That same year the NCCIA also pushed legislation giving state-recognized tribes more social and political sovereignty. One bill, for example, legally honored any marriage sanctioned by a state tribe.[3] According to Greg Richardson, the current executive director, the NCCIA adopted two new areas of emphasis in the early twenty-first century. First, the commission wanted to develop and train future tribal and community leaders. The individuals who directed the organizational movement of the 1960s and 1970s were rapidly aging, and Richardson was concerned about the future. The generation of tribal founders—people like Chief Richardson (Haliwa) and Chief Freeman (Waccamaw)—was no longer able to govern, and Indian communities needed new leaders. In July 2003 Lonnie Revels passed away. Born in Robeson County in the 1930s, Revels moved to Greensboro in the 1960s, where he and his wife, Ruth, helped establish the Guilford Native American Association. Revels, who had a political science degree from Wake Forest University, also was instrumental in forming the NCCIA and served for two terms on the Greensboro City Council in the 1980s. The NCCIA looked for fresh faces to replace Revels, Freeman, Richardson, and others who had worked so hard during the 1960s and 1970s to effect change. After all, the opportunities that many Indians had in the 1990s—opportunities that their grandparents never had—were a direct result of these men and women.[4]

The NCCIA also targeted Native American health-care issues, a longtime problem in many communities. Indians experienced more health problems than other groups, a fact partially attributable to poverty and lack of access to affordable health care. In the late 1990s the life expectancy for Indians was 71.1 years, compared to 76.3 for whites and 75.5 for all races in the state. Native Americans suffered from high rates of asthma, diabetes, heart disease, stroke, and substance abuse. In May 2001 the NCCIA sponsored the first North Carolina American Indian Health Summit, subtitled "Keeping the Circle Healthy." The two-day event included seminars and guest lecturers who spoke on various health issues, from infant care, to proper nutrition, to the prevention of heart disease. The health-care conference subsequently became an annual event.[5]

Despite the loss of Indian-only schools, educational issues remained important to North Carolina Native Americans. The Haliwa-Saponis recently established their own charter school in Halifax County, thus regaining some control over their children's education. As economic and technological changes placed a new premium on college degrees, more Indians enrolled in universities. Many still entered UNC–Pembroke, but some went elsewhere, where they often experienced culture shock and struggled to overcome long-standing stereotypes. "I came here from a three stoplight town," one Robeson County native and University of North Carolina–Chapel Hill student told a reporter. "So coming to this school I felt lonely in that I was different. I was asked if I lived in a teepee—did I have running water."[6] In 2001 there were only about two hundred Indian students at Chapel Hill out of a total enrollment of twenty-five thousand. At UNC–Chapel Hill and other large colleges in the state, American Indians formed support groups to help ease their adjustments, such as the Carolina Indian Circle and Alpha Pi Omega, an all-Indian sorority. "Coming to Carolina was a culture shock," according to one UNC undergrad from the small town of Hollister. "White and Black are the majority on campus. At home, it's not an issue being Native American."[7]

Despite the failures of the 1990s, North Carolina Indians continued to pursue federal recognition. In 2002 Elizabeth Dole opted to run for the Senate seat left vacant by the retirement of fellow Republican Jesse Helms. Dole actively campaigned in Robeson County and, unlike Helms, promised to support Lumbee recognition. Dole won the election and kept her promise in February 2003 by initiating a bill in the Senate to grant the Lumbees full acknowledgment. The Democrat John Edwards, the other North Carolina senator, also supported the legislation. In the House, Mike McIntyre, a Democrat representing southeastern North Carolina, authored a similar bill.

Opponents of Lumbee recognition quickly rallied to attack the proposed legislation. Congressman Charles Taylor, who represented the Cherokees' district in western North Carolina, introduced a competing bill that would require the Lumbees to go through the FAP process. Taylor's legislation also set a time limit, after which the Lumbees would be ineligible for certification. Critics attacked the pro-Lumbee bill using an old argument and a new one. First, they claimed that recognizing more than forty thousand new Indians would cost the government seventy to eighty million dollars each year. Second, opponents contended that if recognized, the Lumbees would push for legalized gaming in eastern North Carolina. In the 1990s the Eastern Band of Cherokees had used their status as a federal tribe to establish gambling on their reservation. Harrah's Casino, which opened in Cherokee in 1997, was a source of controversy in the state. The prospect of a Las Vegas–type casino in eastern North Carolina, traditionally a socially and culturally conservative region, scared many Tar Heels, which was the strategy of Lumbee opponents. Representative Walter Jones Jr., one of the North Carolina delegates who opposed recognition, predicted that "ten years down the road, if there is an attempt to get approval for a casino, it would create a problem that would be almost uncontrollable."[8] William Brooks, president of the North Carolina Family Policy Council, attacked the bill by focusing on the possible side effects of gambling. "As a major part of the economy of the coastal region depends on tourism and retirement, the negative economic impact on the region from gambling would be significant," he contended in April 2004.[9] Moreover, according to Brooks, "Easy access to gambling means that a significant number of citizens would develop a pathological gambling-habit problem."[10]

Supporters of the Lumbees responded to these charges with their own three-prong attack. First, they contended that recognition was about cultural identity and pride, not gambling and money. The financial benefits were significant, but not the primary motivation for pursuing acknowledgment. "I could care less about the money," one Lumbee told a Raleigh reporter in 2003. "I want the recognition as a Native American because of our background and our ancestry."[11] Second, proponents argued that Lumbee certification would be good for the entire region, not just Native Americans. It would spur economic growth in eastern North Carolina, which was struggling in the late 1990s and early 2000s because of the loss of manufacturing jobs to factories overseas. "If this goes through, you'll be able to draw a circle from downtown Pembroke to 50 or 60 miles out, in which the whole landscape will change," claimed the executive director of the NCCIA. "You're talking about jobs, new industry, improved health care and education in a place that desperately needs them. This would help everybody."[12] And finally, supporters refuted the accusation that recognition would lead to casino gambling. "Our folks [Lumbee Indians] live in a very conservative part of North Carolina," the tribal lawyer Arlinda Locklear responded in April 2004. "The tribe has expressed no interest in a casino at all."[13]

For perhaps the first time, the movement to recognize the Lumbees appeared to be gaining widespread support. More than one-half of the representatives in the House cosponsored McIntyre's bill, virtually guaranteeing it would pass if it could get out of committee. Both North Carolina senators supported it, again for the first time. Dole authored an enthusiastic endorsement of Lumbee certification that appeared in the *Raleigh News and Observer* in September 2003. "Now, more than ever," she wrote, "it's time for the federal government to do what's fair and give recognition to the Lumbees."[14] Members of the relevant committees also appeared to be leaning toward supporting the bill. Nick Rahall, ranking member of the House Resources Committee, charged that the Lumbees have been "trapped inside a cruel carnival that never ends . . . the treatment of the Lumbee tribe is starting to make me sick."[15] Eni Faleomavaega, a delegate from American Samoa, noted the bureaucratic problems that the Lumbee faced. "The [FAP] process, in layman's terms, sucks," she succinctly and eloquently stated in April 2004. "It is impractical and does not work."[16]

The North Carolina media also started to back the Lumbees. In 2003 and 2004 several major newspapers, including the *News and Observer* and the *Greensboro News and Record*, published editorials supporting Lumbee acknowledgment. Consequently, optimism spread quickly across Robeson County. In September 2003 a busload of Lumbees went to Washington to lobby before a House committee. "We are so excited . . . that we might finally be seeing the fruits of the hard work that has gone on for 115 years," one woman told a reporter. "We can't help but believe our time is now."[17] For the Lumbees, the significance of federal recognition cannot be overstated. "Recognition will make us free," claimed the Reverend Weldon Lowry. "We'll be just like other Indians."[18]

Other Native Americans in the state also wanted to be "just like other Indians." Because of the potential economic and social benefits, almost every Native American group, even those without state acknowledgment, pursued federal certification in the early 2000s. Recognition partly meant access to funds and participation in special Indian programs, but, according to many, it was mostly about pride, respect, and community solidarity. "The economic benefits of federal recognition cannot be ignored, but perhaps most important are the issues of human dignity and human rights," according to Bruce Jones, former executive director of the NCCIA. "North Carolina's non-reservation Indian people have a right to have their heritage recognized by the federal government."[19]

At the same time, many North Carolina Indians appreciated the problem of placing so much importance on recognition. In effect, government certification meant relying on others for acknowledgment of one's identity, a very disempowering position. Moreover, the process pitted tribe versus tribe in a contest over "Indianness," and the arguments over recognition could be heated. One reaction to state certification of the Occaneechis was illustrative, if extreme. Shortly after the tribe earned acknowledgment, an Occaneechi leader received a threatening letter in the mail. "You like to play American Indian, and that's fine," the letter read. "But here in Hollister, NC, we will not Tolerate it. Keep your Turkey feathers, Jerry curls, and your raggedy Drum teams away from our community." Haliwa tribal leaders quickly dismissed the letter as the opinion of a few individuals, not of the tribe. "That letter in no way, shape, form or fashion was generated by our tribal council or any of the leadership," the Haliwa chief responded. "Whoever did it was not a spokesperson for the tribe."[20] Indeed, the majority of Haliwas did not agree with the sentiment of the letter, but it was symbolic of the contentiousness over recognition within the North Carolina Indian community. Recognition inevitably divided Native Americans into the haves and the have-nots. The process has "created deep divisions between the Indian people of this state," the Occaneechi chief Beverly Payne-Betts complained. "These divisions only serve to hurt Indian people further at a time when we should be striving to work together for the benefit of all Indian people in this state."[21]

The fight over federal acknowledgment alienated North Carolina Native Americans from tribes in other states. When traveling in the West, Cynthia Hunt noted the antipathy toward the Lumbees from other Indians. One Shoshone councilman told her that the Lumbees were not real Indians because they did not live on a reservation, a circular argument at best since a tribe needed recognition in order to establish a reservation. Hunt found little sympathy for the struggles of her people. "The Indians out west can't accept us because we ain't got feathers and beads," she remarked in the mid-1990s. "You can't expect anything from non-Indian society, but you'd expect Indians to empathize, to understand what you're going through. But now they've got a chance to go down on somebody else. I know that I am an Indian, and I want them to acknowledge that I am an Indian."[22]

Modern Native American identity, rightly or wrongly, was partially defined by government acknowledgment. Some Indian tribes and individuals have internalized the process, basing their own definition of Indianness on government authentication. Recognition of tribes was in turn based on reparations, or the belief that the U.S. government owed Native Americans for broken treaties and other past injustices. This presented a problem: could individual Native Americans or unrecognized tribes be "real" Indians? In theory, of course, the answer was yes. Personal identity and tribal eligibility for special benefits were separate issues. Whether the definition was based on biology or culture, one could be an Indian but not a member of an acknowledged tribe. The reality was more complex. In modern America, Indian identity and acknowledgment were interconnected. To most Americans, to be an Indian was to be an enrolled member of a federally recognized tribe. The identity of noncertified Native Americans was therefore constantly questioned, no matter how valid their claim.

The Federal Acknowledgment Process did not recognize this problem; nor was it designed to do so. The BIA established the FAP to recognize Native American tribes that had a historical relationship with the U.S. government. The process was not designed to define identity or certify all Native Americans. But in the 1980s federal acknowledgment became something more. Ultimately, recognition was about defining Indianness: Who were Indians? What did it mean to be Indian? What were tribes? And who decided? These were difficult questions, and the answers had serious ramifications. The BIA and state governments attempted to address these questions through a bureaucratic system of guidelines, which, fairly or not, defined contemporary Indianness. In the late twentieth century, North Carolina Native Americans, like other Indians in the nation, confronted this reality as they always had, by fighting to maintain their identity.

Conclusion

From the late nineteenth to the early twenty-first century, the United States changed dramatically. North Carolina was no exception. Primarily rural and agrarian in the late 1800s, by 2004 North Carolina had become an urban commercial and industrial state. The technological changes alone—automobiles, telephones, airplanes, and computers—transformed the daily lives of every citizen. These material changes were accompanied by changes in racial ideology. Social Darwinism was dead, or at least dormant, replaced by cultural pluralism and a growing belief in racial equality. These changes forced Native Americans in eastern North Carolina to alter their definition of Indianness. In short, Indian identity—or what it meant to be a Native American—changed in the twentieth century. In the early 1900s being Indian in eastern North Carolina meant living in a certain community, being related to certain families, belonging to certain churches, and attending certain schools. By 2000 Indian churches still existed and played important social roles but were less important in terms of identity—individuals who did not go to church could still be Indians. In the 1960s federally mandated integration had closed Indian-only schools, erasing the most definitive external marker of Indianness. Home communities were still important, but Native Americans had moved all over the state, especially into urban areas to find jobs. Family history remained a factor in defining identity, but new elements had also been added to the definition. Being Indian in North Carolina in the twenty-first century meant being an enrolled member of a recognized tribe or organization and regularly participating in cultural events and celebrations. North Carolina Native Americans, in other words, had added new "boundaries" to their definition of Indian identity. Not mere happenstance, these changes were a strategic response to postwar society. In 2004 Native Americans not only needed to protect their identity within their own communities, which was their primary objective before World War II, but they also needed to assert and prove it to outsiders.

From the first day Columbus waded ashore in the "New World," Europeans, and later Americans, failed to understand the diversity of Native American cultures. Whites consistently tried to group all indigenous peoples under one umbrella. But there was no such thing as an "Indian," at least culturally, until the twentieth century. In the post–World War II era, however, Native Americans used the stereotype of the "Indian" to create a generalized identity. In many ways, Native Americans became, for the first time, truly part of the United States. They began to see themselves as a single minority group, rather than just a collection of separate communities and tribes. In other words, they wanted political and economic equality, but they also sought to retain their social and cultural distinctiveness.

The emerging pan-Indianism in the postwar era was based on a combination of biological and cultural factors. Some Native Americans accepted the significance of biology in defining Indianness, despite the fact that traditionally race had nothing to do with identity. But modern Indian identity was also determined by other characteristics, such as lifestyle, tribal membership, and cultural awareness. Race alone did not define Indianness, therefore, but neither did community, kinship, or worldview. In the future, the significance of quantum in defining Indian identity will most likely change, as the number of "full-bloods" decreases rapidly. According to one government study, by 2080 less than 10 percent of those claiming to be Indians will be more than "one-half," and 60 percent will be less than "one-quarter." According to the author Fergus Bordewich, a critic of such biological definitions, "It is plain that the principle, or the pretense, that blood should be a central defining fact of being Indian will soon become untenable."[23]

Despite criticisms to the contrary, political and economic assimilation and Native American identity were not inherent contradictions. Ethnic groups can be part of a pluralistic liberal democracy without giving up their cultural identity. Ethnic groups, in other words, do not have to be segregated in order to survive. Boundaries were needed to define these groups, but these boundaries could be symbolic or ideological, rather than simply geographical. Moreover, individuals could flow across the boundaries—which certainly happened among Indians in North Carolina in the 1960s and 1970s—without threatening the identity of the ethnic group. Consequently, despite stereotypes, contrasting and distinctive social, cultural, economic, and political systems are not necessary to define ethnic boundaries. Even further, the preservation of ethnicity in a large multicultural society is not only possible but perhaps even desirable; ethnic groups unite communities, promote stability, and inculcate values.

Modern Native American identity is a dialectical process involving both internal and external factors. This is not unique to Native Americans but applies to the formation of all group identities. In North Carolina these external and internal forces clashed in the second half of the twentieth century to reshape definitions of Indian identity. The world changed for Native Americans in North Carolina following World War II, but they changed with it. They adopted and employed new boundaries to mark their distinctiveness. In doing so, they were remarkably successful—Native American identity appeared safer in 2004 than at any point in the previous two hundred years. North Carolina Indians honored their past by keeping the circle strong, protecting their identity by reshaping it. As one southern Native American author put it, "We have always been here and we are here forever."[24]

Suggestions for Further Reading

The history of Native Americans in North Carolina is both diverse and vast. Unfortunately, the scholarship fails to capture the richness of Indian history in the state. What the literature lacks in quantity, however, is partially compensated by the overall quality. This bibliography has been divided into two parts to help readers who are interested in learning more about North Carolina Indian history. For complete citations and references, readers should consult the endnotes, which are more detailed.

General
Books

Berry, Brewton. *Almost White*. New York: Macmillan, 1963.

Butler, George E. *The Croatan Indians of Sampson County, North Carolina: Their Origin and Racial Status*. Durham: Seeman Printery, 1916.

Center for Urban Affairs. *Paths toward Freedom: A Biographical History of Blacks and Indians in North Carolina by Blacks and Indians*. Raleigh: North Carolina State University, 1976.

Eliades, David K., and Linda Oxendine. *Pembroke State University: A History*. Columbus GA: Brentwood University Press, 1986.

Milling, Chapman J. *Red Carolinians*. Chapel Hill: University of North Carolina Press, 1940.

Moore, MariJo, ed. *Feeding the Ancient Fires: A Collection of Writings by North Carolina American Indians*. Crossroads Press, 1999.

Perdue, Theda. *Native Carolinians: The Indians of North Carolina*. Raleigh: North Carolina Division of Archives and History, 1985.

Presti, Susan M. *Public Policy and Native Americans in North Carolina: Issues for the 1980s*. Raleigh: North Carolina Center for Public Policy Research Book, 1981.

Rights, Douglas L. *The American Indian in North Carolina*. Winston-Salem: John F. Blair, 1957.

Ross, Thomas E. *American Indians in North Carolina: Geographic Interpretations*. Southern Pines NC: Kara Hollow, 1999.

South, Stanley. *Indians in North Carolina*. Raleigh: State Division of Archives and History, 1972.

Wetmer, Ruth Y. *First on the Land: The North Carolina Indians*. Winston-Salem: John F. Blair, 1975.

Articles, Dissertations, and Unpublished Papers

Alexander, Maxine. "We Are Here Forever: Indians of the South." *Southern Exposure* 13 (1984): 12–15.

Conley, Manuel Arthur. "Indians and Academia: How the Post–World War Two Revival of Interest in Native Americans Influenced the Teaching of Indian History in North Carolina Education." PhD diss., Middle Tennessee State University, 1997.

Dane, J. K., and B. Eugene Griessman. "The Collective Identity of Marginal Peoples: The North Carolina Experience." *American Anthropologist* 74 (June 1972): 694–704.

Greenbaum, Susan. "What's in a Label? Identity Problems of Southern Indian Tribes." *Journal of Ethnic Studies* 19 (Summer 1991): 107–26.

Hazel, Forest. "Black, White and 'Other': The Struggle for Recognition." *Southern Exposure* 13 (1984): 34–37.

Massey, Thomas R. T. "School Desegregation: Its Significance for Native Americans of Eastern North Carolina." Master's thesis, University of North Carolina–Wilmington, 1996.

McIrvin, Ronald R. "The Urban Indian: A Profile of the Greensboro Native American Population." In *Urban Growth and Urban Life*, ed. Warren Jake Wicker. Proceedings of the Third Annual Urban Affairs Conference of the University of North Carolina. Chapel Hill: Urban Studies Council, 1981. The North Carolina Collection.

North Carolina Commission on Indian Affairs. "A Historical Perspective about the Indians of North Carolina and an Overview of the Commission of Indian Affairs." *North Carolina Historical Review* 56 (Spring 1979): 183–87.

Oxendine, Clifton. "Pembroke State College for Indians: Historical Sketch." *North Carolina Historical Review* 22 (1945): 22–33.

Parramore, Thomas C. "With Tuscarora Jack on the Back Path to Bath." *North Carolina Historical Review* (April 1987): 115–38.

Pollitzer, William S. "The Physical Anthropology and Genetics of Marginal People of the Southeastern United States." *American Anthropologist* 74 (June 1972): 719–34.

Price, Margo L. "Native North Carolinians: Then and Now." Master's thesis, University of North Carolina–Chapel Hill, 1990.

Thompson, Edgar T. "The Little Races." *American Anthropologist* 74 (October 1972): 1295–306.

Tribe-Specific
Coharies

Berde, Stuart. *Coharie Reemergence: Attaining Religious and Educational Freedom in Eastern North Carolina, 1850-Present*. Lumbee River Legal Services and the Coharie Intra-Tribal Council, 1982. Copy at State Archives in Raleigh.

———. *Nowhere to Hide: A Theoretical and Documentary Quest into Coharie Indian History*. Lumbee River Legal Services and the Coharie Intra-tribal Council, 1984.

Grady, Don Avasco. *The Coharie Indians of Sampson County, North Carolina: A Collection of Their Oral Folk History*. The North Carolina Collection, 1981.

Wilkins, David. *Walking Upright: The Coharie People of Sampson County*. Raleigh: Division of Archives and History, Department of Cultural Resources, 1980.

Haliwa-Saponis

Everette, James A., Jr. "Claude Richardson: Haliwa-Saponi Carver." *North Carolina Folklore Journal* 40 (1993): 91–96.

Lumbees and Tuscaroras
PUBLISHED

Anderson, Ryan. "Lumbee Kinship, Community, and the Success of the Red Banks Mutual Association." *American Indian Quarterly* 23 (1999): 39–58.

Barton, Bruce. *An Indian Manifesto*. Pembroke: Carolina Indian Voice, 1983.

Barton, Garry Lewis. *The Life and Times of Henry Berry Lowry*. Pembroke: Lumbee, 1979.

Barton, Lew. *The Most Ironic Story in American History: An Authoritative, Documented History of the Lumbee Indians of North Carolina*. Charlotte: Associated Printing, 1967.

Berry, Brewton. *Almost White*. New York: Macmillan, 1963.

Blu, Karen I. *The Lumbee Problem: The Making of an American Indian People*. Cambridge: Cambridge University Press, 1980.

———. *The Lumbee Problem: The Making of an American Indian People*. Lincoln: University of Nebraska Press, 2001.

———. "The Uses of History for Ethnic Identity: The Lumbee Case." In *Currents in Anthropology: Essays in Honor of Sol Tax*, ed. Robert Hinshaw, 271–85. The Hague: Mouton, 1979.

———. "'Where Do You Stay At?' Home Place and Community among the

Lumbee." In *Senses of Place*, edited by Steven Field and Keith Basso, 197–227. Santa Fe: School of American Research, 1997.

Brewington, C. D. *The Five Civilized Indian Tribes in Eastern North Carolina*. Clinton NC: Bass, 1953.

Craven, Charles. "The Night the Klan Died in North Carolina." *True* (March 1975): 61–65.

Dial, Adolph L. "From Adversity to Progress." *Southern Exposure* 13 (1984): 85–89.

————. *The Lumbee*. New York: Chelsea House, 1993.

Dial, Adolph L., and David K. Eliades. *The Only Land I Know: A History of the Lumbee Indians*. San Francisco: Indian Historian, 1975.

Evans, W. McKee. "The North Carolina Lumbees: From Assimilation to Revitalization." In *Southeastern Indians since the Removal Era*, edited by Walter L. Williams. Athens: University of Georgia Press, 1979.

————. *To Die Game: The Story of the Lowry Band, Indian Guerillas of Reconstruction*. Baton Rouge: Louisiana State University Press, 1971.

Gaillard, Frye. "Lumbee Indians." *South Today* 3 (September 1971): 4–5.

Humphreys, Josephine. *Nowhere Else on Earth*. New York: Viking, 2000.

"The Indians of Robeson County." *The State* 18 (April 21, 1951): 3, 22.

Knick, Stanley. *The Lumbee in Context: Toward an Understanding*. Pembroke: Native American Resource Center, 2000.

Lowery, Clarence E. *The Lumbee Indians of North Carolina*. Durham: Christian Publishing, 1960.

Lowry, D. F. "No Mystery." *The State* 20 (December 1952): 24.

Makofsky, Abraham. "Struggling to Maintain Identity: Lumbee Indians in Baltimore." *Anthropological Quarterly* 55 (April 1982): 74–83.

Makofsky, Abraham, and David Makofsky. "Class Consciousness and Culture: Class Identification in the Lumbee Indian Community of Baltimore." *Anthropology Quarterly* 46 (1973): 261–77.

Maynor, Malinda. "Indians Got Rhythm: Lumbee and African American Church Song." *North Dakota Quarterly* 67 (2000): 72–91.

McCulloch, Anne Merline, and David E. Wilkins. "'Constructing' Nations within States: The Quest for Federal Recognition by the Catawba and Lumbee Tribes." *American Indian Quarterly* 19 (Summer 1995): 361–88.

Mooney, James. "Croatans." In *Handbook of American Indians North of Mexico*, edited by Frederick Webb Hodge, 365. Washington DC: Government Printing Office, 1970.

Patterson, Oscar, III. "The Press Held Hostage: Terrorism in a Small North Carolina Town." *American Journalism* 15 (1998): 125–39.

Ross, Thomas E. "The Lumbees: Population Growth of a Non-reservation Indian Tribe." In *A Cultural Geography of Native American Indians*, edited by T. E. Ross and T. G. Moore, 297–309. Boulder: Westview Press, 1987.

————. *One Land, Three Peoples: A Geography of Robeson County.* Southern
Pines NC: Kara Hollow Press, 1993.
Shapiro, Joseph P., and Ronald A. Taylor. "There's Trouble in Robeson County."
U.S. News and World Report, May 2, 1988, 24–27.
Sider, Gerald. *Living Indian Histories: Lumbee and Tuscarora People in North
Carolina.* Chapel Hill: University of North Carolina Press, 2003.
————. "Lumbee Indian Cultural Nationalism and Ethnogenesis." *Dialectical
Anthropology* 1 (1976): 161–72.
————. *Lumbee Indian Histories: Race, Ethnicity, and Indian Identity in the
Southern United States.* Cambridge: Cambridge University Press, 1993.
Smith, Joseph Michael. *The Lumbee Methodists: Getting to Know Them, a Folk
History.* Raleigh: Commission of Archives and History and North Carolina
Methodist Conference, 1990.
Starr, Glenn Ellen. *The Lumbee Indians: An Annotated Bibliography.* Jefferson
NC: McFarland, 1994.
Wilkins, David E. "Breaking Into the Intergovernmental Matrix: The Lumbee
Tribe's Efforts to Secure Federal Acknowledgment." *Publius* 23 (Fall 1993):
123–42.
Wolfram, Walt. "From the Brickhouse to the Swamp." *American Language Re-
view* (July–August 2001): 34–38.
Wolfram, Walt, and Clare Dannenberg. "Dialect in a Tri-ethnic Context: The
Case of Lumbee-American Indian English." *English World-Wide: A Journal
of Varieties of English* 20, no. 2 (1999): 179–216.
Wolfram, Walt, Clare Danneberg, Stanley Knick, and Linda Oxendine. *Fine in
the World: Lumbee Language in Time and Place.* Raleigh: North Carolina State
University, 2002.

UNPUBLISHED

Blu, Karen I. "We People: Understanding Lumbee Indian Identity in a Tri-racial
Situation." PhD diss., University of Chicago, 1972.
Knick, Stanley Graham. "Growing Up Down Home: Health and Growth in the
Lumbee Nation." PhD diss., Indiana University, 1986.
Makofsky, Abraham. "Tradition and Change in the Lumbee Indian Community
of Baltimore." PhD diss., Catholic University, 1971.
Maynor, Malinda. "People and Place: Croatan Indians in Jim Crow Georgia,
1890–1920." Paper presented at 2002 Southern Historical Association annual
convention in Baltimore.
Oxendine, Clifton. "A Social and Economic History of the Indians of Robe-
son County, North Carolina." Master's thesis, George Peabody College for
Teachers, 1934.
Peck, John Gregory. "Urban Station—Migration of the Lumbee Indians." PhD
diss., University of North Carolina–Chapel Hill, 1972.
Ransom, Ronald Gene. "The Tie That Binds: The Grandparent/Grandchild

Relationship among the Lumbee Indians of Robeson County." Master's thesis, University of Arizona, 1989.

Sider, Gerald. "The Political History of the Lumbee Indians of Robeson County, North Carolina: A Case Study of Political Affiliations." PhD diss., New School for Social Research, 1971.

Snow, Claude H., Jr. "An Annotated Transcription of Eight Lumbee Sermons in Upper Robeson County, N.C." Master's thesis, University of North Carolina–Chapel Hill, 1977.

Thompson, Vernon Ray. "A History of the Education of the Lumbee Indians of Robeson County from 1885 to 1970." PhD diss., University of Miami, 1974.

Woods, Ruth Dial. "Growing Up Red: The Lumbee Experience." PhD diss., University of North Carolina–Chapel Hill, 2001.

Zak, Susannah. "A Story of Survival: The Lumbee Indians." Master's thesis, University of North Carolina–Chapel Hill, 1992.

Meherrins

Dawdy, Shannon Lee. "The Secret History of the Meherrin." Master's thesis, College of William and Mary, 1994.

Occaneechis

Nowell, Jeremiah James, Jr. "Red, White and Black: Race Formation and the Politics of American Indian Recognition in North Carolina." PhD diss., University of North Carolina–Chapel Hill, 2000.

Smith, Lisa A. "Hillsborough's Representation of History and the Incorporation of the Occaneechi Story." Honors thesis, University of North Carolina–Chapel Hill, 1994.

PERSON COUNTY INDIANS

Lougee, George. "Origin of Person County Indians." In *The Heritage of Person County*. Vol. 1, edited by M. H. Eaker. Winston-Salem: Hunter 1983.

WACCAMAW-SIOUX

Aldred, Jo E. "'No More Cigar Store Indians': Ethnographic and Historical Representations by and of the Waccamaw-Siouan Peoples and Their Socioeconomic, Legal, and Political Consequences." Master's thesis, University of North Carolina–Chapel Hill, 1992.

Hemming, Jill. "The Craft of Identity: Quilting Traditions in the Waccamaw-Siouan Tribe." Master's thesis, University of North Carolina–Chapel Hill, 1995.

———. "Waccamaw-Siouan Quilts: A Model for Studying Native American Quilting." *Uncoverings* 18 (1997): 189–211.

Lerch, Patricia B. "Articulatory Relationships: The Waccamaw Struggle against Assimilation." In *Sea and Land: Cultural and Biological Adaptations in the*

Southern Coastal Plain, Southern Anthropological Society Proceedings No. 21, edited by James A. Peacock and James C. Sabella, 76–91. Athens: University of Georgia Press, 1988.

———. "Celebrations and Dress: Sources of Native American Identity." In *Anthropologists and Indians in the New South,* edited by Rachel A. Bonney and J. Anthony Paredes, 143–55. Tuscaloosa: University of Alabama Press, 2001.

———. "Pageantry, Parade, and Indian Dancing: The Staging of Identity among the Waccamaw-Sioux." Patricia Lerch Papers, the North Carolina Collection. (Originally published in *Museum Anthropology* 16 (June 1992): 27–33.)

———. "Powwows, Parades and Social Drama among the Waccamaw-Sioux." Patricia Lerch Papers, the North Carolina Collection. (Originally published in *Celebrations of Identity: Multiple Voices in American Ritual Performance,* edited by Pamela R. Frese, 75–92. Westport CT: Bergin and Garvey, 1993).

———. "State-Recognized Indians of North Carolina, Including a History of the Waccamaw Sioux." In *Indians of the Southeastern United States in the Late 20th Century,* edited by J. Anthony Paredes, 44–71. Tuscaloosa: University of Alabama Press, 1992.

———. *Waccamaw Legacy: Contemporary Indians Fight for Survival.* Tuscaloosa: The University of Alabama Press, 2004.

Notes

Introduction: Defining Indian Identity

Opening epigraph from Shannon Lee Dawdy, "The Secret History of the Meherrin" (master's thesis: College of William and Mary, 1994), 130.

1. Michael Omi and Howard Winant, *Racial Formation in the United States from the 1960s to the 1980s* (New York: Routledge and Kegan Paul, 1986), 14–15.

2. Ibid., 12–15; Karen I. Blu, "Region and Recognition," in *Anthropologists and Indians in the New South*, ed. Rachel A. Bonney and J. Anthony Paredes (Tuscaloosa: University of Alabama Press, 2001), 71–88; Michael H. Logan and Stephen D. Ousley, "Hypergamy, Quantum, and Reproductive Success: The Lost Ancestor Reconsidered," in *Anthropologists and Indians*, 187; Hazel W. Hertzberg, *The Search for an American Indian Identity: Modern Pan-Indian Movements* (Syracuse University Press, 1971), 52.

3. Frederik Barth, *Ethnic Groups and Boundaries: The Social Organization of Culture Difference* (Boston: Little, Brown, 1969), 2–38. Kallen started developing his theories on ethnicity and democracy as early as 1915. For more on his work, see Milton R. Konvitz, *The Legacy of Horace M. Kallen* (Cranbury NJ: Associated University Presses, 1987); Horace M. Kallen, *Cultural Pluralism and the American Ideal* (University of Pennsylvania Press, 1956); and Horace M. Kallen, *Culture and Democracy in the United States* (1924; repr., New York: Arno, 1970).

4. Omi and Winant, *Racial Formation*, 23.

5. Fergus M. Bordewich, *Killing the White Man's Indian: Reinventing Native Americans at the End of the Twentieth Century* (New York: Doubleday, 1996), 10–11; Stephen Cornell, *The Return of the Native: American Indian Political Resurgence* (New York: Oxford University Press, 1988).

6. Quotation in Bordewich, *White Man's Indian*, 332; Angela A. Gonzales, "Urban (Trans)Formations: Changes in the Meaning and Use of American Indian Identity," in *American Indians and the Urban Experience*, ed. Susan Lobo and Kurt Peters (Walnut Creek CA: Altamira, 2001), 175.

7. Quotation in Julian H. Steward, "The Changing American Indian," in *The Science of Man in the World Crisis*, ed. Ralph Linton (New York: Columbia University Press, 1945); J. Anthony Paredes, ed., *Indians of the Southeastern United States in the Late Twentieth Century* (Tuscaloosa: University of Alabama Press, 1992).

8. Walter L. Williams, ed., *Southeastern Indians since the Removal Era* (Athens: University of Georgia Press, 1979), 207.

9. Blu, "Region and Recognition," 81.

Chapter 1. Acculturated but Not Assimilated

Opening epigraph from *Greensboro Daily News*, January 19, 1971.

1. Quotation from letter from T. J. Moore to W. L. Moore, August 11, 1890, in O. M. McPherson, *Indians of North Carolina*, 63rd Cong., 3rd sess., December 7, 1914, S. Doc. vol. 4 (Washington DC: Government Printing Office, 1915), 40 (hereafter cited as McPherson report); Memo titled "Indians of Robeson County," May 1, 1936, in John Pearmain, "Report on Condition" (hereafter cited as Pearmain report).

2. Thomas E. Ross, *American Indians in North Carolina: Geographic Interpretations* (Southern Pines NC: Kara Hollow, 1999), 3–35, 164–200; North Carolina Commission of Indian Affairs, "A Historical Perspective about the Indians of North Carolina and an Overview of the Commission of Indian Affairs," *North Carolina Historical Review* 56 (Spring 1979): 177. For more on Indians in the prehistoric Southeast, see Marvin T. Smith, *Archaeology of Aboriginal Culture Change in the Interior Southeast* (Gainesville: University of Florida Press, 1987); and Chester B. DePratter, *Late Prehistoric and Early Historic Chiefdoms in the Southeastern United States* (New York: Garland, 1991).

3. Thomas C. Parramore, "The 'Lost Colony' Found: A Documentary Perspective," *The North Carolina Historical Review* 77 (January 2001): 67–83; David Beers Quinn, *The Lost Colonists: Their Fortune and Probable Fate* (Raleigh: Division of Archives and History, 1984).

4. Christopher Arris Oakley, "The Indian Slave Trade in Coastal North Carolina and Virginia" (master's thesis: University of North Carolina–Wilmington, 1996); Thomas C. Parramore, "With Tuscarora Jack on the Back Path to Bath," *North Carolina Historical Review* (April 1987): 115–38.

5. Oakley, "Indian Slave Trade."

6. Ruth Y. Wetmore, *First on the Land: The North Carolina Indians* (Winston-Salem: John F. Blair, 1975): 164, xvi; Stuart Berde, *Coharie Reemergence: Attaining Religious and Educational Freedom in Eastern North Carolina, 1850-Present* (Lumbee River Legal Services and Coharie Intra-tribal Council, 1982), 9; Don Avasco Grady, *The Coharie Indians of Sampson County, North Carolina: A Collection of Their Oral Folk History* (Chapel Hill: The North Carolina Collection, 1981), 69; Lew Barton, *The Most Ironic Story in American History: An Authoritative, Documented History of the Lumbee Indians of North Carolina* (Charlotte: Associated Printing Corporation, 1967), 90; David Wilkins, *Walking Upright: The Coharie People of Sampson County* (Raleigh: Division of Archives and History, Department of Cultural Resources, 1980), 21.

7. W. McKee Evans, *To Die Game: The Story of the Lowry Band, Indian Guerillas of Reconstruction* (Baton Rouge: Louisiana State University Press, 1971), 1–7.

8. Evans, *To Die Game*, 37–45, 72–76, 119–20. "Lowry" also appears in various sources as "Lowery" and "Lowrie."

9. Ibid., 137–38, 178.

10. Ibid., 198–99.

11. Ibid., 220–52.

12. McPherson report, 27; Gerald M. Sider, *Lumbee Indian Histories: Race, Ethnicity, and Indian Identity in the Southern United States* (Cambridge: Cambridge University Press, 1993), 66–68; Jill Hemming, "The Craft of Identity: Quilting Traditions in the Waccamaw-Siouan Tribe" (master's thesis, University of North Carolina–Chapel Hill,

1995), 31; Ross, *American Indians*, 129, 204; Theda Perdue and Michael D. Green, *The Columbia Guide to American Indians of the Southeast* (New York: Columbia University Press, 2001), 134–35; Evans, *To Die Game*, 99–103, 243. For more on Reconstruction in southeastern North Carolina, see W. McKee Evans, *Ballots and Fence Rails: Reconstruction on the Lower Cape Fear* (Chapel Hill: University of North Carolina Press, 1967). For more on race in the state in the late nineteenth century, see Eric Anderson, *Race and Politics in North Carolina: The Black Second, 1872–1901* (Baton Rouge: Louisiana State University Press, 1981).

13. Sider, *Lumbee Indian Histories*, 82.

14. McPherson report, 25; David Beers Quinn, *The Lost Colonists: Their Fortune and Probable Fate* (Raleigh: Division of Archives and History, 1984); Sider, *Lumbee Indian Histories*, 81–83; Karen I. Blu, *The Lumbee Problem: The Making of an American Indian People* (Cambridge: Cambridge University Press, 1980), 62–65.

15. Sider, *Lumbee Indian Histories*, 169.

16. Ibid., 170.

17. Ibid., 83.

18. Memos titled "Indians of Robeson County," May 1, 1936, and "Indians of Robeson County," April 7, 1936, in Pearmain report; McPherson report, 25; Adolph L. Dial and David K. Eliades, *The Only Land I Know: A History of the Lumbee Indians* (San Francisco: Indian Historian, 1975), 90–93; Perdue and Green, *Columbia Guide*, 136; Blu, *Lumbee Problem*, 62–65; Sider, *Lumbee Indian Histories*, 81. For more on Plains Indians wars, see Robert M. Utley, *The Indian Frontier of the American West, 1846–1890* (Albuquerque: University of New Mexico Press, 1984).

19. Statement of Johnnie P. Bullard, U.S. Congress, *Act to Provide for the Recognition*, 145; David K. Eliades, *Pembroke State University: A History* (Columbus GA: Brentwood University Press, 1986), 10–25; Dial and Eliades, *Only Land I Know*, 90–95; McPherson report, 226–27.

20. Berde, *Coharie Reemergence*, 2–8, 13–22; Grady, *Coharie Indians*, 37, 76–78; Wilkins, *Walking Upright*, 28–29.

21. Waccamaw Siouan Tribe, personal correspondence, August 31, 2002; Patricia B. Lerch, "State-Recognized Indians of North Carolina, Including a History of the Waccamaw Sioux," in *Indians of the Southeastern United States in the Late Twentieth Century*, ed. J. Anthony Paredes (Tuscaloosa: University of Alabama Press, 1992), 59–62.

22. *Charlotte Observer*, November 6, 1925; McPherson report, 26; Jeremiah James Nowell Jr., "Red, White and Black: Race Formation and the Politics of American Indian Recognition in North Carolina" (PhD diss., University of North Carolina–Chapel Hill, 2000), 64; Vernon Ray Thompson, "A History of the Education of the Lumbee Indians of Robeson County from 1885 to 1970" (PhD diss., University of Miami, 1974), 52–78; Ruth Dial Woods, "Growing Up Red: The Lumbee Experience" (PhD diss., University of North Carolina–Chapel Hill, 2001), 75–76.

23. McPherson report, 231.

24. *Robesonian*, September 15, 1985; David K. Eliades and Linda Oxendine, *Pembroke State University: A History* (Columbus GA: Brentwood University Press, 1986), 10–25; Dial and Eliades, *Only Land I Know*, 90–95; Thompson, "History of the Education," 42–45; Manuel Arthur Conley, "Indians and Academia: How the Post–World War Two Revival of Interest in Native Americans Influenced the Teaching of Indian History in North Carolina Education" (PhD diss., Middle Tennessee State University, 1997), 163; McPherson report, 226–31; Woods, "Growing Up Red," 80.

25. Native American Rights Fund, *Waccamaw-Siouan Tribe of North Carolina, a Collection of Historical Documents*, the North Carolina Collection, 1978, Resolution 7153,

February 6, 1950; *Robesonian*, April 16, 1914; Berde, *Coharie Reemergence*, 16–48; Sider, *Lumbee Indian Histories*, 73.

26. Native American Rights Fund, *Waccamaw-Siouan Tribe*; *Robesonian*, September 15, 1985; W. McKee Evans, "The North Carolina Lumbees: From Assimilation to Revitalization," in Walter L. Williams, ed., *Southeastern Indians since the Removal Era* (Athens: University of Georgia Press, 1979), 53–57; Wilkins, *Walking Upright*, 24–29.

27. Interview with Shirley Jacobs Freeman by Jill Hemming, September 28, 1996, G-196, Southern Oral History Program Collection no. 4007, Southern Historical Collection; interview with Brenda Jacobs Moore by Jill Hemming, September 26, 1996, G-200, Southern Oral History Program Collection no. 4007, Southern Historical Collection; Sider, *Lumbee Indian Histories*, 32–33; Eliades and Oxendine, *Pembroke State University*, 129–31; Woods, "Growing Up Red," 73–74.

28. Joseph Michael Smith, *The Lumbee Methodists: Getting to Know Them, a Folk History* (Raleigh: Commission of Archives and History and North Carolina Methodist Conference, 1990), 22; Lumbee River Legal Services, *The Lumbee Petition (for Federal Recognition)* (Pembroke NC: Lumbee River Legal Services, 1987), 1:41–48; Barton, *Most Ironic Story*, 93–96; Berde, *Coharie Reemergence*, 6–21; Grady, *Coharie Indians*, 74–76; Ross, *American Indians*, 124–94.

29. Guy Benton Johnson Papers, folder 1231; interview with Regina Mills by author, October 16, 2000, Rocky Mount NC; *Greensboro Daily News*, August 24, 1958; *Littleton Observer*, April 5, 1958; American Indian Policy Review Commission, *Final Report on Terminated and Non Federally Recognized Indians* (Washington DC: U.S. Government Printing Office, 1976), 178; Joseph Michael Smith, *Lumbee Methodists*, 25.

30. Joseph Michael Smith, *Lumbee Methodists*, 30–35.

31. Johnson Papers, folder 1231; Jack Campisi, *The Haliwa-Saponi Petition for Federal Acknowledgment* (Pembroke NC: Lumbee River Legal Services, 1989), 72, 137–38; Berde, *Coharie Reemergence*, 21. For more on religion and social change in the South and North Carolina, see Christine Leigh Heyrman, *Southern Cross: The Beginnings of the Bible Belt* (New York: A.A. Knopf, 1997); Samuel S. Hill, ed., *Religion in the Southern States: A Historical Study* (Macon GA: Mercer University Press, 1983); and Frederick A. Bode, *Protestantism and the New South: North Carolina Baptists and Methodists in Political Crisis, 1894–1903* (Charlottesville: University Press of Virginia, 1975).

32. Joseph Michael Smith, *Lumbee Methodists*, 24–25; Woods, "Growing Up Red," 62–63.

33. Lerch, "State-Recognized Indians," 50.

34. Campisi, *Haliwa-Saponi Petition*, 72, 137; statement of Ruth Locklear, U.S. Congress, *Act to Provide for the Recognition*, 94; Lumbee River Legal Services, *Lumbee Petition*, 1:41–48; Dial and Eliades, *Only Land I Know*, 106–12.

35. Wilkins, *Walking Upright*, 24; Berde, *Coharie Reemergence*, 3–4, 16–29, 43–48.

36. Freeman interview; Moore interview; Ross, *American Indians*, 124–25, 142–94; Lumbee River Legal Services, *Lumbee Petition*, 1:167–68; Woods, "Growing Up Red," 26, 32, 63.

37. Interview with Priscilla Freeman Jacobs by Jill Hemming, October 7, 1996, G-197, Southern Oral History Program Collection no. 4007, Southern Historical Collection; Woods, "Growing Up Red," 23–24. For more on the concept of domesticity, see Carl N. Degler, *At Odds: Women and the Family from the Revolution to the Present* (Oxford: Oxford University Press, 1980).

38. Ross, *American Indians*, 152; Blu, *Lumbee Problem*, 176; Lerch, "State-Recognized Indians," 50; Joseph Michael Smith, *Lumbee Methodists*, 24.

39. McPherson report, 24; William J. Cooper and Thomas E. Terrill, *The American*

South: A History (New York: McGraw Hill, 1991), 438–39; Paul Escott, *Many Excellent People: Power and Privilege in North Carolina, 1850–1900* (Chapel Hill: University of North Carolina Press, 1985), 175.

40. *Greensboro Daily News*, December 1, 1950; Pearmain report; Lumbee River Legal Services, *Lumbee Petition*, 1:157; Sider, *Lumbee Indian Histories*, 30, 65–68, 153.

41. Memo from Fred Baker to John Collier, July 1, 1935, in Fred A. Baker, "Report on Siouan Tribe" (hereafter cited as Baker report); Perdue and Green, *Columbia Guide*, 134–35; Sider, *Lumbee Indian Histories*, 65–68.

42. Quotation from interview with William Sampson, "Never That Far from Home: Lumbee Men and World War II," Native American Resource Center, http://www.uncp.edu/nativemuseum/; Moore interview; Freeman interview.

43. Memo from Fred A. Baker to John Collier, July 1, 1935, in Baker report; Pearmain report; Woods, "Growing Up Red," 27.

44. Memo from D'Arcy McNickle titled "Indians of Robeson County," April 7, 1936, in Pearmain report; Moore interview; Freeman interview; McPherson report, 24.

45. James Mooney, "Croatans," in *Handbook of American Indians North of Mexico*, ed. Frederick Webb Hodge (Washington DC: Government Printing Office, 1970), 365.

46. Blu, *Lumbee Problem*, 78–82; McPherson report, 230–31.

47. Blu, *Lumbee Problem*, 78–82; McPherson report, 17.

48. McPherson report, 17; "Indians of Robeson County," May 1, 1936, in Pearmain report.

49. McPherson report, 17.

50. "Indians of Robeson County," May 1, 1936, in Pearmain report.

51. Woods, "Growing Up Red," 46–50; Waccamaw Siouan Tribe, personal correspondence, August 31, 2002; *Duplin Times Progress-Sentinel*, October 27, 1983; *Pilot* (Southern Pines), September 6, 1972; interview with Barbara Braveboy-Locklear, "Lumbee—in Touch with the Earth," http://www.ibiblio.org/storytelling/lumbbody.html/ (accessed January 27, 2005); Berde, *Coharie Reemergence*, 28–38. Trickster tales are very common in Native American oral tradition. For more on Cherokee and Native American mythology, see Barbara R. Duncan, *Living Stories of the Cherokee* (Chapel Hill: University of North Carolina Press, 1998); David Leeming and Jake Page, *The Mythology of Native North America* (Norman: University of Oklahoma Press, 1998); and Richard Erdoes and Alfonso Ortiz, eds., *American Indian Trickster Tales* (New York: Viking, 1998).

52. Grady, *Coharie Indians*, 41.

53. *UPI Regional News*, Lexis-Nexis, February 3, 1986.

54. Quotation in ibid., February 3, 1986; *Virginian-Pilot*, January 10, 1986, May 31, 1977; *Raleigh News and Observer*, July 3, 1949, January 29, 1956; *Greensboro Daily News*, March 26, 1950; *Durham Morning Herald*, May 31, 1953, February 27, 1957; Dial and Eliades, *Only Land I Know*, 8–11; Stuart Berde, *Nowhere to Hide: A Theoretical and Documentary Quest into Coharie Indian History* (Lumbee River Legal Services and the Coharie Intra-tribal Council, 1984), 124–31.

55. Bruce Barton, *An Indian Manifesto* (Pembroke: Carolina Indian Voice, 1983), 43; Robeson Historical Drama, Incorporated, "*Strike at the Wind* Official Program" (Braswell Memorial Library, Rocky Mount NC, 1977); Sider, *Lumbee Indian Histories*, 155–58; Blu, *Lumbee Problem*, 43–45, 61, 149–55; Dial and Eliades, *Only Land I Know*, 86, 121. For a fictional account of the Lowry War, see Josephine Humphreys, *Nowhere Else on Earth* (New York: Viking, 2000).

56. AIPRC, *Final Report on Indians*, 164; Ronald Gene Ransom, "The Tie That Binds: The Grandparent/Grandchild Relationship among the Lumbee Indians of Robeson County" (master's thesis, University of Arizona, 1989), 11–15; Lumbee River Legal Ser-

vices, *Lumbee Petition*, 1:157–64, 181; *Raleigh News and Observer*, July 11, 1971, September 18, 1977; Ross, *American Indians*, 104; John Gregory Peck, "Urban Station—Migration of the Lumbee Indians" (PhD diss., University of North Carolina–Chapel Hill, 1972), 119–21; Moore interview; http://www.haliwa-saponi.org/; Grady, *Coharie Indians*, 51, 65; Woods, "Growing Up Red," 23–32.

57. Johnson papers, subseries 5.7, folders 1199–214; Moore interview; confidential interview, tape no. 68, March 15, 1994, courtesy of Walt Wolfram and the North Carolina Language and Life Project; Ross, *American Indians*, 104; Susannah Zak, "A Story of Survival: The Lumbee Indians" (master's thesis, University of North Carolina–Chapel Hill, 1992), 36–37; Ransom, "Tie That Binds," 11–15; *Raleigh News and Observer*, July 11, 1971, September 18, 1977; Evans, *To Die Game*, 57; Sampson interview, in "Never That Far"; Moore interview; Freeman interview; confidential interview, tape no. 1, March 5, 1994, courtesy of Walt Wolfram and the North Carolina Language and Life Project; Lumbee River Legal Services, *Lumbee Petition*, 1:157; Grady, *Coharie Indians*, 51, 65; Woods, "Growing Up Red," 23–32; *Durham Morning Herald*, March 19, 1948.

58. Statement of Adolph Blue, U.S. Congress, *Act to Provide for the Recognition*, 71–76; statement of Ruth Locklear, ibid., 91–94; Johnson papers, subseries 5.7, folders 1199–214; Moore interview; Oxendine interview; Freeman interview; Lumbee River Legal Services, *Lumbee Petition*, 1:157; Grady, *Coharie Indians*, 51, 65; Woods, "Growing Up Red," 23–32; *Durham Morning Herald*, March 19, 1948; Lerch, "State-Recognized Indians," 48.

59. Statement of Adolph Blue, U.S. Congress, *Act to Provide for the Recognition*, 70–76; Blu, *Lumbee Problem*, 82–86; Woods, "Growing Up Red," 51.

60. Angus W. McLean to Josiah Bailey, August 18, 1932, Josiah William Bailey Papers.

61. Memo titled "Indians of Robeson County," May 1, 1936, in Pearmain report.

62. Sider, *Lumbee Indian Histories*, 74–79; Blu, *Lumbee Problem*, 175.

63. Michael Omi and Howard Winant, *Racial Formation in the United States from the 1960s to the 1980s* (New York: Routledge and Kegan Paul, 1986), 14–15.

Chapter 2. From Pitchforks to Time Cards

Opening epigraph from an interview with James Locklear, "Never That Far from Home: Lumbee Men and World War II," Native American Resource Center, http://www.uncp.edu/nativemuseum/.

1. For more on the Depression in North Carolina, see Anthony Badger, *Prosperity Road: The New Deal, Tobacco, and North Carolina* (Chapel Hill: University of North Carolina Press, 1980).

2. Quote from Ruth Dial Woods, "Growing Up Red: The Lumbee Experience" (PhD diss., University of North Carolina–Chapel Hill, 2001), 95; John Pearmain, "Report on Condition" (hereafter cited as Pearmain report).

3. Data drawn from federal census figures accumulated by John Pearmain in Pearmain report.

4. Interview summaries of Jasper Locklear, Heezie Dees, John Strickland, J. W. Wilkins, James Chavis, S. M. Bell, R. M. Lowry, and J. T. Moore in Pearmain report; 1920 and 1930 federal census data from ibid.

5. Quote by A. C. Locklear in ibid; interview summaries of Wash Bell, Ellen Jacobs, D. L. Locklear, Nathaniel Dial, A. C. Locklear, and John R. Oxendine in ibid.

6. Interview summaries of Henry Locklear, Parker Locklear, S. M. Bell, Mrs. J. T. Moore, Shaw Dees, Ellen Jacobs, J. W. Wilkins, and Nathaniel Dial in ibid.

7. Interview summaries of J. T. Moore and Mrs. J. T. Moore in ibid.

8. James C. Cobb, *Industrialization and Southern Society, 1877–1984* (Lexington: Uni-

versity Press of Kentucky, 1984), 52–53; Gilbert C. Fite, *Cotton Fields No More: Southern Agriculture, 1865–1980* (Lexington: University Press of Kentucky, 1984), 233–37. For more on the New Deal and southern agriculture, see Theodore Saloutos, *The American Farmer and the New Deal* (Ames: Iowa State University Press, 1982).

9. Peter Iverson, *"We Are Still Here:" American Indians in the Twentieth Century* (Wheeling IL: Harlan Davidson, 1998), 80–97. For more on John Collier and the IRA, see Lawrence Kelly, *The Assault on Assimilation: John Collier and the Origins of Indian Policy Reform* (Albuquerque: University of New Mexico Press, 1983); and Kenneth Philp, *John Collier's Crusade for Indian Reform, 1920–1954* (Tucson: University of Arizona Press, 1977).

10. Stephen Cornell, *The Return of the Native: American Indian Political Resurgence* (New York: Oxford University Press, 1988), 89.

11. Quotation from John R. Swanton, "Report on Identity of the 'Croatan' Indians," Josiah William Bailey Papers, box 311; Elwood P. Morley, "In Re Cherokee Indians, Robeson County, North Carolina," letter to commissioner of Indian Affairs, 1932, ibid.; Joseph Dixon, secretary of the Interior, to Lynn Frazier, chairman of the Committee on Indian Affairs, January 10, 1934, ibid.; Josiah Bailey to John Collier, August 16, 1932, ibid.; memo titled "Indians of Robeson County, North Carolina," May 1, 1936, in Pearmain report; Joseph Brooks to John Collier, July 8, 1935, in ibid.

12. Clifton Oxendine to Josiah Bailey, February 1, 1934, Josiah William Bailey Papers, box 311; memo titled "Indians of Robeson County, North Carolina," May 1, 1936, in Pearmain report; statement of Johnnie P. Bullard, U.S. Congress, *Act to Provide for the Recognition*, 147–48. There are several letters regarding this issue in the Josiah William Bailey Papers, boxes 310 and 311.

13. Quotation from letter from Dr. F. Lowry to Josiah Bailey, January 21, 1935, Josiah William Bailey Papers, box 311; statement of Johnnie P. Bullard, U.S. Congress, *Act to Provide for the Recognition*, 147–48; Joseph Michael Smith, *The Lumbee Methodists: Getting to Know Them, a Folk History* (Raleigh: Commission of Archives and History and North Carolina Methodist Conference, 1990), 69.

14. Memo titled "Indians of Robeson County, North Carolina," May 1, 1936, in Pearmain report.

15. Ibid.; D'Arcy McNickle to Larouche, November 17, 1937, in Pearmain report; memo from D'Arcy McNickle, E. S. McMahon, and Carl Seltzer to John Collier, January 26, 1937, in ibid.; John Collier to secretary of the Interior, in ibid.

16. John Herrick to Henry Sanderson, September 8, 1935, in ibid.; memo titled "Indians of Robeson County, North Carolina," May 1, 1936, in ibid.; D'Arcy McNickle to Larouche, November 17, 1937, in ibid.; memo from D'Arcy McNickle, E. S. McMahon, and Carl Seltzer to John Collier, January 26, 1937, in ibid.; John Collier to secretary of the Interior, in ibid.; statement of Arlinda Locklear, U.S. Congress, *Act to Provide for the Recognition*, 158.

17. Quotation in memo from D'Arcy McNickle, E. S. McMahon, and Carl Seltzer to John Collier, January 26, 1937, in Pearmain report; Lumbee River Legal Services, *The Lumbee Petition (for Federal Recognition)* (Pembroke NC: Lumbee River Legal Services, 1987), 1:84–87; "Indians of Robeson County, North Carolina" May 1, 1936, in Pearmain report; Gerald M. Sider, *Lumbee Indian Histories: Race, Ethnicity, and Indian Identity in the Southern United States* (Cambridge: Cambridge University Press, 1993), 136–37.

18. Memo from D'Arcy McNickle, E. S. McMahon, and Carl Seltzer to John Collier, January 26, 1937, in Pearmain report.

19. Ibid.

20. Memo from D'Arcy McNickle in "Indians of Robeson County, North Carolina,"

April 7, 1936, in ibid. For more on McNickle, see Dorothy Parker, *Singing an Indian Song: A Biography of D'Arcy McNickle* (Lincoln: University of Nebraska Press, 1992).

21. William Zimmerman Jr. to Fred A. Baker, June 13, 1935, in Fred A. Baker, "Report on Siouan Tribe" (hereafter cited as Baker report).

22. Quotation from Fred A. Baker to John Collier, July 10, 1935, in Baker report; John Collier to James Brooks, June 3, 1935, in ibid.; William Zimmerman Jr. to Fred A. Baker, June 13, 1935, in ibid.; statement of Claude Lowry, U.S. Congress, *Act to Provide for the Recognition*, 151.

23. Memo from Edwin L. Groome to J. M. Stewart, May 1, 1936, in Baker report; exhibits C, G, and J in ibid.; *Charlotte Observer*, May 19, 1940; Ryan Anderson, "Lumbee Kinship, Community, and the Success of the Red Banks Mutual Association," *American Indian Quarterly* 23 (1999): 39–54; Sider, *Lumbee Indian Histories*, 138–39. For more information on the FSA, see Sidney Baldwin, *Poverty and Politics: The Rise and Decline of the Farm Security Administration* (Chapel Hill: University of North Carolina Press, 1967).

24. Guy Benton Johnson Papers, subseries 5.7, folder 1199; Anderson, "Lumbee Kinship," 39–58; *Raleigh News and Observer*, July 7, 1968; Karen I. Blu, *The Lumbee Problem: The Making of an American Indian People* (Cambridge: Cambridge University Press, 1980), 82–86.

25. John Collier to Ella Deloria, November 29, 1940, in Pearmain report; *Raleigh News and Observer*, December 6, 1940, November 28, 1940, December 5, 1941; *Charlotte Observer*, December 5, 1940; Lumbee River Legal Services, *Lumbee Petition*, 1:88–91. Previously, there had been other smaller productions on Indian history in the area, including Paul Green's *The Last of the Lowries* and William Norment Cox's *The Scuffletown Outlaws*, both from the 1920s.

26. *House Resolution 7153*, 81st Cong., *Congressional Record* A886 (February 6, 1950), in Native American Rights Fund, *Waccamaw-Siouan Tribe of North Carolina*; Patricia B. Lerch, "State-Recognized Indians of North Carolina, Including a History of the Waccamaw Sioux," in *Indians of the Southeastern United States in the Late Twentieth Century*, ed. J. Anthony Paredes (Tuscaloosa: University of Alabama Press, 1992), 62.

27. *House Resolution 7153*; American Indian Policy Review Commission, *Final Report on Terminated and Non Federally Recognized Indians* (Washington DC: U.S. Government Printing Office, 1976), 157–59; *Robesonian*, September 15, 1985; Thomas E. Ross, *American Indians in North Carolina: Geographic Interpretations* (Southern Pines NC: Kara Hollow), 144, 192.

28. Jeremiah James Nowell Jr., "Red, White and Black: Race Formation and the Politics of American Indian Recognition in North Carolina" (PhD diss., University of North Carolina–Chapel Hill, 2000), 65–78.

29. Vernon Ray Thompson, "A History of the Education of the Lumbee Indians of Robeson County from 1885 to 1970" (PhD diss., University of Miami, 1974), 53–78; *Charlotte Observer*, May 19, 1940; *Robesonian*, September 9, 1985; data accumulated by John Pearmain from county superintendent's office, in Pearmain report.

30. AIPRC, *Final Report on Indians*, 159; *Robesonian*, September 9, 1985; Ross, *American Indians*, 144, 193; Stuart Berde, *Coharie Reemergence: Attaining Religious and Educational Freedom in Eastern North Carolina, 1850-Present* (Lumbee River Legal Services and Coharie Intra-tribal Council, 1982), 48–50; Thompson, "History of the Education," 53–78; *Charlotte Observer*, November 6, 1925.

31. Don Avasco Grady, *The Coharie Indians of Sampson County, North Carolina: A Collection of Their Oral Folk History* (Chapel Hill: The North Carolina Collection),

38; Ross, *American Indians*, 158–59; Berde, *Coharie Reemergence*, 39–50; Lerch, "State-Recognized Indians," 52.

32. Quotation in Lerch, "State-Recognized Indians," 62–63; confidential interview, tape no. 68, March 15, 1994, courtesy of Walt Wolfram and the North Carolina Language and Life Project; *Greensboro Daily News*, March 30, 1950; *Durham Morning Herald*, March 19, 1948; Native American Rights Fund, *Waccamaw-Siouan Tribe*, February 6, 1950, HR 7153; Brewton Berry, *Almost White* (New York: Macmillan, 1963), 123; *Robesonian*, September 15, 1985; Forest Hazel, "Black, White and 'Other': The Struggle for Recognition," *Southern Exposure* 13 (1984): 37; Berde, *Coharie Reemergence*, 27–35, 70.

33. Data from *The Sixteenth Census of the United States*; *Raleigh News and Observer*, March 18, 1972; Lumbee River Legal Services, *Lumbee Petition*, 1:169, 181; Thompson, "History of the Education," 52–60; Berde, *Coharie Reemergence*, 6, 29, 34, and 134.

34. David K. Eliades and Linda Oxendine, *Pembroke State University: A History* (Columbus GA: Brentwood University Press, 1986), 10–25, 50–57; Adolph L. Dial and David K. Eliades, *The Only Land I Know: A History of the Lumbee Indians* (San Francisco: Indian Historian, 1975), 90–95; Thompson, "History of the Education," 42–47; *Asheville Citizen Times*, September 23, 1950.

35. Quotation in Iverson, *"We Are Still Here,"* 105.

36. Alison Bernstein, *American Indians and World War II: Toward a New Era in Indian Affairs* (Norman: University of Oklahoma Press, 1991), xi.

37. *Greensboro Daily News*, December 1, 1950; *Daily Times*, April 18, 1950; Nowell, "Red, White and Black," 82.

38. UPI *Regional News*, Lexis-Nexis, December 28, 1988; *Lumberton Voice*, July 3, 1946; Dial and Eliades, *Only Land I Know*, 154–56; Lumbee River Legal Services, *Lumbee Petition*, 1:156.

39. *Greensboro Daily News*, January 17, 1971; *Greensboro Record*, July 2 and 4, 1975; confidential interview, tape no. 39, April 19, 1972, courtesy of Walt Wolfram and the North Carolina Language and Life Project; Center for Urban Affairs, *Paths toward Freedom: A Biographical History of Blacks and Indians in North Carolina by Blacks and Indians* (Raleigh: North Carolina State University, 1976), 31.

40. Quotation from interview with James Locklear, "Never That Far from Home"; confidential interview, tape no. 34, November 1972, courtesy of Walt Wolfram and the North Carolina Language and Life Project; *Robesonian*, March 18, 1946; Berde, *Coharie Reemergence*, 53; Lumbee River Legal Services, *Lumbee Petition*, 1:156.

41. *The Fifteenth Census of the United States*; *The Sixteenth Census of the United States*; *The Twentieth Census of the United States*; *Washington Post*, January 8, 1967; Fite, *Cotton Fields No More*, 163; Johnson Papers, box 78, subseries 5.7, folders 1199–214.

42. Cobb, *Industrialization and Southern Society*, 52–53, 96; James C. Cobb, *The Selling of the South: The Southern Crusade for Industrial Development, 1936–1990* (Urbana: University of Illinois Press, 1982, 1993), 1–5; Bruce J. Schulman, *From Cotton Belt to Sunbelt: Federal Policy, Economic Development, and the Transformation of the South, 1938–1980* (New York: Oxford University Press, 1991), 14–20.

43. *The Fifteenth Census of the United States*; *The Seventeenth Census of the United States*; *The Twentieth Census of the United States*; Cobb, *Industrialization and Southern Society*, 96, 108, 140–50; Schulman, *From Cotton Belt to Sunbelt*, 206–12; Dial and Eliades, *Only Land I Know*, 147–56; Paul Luebke, *Tar Heel Politics: Myths and Realities* (Chapel Hill: University of North Carolina Press, 1990), 15, 71–103. For more on the transformation of southern agriculture, see Jack T. Kirby, *Rural Worlds Lost: The American South, 1920–1960* (Baton Rouge: Louisiana State University Press, 1986).

44. AIPRC, *Final Report on Indians*, 165–76; Ronald Gene Ransom, "The Tie That

Binds: The Grandparent/Grandchild Relationship among the Lumbee Indians of Robeson County" (master's thesis, University of Arizona, 1989), 40–52; Roy Parker Jr., *Cumberland County: A Brief History* (Raleigh: Division of Archive and History, 1990).

45. *The Twentieth Census of the United States*; Dial and Eliades, *Only Land I Know*, 96; Bernstein, *American Indians*, 142. For more on the GI Bill, see Keith W. Olson, *The G.I. Bill, the Veterans, and the Colleges* (Lexington: University Press of Kentucky, 1974).

46. Interview with Curt Locklear, "Never That Far from Home."

47. Interview with William Sampson, ibid.; confidential interview, tape no. 39, April 10, 1972, courtesy of Walt Wolfram and the North Carolina Language and Life Project; Berde, *Coharie Reemergence*, 48–53.

48. Quotation from interview with James Locklear, "Never That Far from Home"; interviews with Curt Locklear and William Sampson, ibid.; interview with Dexter Brooks by Susan M. Hunt, March 14 and 21, 1994, J-11, Southern Oral History Program Collection no. 4007, Southern Historical Collection.

Chapter 3. What's in a Name?

Opening epigraph from the *Durham Morning Herald*, May 27, 1973.

1. Data drawn from *The Sixteenth Census of the United States*, *The Eighteenth Census of the United States*, and *The Twentieth Census of the United States*; Thomas E. Ross, *American Indians in North Carolina: Geographic Interpretations* (Southern Pines NC: Kara Hollow), 37, 226.

2. Frederik Barth, *Ethnic Groups and Boundaries: The Social Organization of Culture Difference* (Boston: Little, Brown, 1969), 32–38; *The Seventeenth Census of the United States*; *The Twentieth Census of the United States*; Guy Benton Johnson Papers, box 78, subseries 5.7, folders 1231–32.

3. *Durham Morning Herald*, March 19, 1948; *Raleigh News and Observer*, July 3, 1949; *Greensboro Daily News*, March 26 and 30, 1950.

4. Interview with Brenda Jacobs Moore, September 26, 1996; interview with Shirley Jacobs Freeman, September 28, 1996; interview with Priscilla Freeman Jacobs, October 7, 1996; interview with Dexter Brooks, March 14 and 21, 1994; interview with Carol Brewington by Jill Hemming, October 7, 1996, G-189, Southern Oral History Program Collection no. 4007, Southern Historical Collection; Lumbee River Legal Services, *The Lumbee Petition (for Federal Recognition)* (Pembroke NC: Lumbee River Legal Services, 1987), 1:158; Jack Campisi, *The Haliwa-Saponi Petition for Federal Acknowledgment* (Pembroke NC: Lumbee River Legal Services, 1989), 103–5.

5. William H. Chafe, *Civilities and Civil Rights: Greensboro, North Carolina, and the Black Struggle for Freedom* (Oxford: Oxford University Press, 1980), 48–60. For more on the significance of Brown, see Raymond Wolters, *The Burden of Brown: Thirty Years of School Desegregation* (Knoxville: University of Tennessee Press, 1984); and J. Harvie Wilkinson, *From Brown to Bakke: The Supreme Court and School Integration, 1954–1978* (New York: Oxford University Press, 1979).

6. Chafe, *Civilities and Civil Rights*, 48–60; Bruce J. Schulman, *From Cotton Belt to Sunbelt: Federal Policy, Economic Development, and the Transformation of the South, 1938–1980* (New York: Oxford University Press, 1991), 212.

7. *Raleigh News and Observer*, November 8, 1958.

8. Campisi, *Haliwa-Saponi Petition*, 122; *Raleigh News and Observer*, January 29, 1956, August 18 and 21, 1958; *New York Times*, August 3, 1972; *Durham Morning Herald*, May 31, 1953, January 1, 1977; *Carolina Indian Voice*, July 12, 2001.

9. Terry Sanford, Governor's Papers, General Correspondence, box 83, State Archives;

NOTES TO PAGES 69–73 • 167

W. R. Richardson to Governor Sanford, April 16, 1961; *Durham Morning Herald*, February 22, 1959; *Raleigh News and Observer*, January 8, 1959, November 24, 1962; *Greensboro Daily News*, August 24, 1958, September 21, 1957; Jeremiah James Nowell Jr., "Red, White and Black: Race Formation and the Politics of American Indian Recognition in North Carolina" (PhD diss., University of North Carolina–Chapel Hill, 2000), 269–73; Campisi, *Haliwa-Saponi Petition*, 38, 86–94, 127–33.

10. Campisi, *Haliwa-Saponi Petition*, 19–26, 78–81, 94c-97, 117–28; American Indian Policy Review Commission, *Final Report on Terminated and Non Federally Recognized Indians* (Washington DC: U.S. Government Printing Office, 1976), 152; Ross, *American Indians*, 162–67.

11. Quotation in *Raleigh News and Observer*, May 27, 2001; *Rocky Mount Telegram*, October 27, 1981; Campisi, *Haliwa-Saponi Petition*, 26, 78–80, 94c, 117–28, 141; Nowell, "Red, White and Black," 265–66.

12. James D. Brewington to North Carolina Indian Affairs, May 18, 1979, Department of Indian Affairs, Executive Director's file, Conference and Workshops, 1978–79, box 1; *Fayetteville Observer*, August 27, 1984; David Wilkins, *Walking Upright: The Coharie People of Sampson County* (Raleigh: Division of Archives and History, Department of Cultural Resources, 1980), 31–36; Don Avasco Grady, *The Coharie Indians of Sampson County, North Carolina: A Collection of Their Oral Folk History* (Chapel Hill: The North Carolina Collection), 2, 47, 39, and 51; Stuart Berde, *Coharie Reemergence: Attaining Religious and Educational Freedom in Eastern North Carolina, 1850-Present* (Lumbee River Legal Services and Coharie Intra-tribal Council, 1982), 11–12. There are actually two Coharie rivers, the Great Coharie, the largest and more significant, and the Little Coharie.

13. Patricia B. Lerch, "State-Recognized Indians of North Carolina, Including a History of the Waccamaw Sioux," in *Indians of the Southeastern United States in the Late Twentieth Century*, ed. J. Anthony Paredes (Tuscaloosa: University of Alabama Press, 1992), 55–57; Native American Rights Fund, *Waccamaw-Siouan Tribe of North Carolina, a Collection of Historical Documents*, the North Carolina Collection.

14. James E. Alexander to Frank Speck, November 2, 1949; *House Resolution 7153*, 81st Cong., *Congressional Record* A886 (February 6, 1950); and letter from Dale Doty, August 7, 1950, all in Native American Rights Fund, "Waccamaw-Siouan Tribe"; *Greensboro Daily News*, December 1, 1950; *Asheville Citizen-Times*, April 27, 1950; Lerch, "State-Recognized Indians," 63–64.

15. Shannon Lee Dawdy, "The Secret History of the Meherrin" (master's thesis: College of William and Mary, 1994), 5, 72; Ross, *American Indians*, 200–209; Meherrin Indian Tribe, personal correspondence, August 15, 2002; Nowell, "Red, White and Black," 84–102.

16. D. F. Lowry, "No Mystery," *The State* 20 (December 1952): 24.

17. Quotation in *Raleigh News and Observer*, March 30, 1951; statement of Claude Lowry, U.S. Congress, *Act to Provide for the Recognition*, 150–54; *Raleigh News and Observer*, July 3, 1949, January 10, 1952, February 5 and 26, 1953; *Greensboro Daily News*, April 1, 1951; Johnson Papers, box 78, subseries 5.7, folders 1199–214 and 1231–32; Lumber River Legal Services, *Lumbee Petition*, 1:52–95; James E. Chavis to Josiah Bailey, March 23, 1934, Josiah Bailey Papers, box 311; Joseph Michael Smith, *The Lumbee Methodists: Getting to Know Them, a Folk History* (Raleigh: Commission of Archives and History and North Carolina Methodist Conference, 1990), 69. There are some references from the early 1900s to the "Lumbee River," but there is no proof that colonial-era tribes used this name.

18. The exact vote varies from source to source, but all agree that the vote was approximately twenty-one hundred to thirty-five.

19. *Raleigh News and Observer*, March 30, 1951, January 10, 1952, February 5, 1952, February 26, 1953; *Greensboro Daily News*, April 1, 1951; Johnson Papers, box 78, subseries 5.7, folders 1199–214 and 1231–32; Lumbee River Legal Services, *Lumbee Petition*, 1:93–95.

20. Alison Bernstein, *American Indians and World War II: Toward a New Era in Indian Affairs* (Norman: University of Oklahoma Press, 1991), 159–66; Larry Burt, *Tribalism in Crisis: Federal Indian Policy, 1953–1961* (Albuquerque: University of New Mexico Press, 1982), ix-5; Donald Fixico, *Termination and Relocation: Federal Indian Policy, 1945–1960* (Albuquerque: University of New Mexico Press, 1986), 183–86.

21. Fixico, *Termination and Relocation*, 183–86, 119; James S. Olson Raymond Wilson, *Native Americans in the Twentieth Century* (Urbana: University of Illinois Press, 1984), 137–40; Bernstein, *American Indians*, 161–62.

22. Russell Thornton, *Studying Native America*, (Madison: University of Wisconsin Press, 1998), 30; Alvin M. Josephy Jr., *The Indian Heritage of America* (Boston: Houghton Mifflin, 1968, 1992), 135; Bernstein, *American Indians*, 148, 168–69. For more on Indian urbanization, see Susan Lobo and Kurt Peters, *American Indians and the Urban Experience* (Walnut Creek CA: Altamira, 2001); and Elaine Neils, *Reservation to City: Indian Migration and Federal Relocation* (Chicago: University of Chicago Press, 1971).

23. John Finger, *Cherokee Americans: The Eastern Band of Cherokees in the Twentieth Century* (Lincoln: University of Nebraska Press, 1991), 111–24, 154–59. For a detailed look at the Menominees, see Nicholas C. Peroff, *Menonominee Drums: Tribal Termination and Restoration* (Norman: University of Oklahoma Press, 1982).

24. Stephen Cornell, *The Return of the Native: American Indian Political Resurgence* (New York: Oxford University Press, 1988), 125. Cornell discusses the relationship between Termination and an emerging supratribal identity in detail on pages 124–46.

25. AIPRC, *Final Report on Indians*, 171.

26. Interview with Dexter Brooks; *Charlotte Observer*, May 2, 1977; Fergus M. Bordewich, *Killing the White Man's Indian: Reinventing Native Americans at the End of the Twentieth Century* (New York: Doubleday, 1996), 65.

27. *Washington Post*, January 26, 1958; *Durham Morning Herald*, January 26, 1958; *New York Times*, January 17, 1958; *Raleigh News and Observer*, January 26, 1958.

28. Charles Craven, "The Night the Klan Died in North Carolina," *True* (March 1975): 61–65; *Washington Post*, January 26, 1958; *Durham Morning Herald*, January 26, 1958; *New York Times*, January 17, 1958; *Raleigh News and Observer*, January 26, 1958.

29. Interview with William Sampson, "Never That Far from Home: Lumbee Men and World War II," Native American Resource Center, http://www.uncp.edu/nativemuseum/.

30. Interview with James Locklear, ibid.

31. Craven, "Night the Klan Died," 61.

32. *Newsweek*, January 27, 1958, 27.

33. Quotation in Craven, "Night the Klan Died," 65; *Greensboro Daily News*, January 17, 1971; *Fayetteville Observer*, January 5, 1959; Adolph L. Dial and David K. Eliades, *The Only Land I Know: A History of the Lumbee Indians* (San Francisco: Indian Historian, 1975), 159–62; Ruth Dial Woods, "Growing Up Red: The Lumbee Experience" (PhD diss., University of North Carolina–Chapel Hill, 2001), 100.

34. Johnson Papers, box 78, subseries 5.7, folders 1199–214.

35. Ibid., folders 1231–32; *Raleigh News and Observer*, August 4, 1972; *Greensboro Daily News*, March 26, 1950.

36. *Raleigh News and Observer*, August 4, 1972.

37. Quotation in Johnson Papers, box 78, subseries 5.7, folders 1231–32; Brewton Berry, *Almost White* (New York: Macmillan, 1963); J. K. Dane and B. Eugene Griessman, "The Collective Identity of Marginal Peoples: The North Carolina Experience," *Amer-*

ican Anthropologist 74 (June 1972): 694–704; Edgar T. Thompson, "The Little Races," *American Anthropologist* 74 (October 1972): 1295–306; William S. Pollitzer, "The Physical Anthropology and Genetics of Marginal People of Southeastern United States," *American Anthropologist* 74 (June 1972): 719–34; Calvin L. Beale, "An Overview of the Phenomenon of Mixed Racial Isolates in the United States," *American Anthropologist* 74 (June 1972): 704–10.

38. "By-Laws of the Haliwa-Saponi Indian Tribe," in Campisi, *Haliwa-Saponi Petition*; Lumbee River Legal Services, *Lumbee Petition*, 1:232; statement of Ruth Locklear, U.S. Congress, *Act to Provide for the Recognition*, 84–95.

39. James S. Olson and Raymond Wilson, *Native Americans in the Twentieth Century* (Urbana: University of Illinois Press, 1984), 148.

40. Bernstein, *American Indians*, 159–66.

Chapter 4. Protests and Powwows

Opening epigraph from the *Fayetteville Observer*, September 13, 1970.

Second epigraph from Bruce Barton, *An Indian Manifesto* (Pembroke: Carolina Indian Voice, 1983), 3.

1. Quotation in Steven Mintz, *Native American Voices: A History and Anthology* (New York: Brandywine, 1995, 2000), 174.

2. Ibid., 173–74.

3. For more on the Indian political movement, see Paul Chaat Smith and Robert Allen Warrior, *Like a Hurricane: The Indian Movement from Alcatraz to Wounded Knee* (New York: Free, 1996); and Vine Deloria Jr., *Behind the Trail of Broken Treaties* (Austin: University of Texas Press, 1974, 1985).

4. Interview with Shirley Jacobs Freeman by Jill Hemming, September 28, 1996, G-196, Southern Oral History Program Collection no. 4007, Southern Historical Collection; interview with Priscilla Freeman Jacobs by Jill Hemming, October 7, 1996, G-197, ibid.; *Greensboro Daily News*, January 19, 1971; Adolph L. Dial and David K. Eliades, *The Only Land I Know: A History of the Lumbee Indians* (San Francisco: Indian Historian, 1975), 163–72; Ruth Dial Woods, "Growing Up Red: The Lumbee Experience" (PhD diss., University of North Carolina–Chapel Hill, 2001), 122.

5. Quotation in *Greensboro Daily News*, January 19, 1971; *Raleigh News and Observer*, May 21, 1967, September 4, 1970, August 31, 1971.

6. Quotation in *Fayetteville Observer*, September 13, 1970; interview with Dexter Brooks by Susan M. Hunt, March 14 and 21, 1994, J-11, Southern Oral History Program Collection no. 4007, Southern Historical Collection; Lumbee River Legal Services, *The Lumbee Petition (for Federal Recognition)* (Pembroke NC: Lumbee River Legal Services, 1987), 1:104–6; *Raleigh News and Observer*, September 4, 1970, September 28, 1970, August 31, 1971, January 9, 1972, March 9, 1973.

7. *New York Times*, September 13, 1970; *Raleigh News and Observer*, September 12, 1970, September 14, 1970; *Fayetteville Observer*, September 13, 1970.

8. Brooks interview; *Raleigh News and Observer*, September 4 and 28, 1970, August 31, 1971, January 9, 1972, March 9, 1973.

9. Quotation from Daystar Dial, in *Feeding the Ancient Fires: A Collection of Writings by North Carolina Indians*, ed. MariJo Moore (Crossroads, 1999), 59–60; interview with Brenda Jacobs Moore by Jill Hemming, September 26, 1996, G-200, Southern Oral History Program Collection no. 4007, Southern Historical Collection; Priscilla Freeman Jacobs interview; Jack Campisi, *The Haliwa-Saponi Petition for Federal Acknowledgment* (Pembroke NC: Lumbee River Legal Services, 1989), 94; Thomas E. Ross, *American Indians*

in North Carolina: Geographic Interpretations (Southern Pines NC: Kara Hollow), 144, 159, 170.

10. *Greensboro Record*, July 3, 1975.

11. Quotation in ibid.; Brooks interview; interview with Regina Mills by author, October 16, 2000, Rocky Mount NC; Lumbee River Legal Services, *Lumbee Petition*, 1:180.

12. Dial and Eliades, *Only Land I Know*, 96–105; David K. Eliades and Linda Oxendine, *Pembroke State University: A History* (Columbus GA: Brentwood University Press, 1986), 58–74.

13. Quote in Eliades and Oxendine, *Pembroke State University*, 92; *Raleigh News and Observer*, July 14, 1972, March 11, 1973; Lumbee River Legal Services, *Lumbee Petition*, 1:111. The campus also received a new auditorium in 1975.

14. *Raleigh News and Observer*, May 12, 1979; *Greensboro Daily News*, June 23, 1979, July 24, 1979; Eliades and Oxendine, *Pembroke State University*, 73–78, 90.

15. For more on the African American civil rights movement, see Harvard Sitkoff, *The Struggle for Black Equality, 1954–1980* (New York: Hill and Wang, 1981); Stokely Carmichael, *Black Power: The Politics of Liberation in America* (New York: Random House, 1967); and August Meier, CORE: A STUDY IN THE CIVIL RIGHTS MOVEMENT, 1942–1968 (New York: Oxford University Press, 1973).

16. Gerald M. Sider, *Lumbee Indian Histories: Race, Ethnicity, and Indian Identity in the Southern United States* (Cambridge: Cambridge University Press, 1993), 95–107; Dial and Eliades, *Only Land I Know*, 163–72; Karen I. Blu, *The Lumbee Problem: The Making of an American Indian People* (Cambridge: Cambridge University Press, 1980), 100–106.

17. Sider, *Lumbee Indian Histories*, 95–107; Blu, *Lumbee Problem*, 100–106.

18. Quotation from confidential interview, tape no. 34, November 1972, courtesy of Walt Wolfram and the North Carolina Language and Life Project; *Raleigh News and Observer*, April 12, 1978, April 22, 1973; *Durham Morning Herald*, October 20, 1971; April 22, 1973, April 22, 1974; Sider, *Lumbee Indian Histories*, 24–43, 95–101; Blu, *Lumbee Problem*, 90–93, 100, 127. Sider's *Lumbee Indian Histories* and Blu's *Lumbee Problem* are both important works regarding the Indians of Robeson County. Both have also been recently expanded and republished. Sider's work, which has been renamed *Living Indian Histories: Lumbee and Tuscarora People in North Carolina*, was republished by the University of North Carolina Press in 2003. Blu's book was republished by University of Nebraska Press in 2001.

19. Sider, *Lumbee Indian Histories*, 32, 45–48, 96.

20. Statement of Adolph Blue, U.S. Congress, *Act to Provide for the Recognition*, 71; *Raleigh News and Observer*, April 11, 1973, September 18, 1974.

21. *Raleigh News and Observer*, April 12, 1978, April 22, 1973; *Durham Morning Herald*, April 22, 1973, April 22, 1974; Blu, *Lumbee Problem*, 73, 90–93, 100, 127.

22. *Raleigh News and Observer*, January 9, 1972.

23. Sider discusses this throughout *Lumbee Indian Histories*. In particular, see chap. 8 and the conclusion.

24. Stephen Cornell, *The Return of the Native: American Indian Political Resurgence* (New York: Oxford University Press, 1988), 149–63.

25. Sider, *Lumbee Indian Histories*, chap. 6; Blu, *Lumbee Problem*, chap. 3.

26. Statement of Ruth Locklear, U.S. Congress, *Act to Provide for the Recognition*, 95; *Greensboro Daily News*, January 19, 1971; *Raleigh News and Observer*, May 25, 1970, January 9, 1972, October 31, 1972, November 1, 1972, March 9, 1973, March 11, 1973, August 6, 1971, March 21, 1973, May 13 and 17, 1973; Ross, *American Indians*, 214–19; Dial and Eliades, *Only Land I Know*, 116–17; Eliades and Oxendine, *Pembroke State University*, 163–66.

27. Sider, *Lumbee Indian Histories*, 118–23.

28. Flyer, Robeson County Indian Movement and Chief Howard Brooks of the United Tuscarora People, "North Carolina's Indians Need Your Help Now," April 10, 1973.

29. *Durham Morning Herald*, April 10, 1974; *News and Observer*, May 25, 1970, January 9, 1972, October 31, 1972, November 1, 1972, March 9 and 11, 1973, August 6, 1971, March 21, 1973, May 13 and 17, 1973; April 5, 9, 11, 14, and 17, 1973; Dial and Eliades, *Only Land I Know*, 116–17.

30. Sider, *Lumbee Indian Histories*, 116–21; Dial and Eliades, *Only Land I Know*, 116–17.

31. *Chapel Hill Herald*, August 7, 1988.

32. Quotation from confidential interview, tape no. 39, April 10, 1972, courtesy of Walt Wolfram and the North Carolina Language and Life Project; interview with Greg Richardson by author, June 28, 2001, Raleigh. For more on King and his philosophy of resistance, see Taylor Branch, *Parting the Waters: America in the King Years, 1954–1963* (New York: Simon and Schuster, 1988); and *Pillar of Fire: America in the King Years, 1963–1965* (New York: Simon and Schuster, 1998).

33. Michael Harrington, *The Other America: Poverty in the United States* (New York: Macmillan, 1962).

34. For more on LBJ and the Great Society, see Doris Kearns Goodwin, *Lyndon Johnson and the American Dream* (New York: Harper and Row, 1976); and Robert Dallek, *Flawed Giant: Lyndon Johnson and His Times, 1961–1973* (New York: Oxford University Press, 1998).

35. James E. Holshouser, Governor's Papers, box 163, State Archives of North Carolina; *Raleigh News and Observer*, October 1, 1972, March 31, 1973; American Indian Policy Review Commission, *Final Report on Terminated and Non Federally Recognized Indians* (Washington DC: U.S. Government Printing Office, 1976), 155–66.

36. Quotation in Woods, "Growing Up Red," 134.

37. Statement of Adolph Blue, U.S. Congress, *Act to Provide for the Recognition*, 79; Lumbee River Legal Services, *Lumbee Petition*, 1:116–17, 208–27; *Raleigh News and Observer*, August 28, 1988; AIPRC, *Final Report on Indians*, 161–64; Sider, *Lumbee Indian Histories*, 260–68; Woods, "Growing Up Red," 134–36, 162.

38. Moore interview; Jacobs interview; Patricia B. Lerch, "State-Recognized Indians of North Carolina, Including a History of the Waccamaw Sioux," in *Indians of the Southeastern United States in the Late Twentieth Century*, ed. J. Anthony Paredes (Tuscaloosa: University of Alabama Press, 1992), 52–66; AIPRC, *Final Report on Indians*, 164.

39. William Sampson, "Never That Far from Home: Lumbee Men and World War II," Native American Resource Center, http://www.uncp.edu/nativemuseum/.

40. Quotation in *Greensboro Record*, July 2, 1975; *The Fifteenth Census of the United States*; *The Twentieth Census of the United States*; *Greensboro Record*, January 1, 1971, July 4, 1975; Ronald R. McIrvin, "The Urban Indian: A Profile of the Greensboro Native American Population," in *Urban Growth and Urban Life*, ed. Warren Jake Wicker, 422–25 (Chapel Hill: Urban Studies Council, 1981).

41. *Baltimore Sun*, June 27, 1966; John Gregory Peck, "Urban Station—Migration of the Lumbee Indians" (PhD diss., University of North Carolina–Chapel Hill, 1972), 1–7; *Washington Post*, January 8, 1967; Abraham Makofsky, "Struggling to Maintain Identity: Lumbee Indians in Baltimore," *Anthropological Quarterly* 55 (April 1982): 74–83.

42. Quotation in *Greensboro Record*, July 2, 1975; Freeman interview; AIPRC, *Final Report on Indians*, 155, 166; *Raleigh News and Observer*, October 1, 1972, March 31, 1972.

43. Quotation in *Greensboro Record*, July 2, 1975; ibid., July 4, 1975; *Greensboro Daily News*, January 15, 1978; AIPRC, *Final Report on Indians*, 174; McIrvin, "Urban Indian," 419–25.

44. For more on urban Indians, see Susan Lobo and Kurt Peters, *American Indians and the Urban Experience* (Walnut Creek CA: Altamira, 2001); and Alan L. Sorkin, *The Urban American Indian* (Lexington MA: Lexington Books, 1978).

45. Quotation from copy of North Carolina Senate Bill 642, establishing North Carolina Commission of Indian Affairs, in Robert W. Scott, Governor's Papers, Appointments, 1969–72, box 573.13, State Archives; statement of Adolph Blue, U.S. Congress, *Act to Provide for the Recognition*, 82; *Durham Morning Herald*, January 1, 1977; *Raleigh News and Observer*, March 18, 1972.

46. Richardson interview; statement of Adolph Blue, U.S. Congress, *Act to Provide for the Recognition*, 82; *Greensboro Daily News*, January 15, 1978; North Carolina Department of Administration, Division of Indian Affairs, Executive Director's Subject File, 1973–78, box 1.

47. Most southern states now have Indian commissions. Louisiana led the way, establishing its commission in 1970, followed by N.C. (1971), Fla. (1974), Ala. (1975), Va. (1983), and Ga. (1992).

48. Roscoe Jacobs Sr. to Governor Holshouser, August 27, 1975, in James E. Holshouser, Governor's Papers, box 163, 399.

49. Fergus M. Bordewich, *Killing the White Man's Indian: Reinventing Native Americans at the End of the Twentieth Century* (New York: Doubleday, 1996), 159.

50. Philip J. Deloria, *Playing Indian* (New Haven: Yale University Press, 1998), 154–68; Bordewich, *White Man's Indian*, 204–39.

51. Great debate surrounds Krech's work. For more on his conclusions, see Shepard Krech III, *The Ecological Indian: Myth and History* (New York: W. W. Norton, 1999).

52. Alfred W. Crosby, review of *The Ecological Indian: Myth and History*, by Shepard Krech, in *Ethnohistory* 49:3 (Summer 2002): 717.

53. Clyde Ellis, review of *The Ecological Indian: Myth and History*, by Shepard Krech, in ibid., 719.

54. Chris Paci, review of *The Ecological Indian: Myth and History*, by Shepard Krech, on H-AmIndian, H-Net Reviews (May 2002), http://www.h-net.org/reviews/ (accessed January 27, 2005).

55. Louis S. Warren, review of *The Ecological Indian: Myth and History*, by Shepard Krech, in *Ethnohistory* 49:3 (Summer 2002): 721.

56. Richard White, "Dead Certainties," *The New Republic* 222 (January 24, 2000): 49.

57. For more on Indians and Hollywood, see Peter C. Rollins and John E. O'Connor, eds., *Hollywood's Indian: The Portrayal of the Native American in Film* (Lexington: University Press of Kentucky, 1998).

58. Freeman interview; *Greensboro Daily News*, January 17, 1971; *Fayetteville Observer*, October 21, 1979; Woods, "Growing Up Red," 40–41. For more, see A. Everette James Jr., "Claude Richardson: Haliwa-Saponi Carver," *North Carolina Folklore Journal* 40 (1993): 91–96; and Paul K. Vestal Jr., "Herb Workers in Scotland and Robeson Counties," *North Carolina Folklore Journal* 21 (1973): 166–70; Jill Hemming, "The Craft of Identity: Quilting Traditions in the Waccamaw-Siouan Tribe" (master's thesis, University of North Carolina–Chapel Hill, 1995).

59. Moore interview, September 26, 1996; confidential interview, tape no. 34, 1972, courtesy of Walt Wolfram and the North Carolina Language and Life Project; *Raleigh News and Observer*, February 14, 1972; Ross, *American Indians*, 158, 171.

60. *Greensboro Daily News*, January 17, 1971, September 15, 1972; *Chapel Hill News*, June 13, 1976; Robeson Historical Drama, Incorporated, "*Strike at the Wind* Official Souvenir Program," the North Carolina Collection, 1984.

61. Quotation in *Raleigh News and Observer*, April 12, 1978, April 22, 1973; *Durham Morning Herald*, April 22, 1973, April 22, 1974; Haliwa-Saponi Indian Tribe, Incorporated, *Haliwa Indian Powwow Program*, 1967; *Rocky Mount Telegram*, April 22, 1969; Campisi, *Haliwa-Saponi Petition*, 30, 67, 99–102.

62. Quotation in Lerch, "State-Recognized Indians," 71; Freeman interview; Hemming, "Craft of Identity," 35–37; Patricia B. Lerch, "Powwows, Parades and Social Drama among the Waccamaw-Sioux," Patricia Lerch Research Papers, the North Carolina Collection, 75–81; Patricia B. Lerch, "Celebrations and Dress: Sources of Native American Identity," in *Anthropologists and Indians in the New South*, ed. Rachel A. Bonney and J. Anthony Paredes, 145–54 (Tuscaloosa: University of Alabama Press, 2001); *Raleigh News and Observer*, July 5 and 6, 1970; Lumber River Legal Services, *Lumbee Petition*, 1:171.

63. Joane Nagel, *American Indian Ethnic Renewal: Red Power and the Resurgence of Identity and Culture* (New York: Oxford University Press, 1996), 12.

64. Alvin M. Josephy Jr., *The Indian Heritage of America* (Boston: Houghton Mifflin, 1968, 1992), 30; Hazel W. Hertzberg, *The Search for an American Indian Identity: Modern Pan-Indian Movements* (Syracuse University Press, 1971), 320–23; Nagel, *American Indian Ethnic Renewal*, 6–7, 13, 130, 140.

65. Ronald W. Walters, *Pan Africanism in the African Diaspora: An Analysis of Modern Afrocentric Political Movements* (Detroit: Wayne State University Press, 1993), quotation 356, 55–84, 355–76.

Chapter 5. Consolidation and the Search for Validation

Opening epigraph from *UPIRegional News*, Lexis-Nexis, March 15, 1987.

1. James G. Martin, Governor's Papers, Speeches, "Speech at Indian Unity Conference," box 3, State Archives; *Daily Advance (Elizabeth City)*, February 13, 1983, June 20, 1983; *Greensboro News and Record*, October 22, 1999.

2. Quotation from Don Avasco Grady, *The Coharie Indians of Sampson County, North Carolina: A Collection of Their Oral Folk History* (Chapel Hill: The North Carolina Collection), 81; *The Twentieth Census of the United States*.

3. Interview with Brenda Jacobs Moore by Jill Hemming, September 26, 1996, G-200, Southern Oral History Program Collection no. 4007, Southern Historical Collection.

4. Patricia B. Lerch, "Celebrations and Dress: Sources of Native American Identity," in *Anthropologists and Indians in the New South*, ed. Rachel A. Bonney and J. Anthony Paredes (Tuscaloosa: University of Alabama Press, 2001), 147.

5. Interview with Shirley Jacobs Freeman by Jill Hemming, September 28, 1996, G-196, Southern Oral History Program Collection no. 4007, Southern Historical Collection; *Raleigh News and Observer*, January 30, 1985; *Fayetteville Observer*, August 27, 1984; Jack Campisi, *The Haliwa-Saponi Petition for Federal Acknowledgment* (Pembroke NC: Lumbee River Legal Services, 1989), 106–7, 134–35.

6. Statement of Adolph Blue, U.S. Congress, *Act to Provide for the Recognition*, 82; Lumbee River Legal Services, *The Lumbee Petition (for Federal Recognition)* (Pembroke NC: Lumbee River Legal Services, 1987), 1:162–65, 224; Helen Rountree, "Indian Virginians on the Move," in *Indians of the Southeastern United States in the Late Twentieth Century*, ed. J. Anthony Paredes (Tuscaloosa: University of Alabama Press, 1992), 11–12.

7. Telegram from Buffalo Tiger, chairman of the Miccosukee Tribe of Indians of Florida, to Congressman Lloyd Meeds, in Ruth Dial Woods, *Testimony: Indian Definition Study* (The North Carolina Collection, 1974), 29.

8. Quotation from telegram from John A. Crow to Congressman Lloyd Meeds, copy in Woods, *Testimony*, appendix.

9. American Indian Press Association, press release, copy in ibid.

10. *Raleigh News and Observer*, August 7, 1978; Lumbee River Legal Services, *Lumbee Petition*, 1:162–64, 223; Gerald M. Sider, *Lumbee Indian Histories: Race, Ethnicity, and Indian Identity in the Southern United States* (Cambridge: Cambridge University Press, 1993), 268.

11. *Raleigh News and Observer*, August 7, 1978; Lumbee River Legal Services, *Lumbee Petition*, 1:162–64, 223; Sider, *Lumbee Indian Histories*, 268–69.

12. North Carolina Department of Administration, Division of Indian Affairs, Executive Director, Conferences and Workshops, 1978–79, box 2; Lumbee River Legal Services, *Lumbee Petition*, 1:166, 225; *Raleigh News and Observer*, March 6, 1982; *Rocky Mount Telegram*, March 3, 2001; statement of Adolph Blue, U.S. Congress, *Act to Provide for the Recognition*, 78–83.

13. Program for "First Annual North Carolina Indian Youth Conference," June 12–14, 1980, North Carolina Collection; *Asheville Citizen-Times*, November 24, 1996; *Charlotte Observer*, December 3, 1990.

14. Interview with Dexter Brooks by Susan M. Hunt, March 14 and 21, 1994, J-11, Southern Oral History Program Collection no. 4007, Southern Historical Collection; *Greensboro News and Record*, June 19, 1994; *Hamlet News*, July 23, 1981; North Carolina Division of Archives and History, pamphlet titled "Archaeology in North Carolina—Recent Legislation," North Carolina Collection, n.d.

15. Statement of Adolph Blue, U.S. Congress, *Act to Provide for the Recognition*, 78–83; Sider, *Lumbee Indian Histories*, 271; *Greensboro News and Record*, May 25, 2003; *Rocky Mount Telegram*, December 3, 2000.

16. North Carolina Commission of Indian Affairs, *Annual Report, 1998–1999* (Raleigh: North Carolina Department of Administration, 1999); NCCIA, *Annual Report, 1999–2000* (Raleigh: North Carolina Department of Administration, 1999); *Asheville Citizen-Times*, November 24, 1996; *Charlotte Observer*, December 3, 1990.

17. NCCIA, *Annual Report, 1998–1999*; NCCIA, *Annual Report, 1999–2000*; interview with Greg Richardson by author, June 28, 2001, Raleigh; NCCIA, *Indian Times* (Fall 2000 and Winter–Spring 2000); North Carolina Department of Administration, Division of Indian Affairs, Executive Director's Subject File, 1973–78, box 1.

18. *The Twenty-first Census of the United States*; *Greensboro News and Record*, May 25, 2003; *Rocky Mount Telegram*, December 3, 2000.

19. AP State and Local Wire, Lexis-Nexis, Nov 23, 1999; Sider, *Lumbee Indian Histories*, 62–68.

20. UPI *Regional News*, Lexis-Nexis, March 15, 1987.

21. Freeman interview.

22. Confidential interview, tape no. 33, November 27, 1972, courtesy of Walt Wolfram and the North Carolina Language and Life Project; *Greensboro News and Record*, March 21, 1998, June 12, 1998, October 22, 1999; *Raleigh News and Observer*, December 29, 1998.

23. *Greensboro News and Record*, March 21, 1998, June 12, 1998, March 20, 1999, October 22, 1999, November 2, 2000, August 28, 2000.

24. *Chapel Hill News*, August 7, 1988; *Chapel Hill Herald*, July 1, 1900; *Raleigh News and Observer*, March 21, 1991, December 29, 2001; Jeremiah James Nowell Jr., "Red, White and Black: Race Formation and the Politics of American Indian Recognition in North Carolina" (PhD diss., University of North Carolina–Chapel Hill, 2000), 101–17.

25. *Fayetteville Observer*, August 27, 1984; *Carolina Indian Voice*, July 12, 2001; *Rocky Mount Telegram*, July 6, 2001; *Raleigh News and Observer*, December 29, 1998.

26. Patricia B. Lerch, "Powwows, Parades and Social Drama among the Waccamaw-Sioux" (Patricia Lerch Research Papers, the North Carolina Collection), 89.

27. Author's field notes, OBSN Powwow, June 8, 2001; North Carolina Department of Administration, Division of Indian Affairs, Executive Director File, Conferences and Workshops, 1978–1979; *Chapel Hill Herald*, August 11, 1996, June 9, 2000; *Raleigh News and Observer*, June 11, 2000; *Wilmington Star-News*, October 15, 1989.

28. Quotation in *Raleigh News and Observer*, July 2, 2000; Freeman interview.

29. *Durham Herald-Sun*, February 23, 1997, September 26, 1997, February 20, 1998; *Raleigh News and Observer*, February 20, 2000; *Greensboro News and Record*, November 5, 2000, September 13, 2001.

30. Quotation from Merv G. Hayes, "A Letter," in *Feeding the Ancient Fires: A Collection of Writings by North Carolina Indians*, ed. MariJo Moore (Crossroads, 1999), 76; author's field notes, OBSN Powwow, June 8, 2001; *Wilmington Star-News*, October 15, 1989, November 10, 2002; *Chapel Hill Herald*, August 11, 1996, June 9, 2000; *Raleigh News and Observer*, July 2, 1977, June 11, 2000.

31. Robert DesJarlait, "The Contest Powwow versus the Traditional Powwow and the Role of the Native American Community," *Wicazo Review* (Spring 1997): 115–27.

32. Quotation from Moore interview; Campisi, *Haliwa-Saponi Petition*, 37–38; Patricia B. Lerch, "Pageantry, Parade, and Indian Dancing: The Staging of Identity among the Waccamaw-Sioux" (Patricia Lerch Papers, the North Carolina Collection), 33.

33. Mark Mattern, "The Powwow as a Public Arena for Negotiating Unity and Diversity in American Indian Life," *American Indian Culture and Research Journal* 20 (1996): 183.

34. Ibid., 183–98; *Raleigh News and Observer*, January 24, 2001; *Durham Herald-Sun*, November 28, 1999.

35. *Raleigh News and Observer*, June 11, 2000.

36. Walt Wolfram and Clare Dannenberg, "Dialect in a Tri-ethnic Context: The Case of Lumbee-American Indian English," *English World-Wide: A Journal of Varieties of English* 20 (1999): 179–216; Walt Wolfram, "From the Brickhouse to the Swamp," *American Language Review* (July–August 2001): 34–38.

37. Quotation in Wolfram and Dannenberg, "Dialect," 211. For more on the connection between Lumbee identity and their language, see Walt Wolfram, Clare Danneberg, Stanley Knick, and Linda Oxendine, *Fine in the World: Lumbee Language in Time and Place* (Raleigh: North Carolina State University, 2002).

38. *Raleigh News and Observer*, July 30, 2000.

39. Ibid., July 30, 2000, April 21, 2001; UPI *Regional News*, Lexis-Nexis, August 31, 1981.

40. Quotation in Oscar Patterson III, "The Press Held Hostage: Terrorism in a Small North Carolina Town" *American Journalism* 15 (1998): 131; UPI *Regional News*, Lexis-Nexis, October 19, 1988.

41. Patterson, "Press Held Hostage," 125–36; Joseph P. Shapiro and Ronald A. Taylor, "There's Trouble in Robeson County," *U.S. News and World Report* (May 2, 1988): 24–27; Sider, *Lumbee Indian Histories*, 248.

42. Patterson, "Press Held Hostage," 125–36; *Chapel Hill News*, August 7, 1988.

43. Shapiro and Taylor, "There's Trouble," 24–27; *Chapel Hill News*, August 7, 1988; Sider, *Lumbee Indian Histories*, 130, 248; Patterson, "Press Held Hostage," 125–36; *Chapel Hill Herald*, September 15, 2002.

44. Patterson, "Press Held Hostage," 125–36; Shapiro and Taylor, "There's Trouble," 24–27.

45. Lew Barton, *The Most Ironic Story in American History: An Authoritative, Documented History of the Lumbee Indians of North Carolina* (Charlotte: Associated Printing

Corporation, 1967), 88; Anne Merline McCulloch and David E. Wilkins, "'Constructing' Nations within States: The Quest for Federal Recognition by the Catawba and Lumbee Tribes," *American Indian Quarterly* 19 (Summer 1995): 361; Sharon O'Brien, *American Indian Tribal Governments* (Norman: University of Oklahoma Press, 1989), 90.

46. Fergus M. Bordewich, *Killing the White Man's Indian: Reinventing Native Americans at the End of the Twentieth Century* (New York: Doubleday, 1996), 18, 84; Peter Iverson, *"We Are Still Here:" American Indians in the Twentieth Century* (Wheeling IL: Harlan Davidson, 1998), 158–59; Nagel, *American Indian Ethnic Renewal*, 123, 226; Josephy, *Indian Heritage of America*, 363.

47. For more on Native American tribal sovereignty, see George S. Grossman, "Indians and the Law," in *New Directions in American Indian History*, ed. Colin G. Calloway (Norman: University of Oklahoma Press, 1988), 97–126; Rennard Strickland, "The Eagle's Empire: Sovereignty, Survival, and Self-Governance in Native American Law and Constitutionalism," in *Studying Native America*, ed. Russell Thornton (Madison: University of Wisconsin Press, 1998), 247–68.

48. *Fayetteville Observer Times*, April 18, 1980; Bordewich, *White Man's Indian*, 79–80; McCulloch and Wilkins, "'Constructing' Nations within States," 361–63; George Roth, "Federal Tribal Recognition in the South," in *Anthropologists and Indians in the New South*, ed. J. Anthony Paredes and Rachel A. Bonney, 49–50 (Tuscaloosa: University of Alabama Press, 2001).

49. *Raleigh News and Observer*, May 27, 2001.

50. Statement of Leola Locklear, U.S. Congress, *Act to Provide for the Recognition*, 186.

51. *Charlotte Observer*, January 5, 1980; *Fayetteville Observer Times*, April 18, 1980; *Raleigh News and Observer*, August 28, 1988, May 27, 2001; *Daily Tar Heel*, November 11, 1992.

52. *Greensboro News and Record*, July 19, 1998; NCCIA, *Annual Report, 1998–99*; Patricia B. Lerch, "State-Recognized Indians of North Carolina, Including a History of the Waccamaw Sioux," in *Indians of the Southeastern United States in the Late Twentieth Century*, ed. J. Anthony Paredes (Tuscaloosa: University of Alabama Press, 1992), 52–54.

53. Quotation in *Chapel Hill Herald*, February 25, 2000; ibid., July 21, 1998; Shannon Lee Dawdy, "The Secret History of the Meherrin" (master's thesis: College of William and Mary, 1994), 5.

54. *Chapel Hill Herald*, September 29, 2001.

55. Quotation in *Rocky Mount Telegram*, December 30, 2001; Richardson interview; *Chapel Hill Herald*, September 29, 2001.

56. *Greensboro News and Record*, July 19, 1998, August 26, 1995; *Raleigh News and Observer*, March 24, 1998, December 12, 1998, June 11, 2000, September 1, 2001; *Chapel Hill Herald*, June 4, 1994, July 21, 1998; Nowell, "Red, White and Black," 84–102, 120–21, 156–63.

57. *Greensboro News and Record*, July 26, 1995.

58. *Chapel Hill Herald*, September 29, 2001, June 4, 1994, July 21, 1998, February 25, 2000; *Greensboro News and Record*, July 26, 1995, July 19, 1998; *Raleigh News and Observer*, September 1, 2001, December 12, 1998.

59. *Greensboro News and Record*, July 19, 1998.

60. Quotation in ibid.; *Chapel Hill Herald*, July 21, 1998, September 29, 2001; *Raleigh News and Observer*, June 11, 2000.

61. *Greensboro News and Record*, November 10, 1999, March 19, 2000; *Raleigh News and Observer*, March 24, 1998, June 11, 2000, December 12, 1998, September 1, 2001; *Chapel Hill Herald*, July 21, 1998, February 25, 2000, September 7 and 29, 2001.

62. *Rocky Mount Telegram*, December 30, 2001.

63. Thomas N. Tureen to Governor Holshouser, February 20, 1973; memo from Louis R. Bruce to Governor Holshouser, September 27, 1972; and Charles Eurley to Governor Holshouser, January 10, 1973, all in James E. Holshouser, Governor's Papers, box 163, State Archives; *News and Observer*, March 21, 1973, May 17, 1973; Sider, *Lumbee Indian Histories*, 131, 132–37, 265–66; statement of Ruth Locklear, U.S. Congress, *Act to Provide for the Recognition*, 95.

64. Quotation in *Durham Herald-Sun*, April 15, 2000; *Asheville Citizen-Times*, November 22, 1982; *Charlotte Observer*, November 21, 1982; *Rocky Mount Telegram*, April 15, 2000; Sider, *Lumbee Indian Histories*, 17–18, 255; *Raleigh News and Observer*, December 16, 1989.

65. Lumbee River Legal Services, *Lumbee Petition*, 1:41–48, 104–14, 159–68, 204, 234; statement of Adolph Blue, U.S. Congress, *Act to Provide for the Recognition*, 78–83; statement of Ruth Locklear, ibid., 84–95; *Fayetteville Observer-Times*, April 18, 1980; *Charlotte Observer*, December 17, 1987; *Raleigh News and Observer*, August 12, 1988; Sider, *Lumbee Indian Histories*, 271–73.

66. U.S. Congress, *Act to Provide for the Recognition*, 1–3.

67. Statement of Jack Campisi, ibid., 99.

68. Statements of Adolph Blue, Ruth Locklear, Jack Campisi, Claude Lowry, ibid., 70–154; Governor James G. Martin to George Miller, chairman House Interior and Insular Affairs Committee, July 30, 1991, in ibid., 265; testimony of Glenn Miller, chairman of Menominee Indian Tribe of Wisconsin, in ibid., 249; Tribal Resolution of Mashantucket Pequots of Connecticut, in ibid., 255.

69. Statement of Ronald Eden, Office of Tribal Services, Bureau of Indian Affairs, Department of the Interior, in ibid., 41; statement of Leola Locklear, ibid., 185–89; statement of George Waters, ibid., 192–205; Bernard Bouschor, tribal chairman, the Sault Ste. Marie Tribe of Chippewa Indians, to Senator Daniel K. Inouye, in ibid., 226; *Durham Herald-Sun*, June 20, 1994; Sider, *Lumbee Indian Histories*, 273–78.

70. McCulloch and Wilkins, "'Constructing' Nations within States," 361–88; David E. Wilkins, "Breaking Into the Intergovernmental Matrix: The Lumbee Tribe's Efforts to Secure Federal Acknowledgment," *Publius* 23 (Fall 1993): 123–42.

71. *Raleigh News and Observer*, December 31, 2000.

72. *Durham Herald-Sun*, June 30, 1994.

73. *Wilmington Star-News*, June 5, 2000; AP State and Local Wire, Lexis-Nexis, July 9, 2000, January 13, 1999; *Atlanta Journal Constitution*, July 31, 2000; *Raleigh News and Observer*, August 27, 1999.

74. Quotation from Lumbee Constitution, http://www.lumbee.org/; *Wilmington Star-News*, April 27, 1999, June 5, 2000; *Raleigh News and Observer*, December 31, 2000; *Rocky Mount Telegram*, May 28, 2001; *Durham Morning Herald*, April 15, 2001.

75. Quotation in *Raleigh News and Observer*, December 31, 2000; Richardson interview.

76. Terry P. Wilson, "Blood Quantum: Native American Mixed Bloods," in *Racially Mixed People in American*, ed. Maria P. P. Root (Newbury Park CA: Sage Publications, 1992), 108–25.

77. Karen I. Blu, "Region and Recognition," in *Anthropologists and Indians in the New South*, ed. Rachel A. Bonney and J. Anthony Paredes (Tuscaloosa: University of Alabama Press, 2001), 78–84; Raymond D. Fogelson, "Perspectives on Native American Identity," in *Studying Native America: Problems and Prospects*, ed. Russell Thornton (Madison: University of Wisconsin Press, 1998), 44.

78. *Raleigh News and Observer*, August 28, 1988.

79. Interview with Regina Mills by author, October 16, 2000, Rocky Mount NC; Wilson, "Blood Quantum," 80, 120; Bordewich, *White Man's Indian*, 329; Russell Thornton, "The Demography of Colonialism and 'Old' and 'New' Native Americans," in *Studying Native America: Problems and Prospects*, ed. Russell Thornton (Madison: University of Wisconsin Press, 1998), 31; Lumbee River Legal Services, *Lumbee Petition*, 1:232.

80. Mills interview; Campisi, *Haliwa-Saponi Petition*, 80, 120: Lumbee River Legal Services, *Lumbee Petition*, 1:232; *Raleigh News and Observer*, August 28, 1988; Karen I. Blu, *The Lumbee Problem: The Making of an American Indian People* (Cambridge: Cambridge University Press, 1980), 109–70.

Conclusion: Keeping the Circle Strong

Opening epigraph from the *Greensboro News and Record*, October 1, 1998.

1. Figures from http://www.census.gov/.

2. *The Twenty-first Census of the United States*; *Greensboro News and Record*, May 25, 2003.

3. *Carolina Indian Voice*, July 12, 2000; North Carolina Commission of Indian Affairs, *Annual Report, 1999–2000*.

4. Interview with Greg Richardson by author, June 28, 2001, Raleigh; *Greensboro News and Record*, July 14, 2003.

5. Richardson interview; North Carolina Commission of Indian Affairs, *Health and Wellness Manual* (Raleigh: North Carolina Department of Administration, 2000); Stanley Graham Knick, "Growing Up Down Home: Health and Growth in the Lumbee Nation" (PhD diss., Indiana University, 1986).

6. *Raleigh News and Observer*, January 24, 2001.

7. Quotation in ibid.

8. *Charlotte Observer*, April 2, 2004.

9. *Wilmington Star-News*, April 5, 2004.

10. Quotation in *Winston-Salem Journal*, April 1, 2004; AP State and Local Wire, April 25, 2004.

11. *Raleigh News and Observer*, September 21, 2003.

12. Ibid.

13. Quotation in *Greensboro News and Record*, May 18, 2004; *Raleigh News and Observer*, September 21, 2003.

14. *Raleigh News and Observer*, September 21, 2003.

15. *Wilmington Star-News*, April 5, 2004.

16. Quotation in *Winston-Salem Journal*, April 2, 2004; *Charlotte Observer*, April 2, 2004.

17. *Raleigh News and Observer*, September 21, 2003.

18. Quotation in Fergus M. Bordewich, *Killing the White Man's Indian: Reinventing Native Americans at the End of the Twentieth Century* (New York: Doubleday, 1996), 92; *Greensboro News and Record*, March 30, 2003, September 12, 2003; *Raleigh News and Observer*, September 21, 2003, May 24, 2004; *Wilmington Star-News*, April 6, 2004.

19. *Greensboro Daily News*, August 11, 1978.

20. *Chapel Hill Herald*, April 18, 2002.

21. Quotation in ibid., September 29, 2001; ibid., April 18, 2002.

22. Quotation in Bordewich, *White Man's Indian*, 62; *Raleigh News and Observer*, September 18, 1977.

23. Quotation in Bordewich, *White Man's Indian*, 329; Russell Thornton, "The Demog-

raphy of Colonialism and 'Old' and 'New' Native Americans," in *Studying Native America: Problems and Prospects*, ed. Russell Thornton (Madison: University of Wisconsin Press, 1998), 31.

24. Maxine Alexander, "We Are Here Forever: Indians of the South," *Southern Exposure* 13 (1984): 15.

Bibliographical Essay

The primary Native American groups examined in this study lack federal recognition. Consequently, the official documentary evidence is somewhat sparse. Nevertheless, several libraries and archives in North Carolina have valuable sources. At the State Archives in Raleigh, the Governor's Papers proved more helpful than initially expected, as did the official papers of the North Carolina Commission of Indian Affairs, though the latter remain poorly organized and cataloged. The NCCIA also publishes a newsletter and annual reports, both of which are available at the North Carolina State Library, which is adjacent to the archives. The North Carolina Collection and the Southern Historical Collection, both at the University of North Carolina at Chapel Hill, contain relevant material. The card catalog at the North Carolina Collection is a treasure of various sources. At the Southern Historical Collection, the Guy Benton Johnson Papers (Southern Historical Collection, Collection 3826, University of North Carolina–Chapel Hill) are important to anyone interested in race in the state. In Durham, the Josiah William Bailey Papers (Collection 274, Rare Book, Manuscript, and Special Collections Library, Duke University, Durham, North Carolina) are worthy of special mention because of the various documents from the 1930s dealing with recognition.

Federal records, both published and unpublished, contain important information on North Carolina Indians. The National Archives and Records Administration in Washington DC, has several documents and reports relating to North Carolina Indians during the twentieth century. The John Pearmain report ("Report on Condition of the Indians of Robeson County, North Carolina," records group 75, Records of the Bureau of Indian Affairs) and the Fred A. Baker report ("Report on Siouan Tribe of Indians of Robeson County North Carolina," records group 75, Records of the Bureau of Indian Affairs) have valuable information from the 1930s. Federal census records also are an excellent source of data, particularly for the post-1960 era, when the bureau began keeping detailed records on Native Americans in North Carolina. In addition, many published government reports, documents, and studies are useful. In particular, see American Indian Policy Review Commission, *Final Report on Terminated and Non Federally Recognized Indians* (Washington, DC: U.S. Government Printing Office, 1976); O. M. McPherson, *Indians of North Carolina*, 63rd Cong., 3rd sess., December 7, 1914, S. Doc. vol. 4 (Washington DC: Government Printing Office, 1915); and Native American Rights Fund, *Waccamaw-Siouan Tribe of North Carolina, a Collection of Historical Documents* (copy in the North Carolina Collection, 1978).

Although media coverage was sparse prior to the 1970s, several newspapers in North Carolina have done a good job of covering Native Americans in the state over the past thirty years. Especially useful are the *Asheville Citizen; Carolina Indian Voice* (Pembroke NC); *Charlotte Observer; Durham Herald; Greensboro News and Record; Morning Star* (Wilmington); *News and Observer* (Raleigh); and *Robesonian* (Lumberton). The North Carolina Collection in Chapel Hill has an excellent, but not complete, clippings file that covers the last twenty-five years.

Much of the history of North Carolina Indians remains undocumented. Therefore, oral history is a valuable tool for anyone interested in the subject. The Southern Oral History Project, which is part of the Southern Historical Collection, has relevant interviews with American Indians. Walt Wolfram, a linguist at North Carolina State University in Raleigh, has also conducted numerous interviews with Robeson County Indians as part of the North Carolina Language and Life Project.

In dealing with contemporary issues, there is no substitute for personal interaction. Anyone interested in North Carolina Indian history must eventually visit all of these communities, but especially Robeson County. In addition to getting a sense of the place that Lumbees call home, one can access several valuable collections. On the campus of the University of North Carolina at Pembroke, the Sampson-Livermore Library and the Native American Resource Center have helpful materials. Old Main, which houses the center, is also home to the university's American Indian Studies Department, which is chaired by Linda Oxendine. The county has several other places of interest, including the Indian Educational Resource Center.

In pursuing government recognition, tribal groups in North Carolina conducted copious research on Indian history in the state. They subsequently assembled detailed petitions for acknowledgment that included valuable supporting documents and appendices. These petitions were obviously designed to earn certification, and therefore should be read and used carefully, but are nonetheless very helpful. Several libraries in the state have copies of these. In particular, see Jack Campisi, *The Haliwa-Saponi Petition for Federal Acknowledgment*

(Lumbee River Legal Services, 1989, copy at State Archives of North Carolina); and Lumbee River Legal Services, *The Lumbee Petition (for Federal Recognition)* (Pembroke NC: Lumbee River Legal Services, 1987). Also, the records of the U.S. Congress contain valuable information regarding the pursuit of federal recognition by North Carolina Indians. As an example, refer to U.S. Congress, *Act to Provide for the Recognition of the Lumbee Tribe of Cheraw Indians of North Carolina,*" joint hearing on HR 1426, *Lumbee Recognition Act,* and S 1036, *Lumbee Recognition Act,* 102nd Cong., 1st sess., (Washington DC: Government Printing Office, 1993).

In recent years the popularity of the World Wide Web, no longer simply the domain of technophiles, has skyrocketed, and Native Americans were not immune to the Internet fever that gripped Americans. Almost every Indian community and group in North Carolina now has its own web site. These sites are excellent examples of how North Carolina Indians express their unique cultural and social identity. Some tribes and organizations build and maintain their own sites, while others contract the work to webmasters. But in both cases, web sites allow North Carolina Indians to exhibit their identity directly to outsiders without a filter. Although not always completely historically accurate, the sites nevertheless are illustrations of how North Carolina Indians define themselves culturally and socially. Some of the more interesting and useful ones are www.doa.state.nc/us.cia/indian/ (North Carolina Commission of Indian Affairs); www.indiantrail.com/mnaa.htm/ (Metrolina Native American Association); www.guilfordnative.org/ (Guilford Native American Association); www.haliwa-saponitribe.com/ (Haliwa-Saponi Tribal Website); www.lumbee.org/ (Lumbee Regional Development Association); www.lumbeetribe.com/ (official site of the Lumbee Indian tribe); www.occaneechi-saponi.org/ (Occaneechi Band of the Saponi Nation); and www.tnasweb.org/ (Triangle Native American Society).

The way scholars wrote about race, ethnicity, and cultural identity changed dramatically after World War II. The horrors of Nazi Germany finally killed Social Darwinism, and in its place, cultural pluralism emerged as the dominant ideology. For more on this important change, see Fredrik Barth, ed., *Ethnic Groups and Boundaries: The Social Organization of Culture Difference* (Boston: Little, Brown, 1969); Horace M. Kallen, *Cultural Pluralism and the American Ideal* (Philadelphia: University of Pennsylvania Press, 1956); and Gunnar Myrdal, *An American Dilemma: The Negro Problem and Modern Democracy* (New York: Harper, 1944).

The theories of Barth, Kallen, and Myrdal, accompanied by the burgeoning civil rights movement, influenced the way that scholars wrote about Native Americans in the postwar years. Initially, this new work concentrated on the eighteenth and nineteenth centuries. In recent years, however, academicians have started examining contemporary Indian history. For more on twentieth-century Native Americans, see Alison R. Bernstein, *American Indians and World War II: Toward a New Era in Indian Affairs* (Norman: University of Oklahoma Press, 1991); Vine Deloria Jr., ed., *American Indian Policy in the Twentieth Century* (Norman: University of Oklahoma Press, 1985); Peter Iverson, *"We Are Still Here": American Indians in the Twentieth Century* (Wheeling IL: Harlan Davidson, 1998); and James S. Olson and Raymond Wilson, *Native Americans in the Twentieth Century* (Urbana: University of Illinois Press, 1984).

Within the broader field of Native American studies, some scholars tackled the difficult question of Indian identity. Authors examining Indianness have had to deal with several complicated questions, such as what it means to be Indian and whether Indianness is biological or cultural. The answers to these questions, and others, were vital to the larger understanding of both Indian and American history. For more, see Fergus M. Bordewich, *Killing the White Man's Indian: Reinventing Native Americans at the End of the Twentieth Century* (New York: Doubleday, 1996); Philip J. Deloria, *Playing Indian* (New Haven: Yale University Press, 1998); and Joane Nagel, *American Indian Ethnic Renewal: Red Power and the Resurgence of Identity and Culture* (New York: Oxford University Press, 1996). For a general look at recent studies in identity, race, and ethnicity, refer to Michael Hughey, ed., *New Tribalisms: The Resurgence of Race and Ethnicity* (New York: New York University Press, 1998); Michael Omi and Howard Winant, *Racial Formation in the United States from the 1960s to the 1980s* (New York: Routledge and Kegan Paul, 1986); Eugeen Roosens, *Creating Ethnicity: The Process of Ethnogenosis* (Newbury Park CA: Sage Publications, 1989); and Warner Sollors, ed., *The Invention of Ethnicity* (New York: Oxford University Press, 1989). For a more critical view of contemporary Native American identity, see James A. Clifton, ed., *The Invented Indian: Cultural Fictions and Government Policies* (New Brunswick: Transaction Publishers, 1990).

The period from 1929 to 1945 was a time of tremendous change for North Carolina Indians. This was partially the product of the economic transformation occurring across the South. On the eve of the Great Depression, most North Carolinians, and most southerners, were farmers; but by the 1960s only a few Tar Heels still worked the land. For more on the effects of the changing economy in North Carolina and the South, see Jack T. Kirby, *Rural Worlds Lost: The American South, 1920–1960* (Baton Rouge: Louisiana State University Press, 1986); Anthony Badger, *Prosperity Road: The New Deal, Tobacco, and North Carolina* (Chapel Hill: University of North Carolina Press, 1980); James C. Cobb, *The Selling of the South: The Southern Crusade for Industrial Development, 1936–1990* (Urbana: University of Illinois Press, 1993, 1982) and *Industrialization and Southern Society, 1877–1984* (Lexington: University Press of Kentucky, 1984); Gilbert Fite, *Cotton Fields No More: Southern Agriculture, 1865–1980* (Lexington: University Press of Kentucky, 1984); and Bruce J. Schulman, *From Cotton Belt* to *Sunbelt: Federal Policy, Economic Development, and the Transformation of the South, 1938–1980* (New York: Oxford University Press, 1991).

Native American churches were vital to the preservation of Indian identity in North Carolina. By the middle of the nineteenth century, most Native Americans in the state had converted to Evangelical Christianity. For more on religion in North Carolina and the South, refer to Frederick A. Bode, *Protestantism and the New South: North Carolina Baptists and Methodists in Political Crisis, 1894–1903* (Charlottesville: University Press of Virginia, 1975); Christine Leigh Heyrman, *Southern Cross: The Beginnings of the Bible Belt* (New York: A. A. Knopf, 1997); and Samuel S. Hill, ed., *Religion and the Solid South* (Nashville: Abingdon Press, 1972).

Native American schools, like churches, helped protect and maintain Indian identity in North Carolina during the twentieth century. New federal legislation, however, led to integration and the end of Indian-only schools in the 1960s and 1970s. For school integration, see William H. Chafe, *Civilities and Civil Rights: Greensboro, North Carolina, and the Black Struggle for Freedom* (New York: Oxford University Press, 1980); J. Harvie Wilkinson, *From Brown to Bakke: The Supreme Court and School Integration, 1954–1978* (New York: Oxford University Press, 1979); and Raymond Wolters, *The Burden of Brown: Thirty Years of School Desegregation* (Knoxville: University of Tennessee Press, 1984).

In the post–World War II era, thousands of Native Americans moved from their reservations and home communities to metropolitan areas. Indian urbanization remains a relatively unexplored topic, especially for nonrecognized tribes in the South. See Susan Lobo and Kurt Peters, *American Indians and the Urban Experience* (Walnut Creek CA: Altamira Press, 2001); Elaine Neils, *Reservation to City: Indian Migration and Federal Relocation* (Chicago: University of Chicago Press, 1971); and Alan L. Sorkin, *The Urban American Indian* (Lexington MA: Lexington Books, 1978).

The Native American cultural renaissance was also an important postwar phenomenon. The powwow was the most visible representation of cultural revival. For more on the contemporary powwow movement, see David Whitehorse, *Pow-wow: The Contemporary Pan-Indian Celebration* (Publications in American Indian Studies No. 5, San Diego: San Diego State University, 1988; Robert DesJarlait, "The Contest Powwow versus the Traditional Powwow and the Role of the Native American Community," *Wicazo Review* (Spring 1997): 115–27; and Mark Mattern, "The Powwow as a Public Arena for Negotiating Unity and Diversity in American Indian Life," *American Indian Culture and Research Journal* 20 (1996): 183–201.

"Blood quantum" remains a very controversial issue among both scholars and Native Americans. For many, the topic is uncomfortable but nevertheless important. For interesting discussions of blood quantum, see Circe Sturm,

Blood Politics: Race, Culture, and Identity in the Cherokee Nation of Oklahoma (Berkeley: University of California Press, 2002); Erik M. Zissu, *Blood Matters: The Five Civilized Tribes and the Search for Unity in the Twentieth Century* (New York: Routledge, 2001); Pauline Strong and Barrik Van Winkle, "'Indian Blood': Reflections on the Reckoning and Refiguring of Native North American Identity," *Cultural Anthropology* 11 (1996): 547–76; and Terry P. Wilson, "Blood Quantum: Native American Mixed Bloods," in *Racially Mixed People in America*, edited by Maria P. P. Root, 108–25 (Newbury Park CA: Sage Publications, 1992).

The twentieth-century story of North Carolina Indians was not unique. Other Native Americans in the South went through similar experiences, and authors have examined Indian tribes and communities in other states. In particular, see Rachel A. Bonney and J. Anthony Paredes, ed., *Anthropologists and Indians in the New South* (Tuscaloosa: University of Alabama Press, 2001); Jesse Burt and Robert B. Ferguson, *Indians of the Southeast: Then and Now* (Nashville: Abingdon Press, 1973); J. Anthony Paredes, ed., *Indians of the Southeastern United States in the Late Twentieth Century* (Tuscaloosa: University of Alabama Press, 1992); Theda Perdue and Michael D. Green, *The Columbia Guide to American Indians of the Southeast* (New York: Columbia University Press, 2001); Frank W. Porter III, ed., *Strategies for Survival: American Indians in the Eastern United States* (New York: Greenwood Press, 1986); Helen Rountree, *Pocahontas's People: The Powhatan Indians of Virginia through Four Centuries* (Norman: University of Oklahoma Press, 1990); and Walter L. Williams, ed., *Southeastern Indians since the Removal Era* (Athens: University of Georgia Press, 1979).

Index

Return of the Native (Cornell), 5
Revels, James, 85
Revels, Lindsey, 44
Revels, Lonnie, 96, 141
Revels, Ronald, 94
Revels, Ruth, 96, 107, 114, 141
Reynolds, Malvina, 77
Ricefield NC, 70
Richardson, Arnold, 115
Richardson, Greg, 70, 127, 140–41
Richardson, Patricia, 115
Richardson, W. R. Talking Eagle, 69–70, *71*,
   81–82, 97, 103, 141
Roanoke Island NC, 36
Robeson County Historical Drama, Inc.
   (RCHD), 102
The Robesonian, 124–25
Rocky Mount NC, 69
Rogers, Elias, 91
Roosevelt, Franklin D., 44, 57, 93
Rose, Charlie, 133
Rountree, Helen, 110

Sampson, William, 32, 77, 95
Sampson County Indian Association, 70. *See
   also* Coharie Indians
Sanford, Terry, 133
Saponi Indians, 15–16, 69
Sargent, William, 92
Schierbeck, Helen, 110
Schulman, Bruce, 59
Scott, Kerr, 59
Scott, Robert, 97
Secotan Indians, *16*
Seeger, Pete, 77
Seltzer, Carl C., 49–51, 62, 131–32
Servicemen's Readjustment Act (1944), 60, 85
sharecropping, 30–33, 40
Sharpe, Bill, 66
Sider, Gerald, 88–90
Siouan Tribal Lodge, 47
slavery (of Indians), 17
Smith, Dolores, 130–31
Smithsonian Institute, 33, 48, 115
Southern Christian Leadership Conference
   (SCLC), 87–88, 91
Spencer, Herbert, 2–3
The State, 72
Steward, Julian H., 9
Stewertsville NC, 37
Strickland, W. J., 110
Strike at the Wind (Umberger), 102–3
Sumner, William Graham, 2–3
Swanton, John R., 48

Tar River Festival (Rocky Mount NC), 122
Taylor, Carl, 52
Taylor, Charles, 142
Termination, 73–80
Thom, Mel, 82
Thompson, Samuel, 54
Triangle Native American Association
   (TNAA), 118, 129
Turner, Nat, 18
Tuscarora Indians, *11*, 13, 15, *16*, 17, 36, 39, 69–
   70, 89–92, 124, 131–32, 139; activism of,
   89–93; and East Carolina Tuscarora Indian
   Organization (ECTIO), 89, 131
Tuteloe Indians, *16*, 69

Umberger, Randolph, 102
United South and Eastern Tribes (USET), 130
United Tribes of North Carolina (UTNC), 111
University of North Carolina, Chapel Hill
   (UNC-CH), 36, 141–42
University of North Carolina, Pembroke, 23–
   25, *26*, 36, 48, 53, 55–56, 141; and consoli-
   dation into UNC, 85–86; and Old Main, 25,
   85–87, *86*
Unto These Hills (Hunter), 102
U.S. News and World Report, 125

Vizenor, Gerald, 99
Volunteers in Service to America (VISTA), 93
Voting Rights Act (1965), 87

Waccamaw-Sioux Indians, *11*, 12, 15, *16*, 72, 80,
   97–98, 111–12, 114–15, 128, 131, 139; federal
   recognition of, 70–71; powwows of, 103–4,
   117; and Waccamaw Sioux Development
   Association (WSDA), 94, 113
Walters, Ronald, 105
Warren, Louis S., 100–101
Warrior, Clyde, 82
Weapemeoc Indians, 15, *16*, 17
Welch, James, 99
Wheeler-Howard Act. *See* Indian Reorganiza-
   tion Act (1934)
White, John, 15, 22, 34, 36
White, Richard, 101
White, Wesly, 132
Wilkins, David E., 134
Williams, Walter L., 9–10
Wilson, Raymond, 79
Winant, Howard, 4–5
Wolfram, Walt, 122–23
Woods, Ruth, 82, 94
World War II, 56–62

Zimmerman, William, Jr., 51

In the Indians of the Southeast Series

*William Bartram on the
Southeastern Indians*
Edited and annotated by
Gregory A. Waselkov and
Kathryn E. Holland Braund

Deerskins and Duffels
*The Creek Indian Trade with
Anglo-America, 1685–1815*
By Kathryn E. Holland Braund

Searching for the Bright Path
*The Mississippi Choctaws from
Prehistory to Removal*
By James Taylor Carson

Demanding the Cherokee Nation
*Indian Autonomy and American
Culture, 1830–1900*
By Andrew Denson

Cherokee Americans
*The Eastern Band of Cherokees
in the Twentieth Century*
By John R. Finger

Creeks and Southerners
*Biculturalism on the Early American
Frontier*
By Andrew K. Frank

Choctaw Genesis, 1500–1700
By Patricia Galloway

The Southeastern Ceremonial Complex
Artifacts and Analysis
The Cottonlandia Conference
Edited by Patricia Galloway
Exhibition Catalog by David H. Dye
and Camille Wharey

*The Invention of the Creek Nation,
1670–1763*
By Steven C. Hahn

An Assumption of Sovereignty
*Social and Political Transformation
among the Florida Seminoles, 1953–1979*
By Harry A. Kersey Jr.

The Caddo Chiefdoms
Caddo Economics and Politics, 700–1835
By David La Vere

Keeping the Circle
*American Indian Identity in Eastern
North Carolina, 1885–2004*
By Christopher Arris Oakley

*Choctaws in a Revolutionary Age,
1750–1830*
By Greg O'Brien

Cherokee Women
Gender and Culture Change, 1700–1835
By Theda Perdue

The Brainerd Journal
A Mission to the Cherokees, 1817–1823
Edited and introduced by Joyce B.
Phillips and Paul Gary Phillips

The Cherokees
A Population History
By Russell Thornton

Buffalo Tiger
A Life in the Everglades
By Buffalo Tiger and Harry A. Kersey Jr.

*American Indians in the Lower
Mississippi Valley*
Social and Economic Histories
By Daniel H. Usner Jr.

Powhatan's Mantle
Indians in the Colonial Southeast
Edited by Peter H. Wood, Gregory A.
Waselkov, and M. Thomas Hatley

Creeks and Seminoles
*The Destruction and Regeneration
of the Muscogulge People*
By J. Leitch Wright Jr.